TEN
DECISIONS

TEN DECISIONS

Canada's Best, Worst, and Most Far-Reaching Decisions of the Second World War

LARRY D. ROSE

DUNDURN
TORONTO

Copyright © Larry D. Rose, 2017

All rights reserved. No part of this publication may be reproduced, stored in a retrieval system, or transmitted in any form or by any means, electronic, mechanical, photocopying, recording, or otherwise (except for brief passages for purpose of review) without the prior permission of Dundurn Press. Permission to photocopy should be requested from Access Copyright.

Cover image: Courtesy of the author
Printer: Webcom

Library and Archives Canada Cataloguing in Publication

Rose, Larry D., author
    Ten decisions : Canada's best, worst, and most far-reaching decisions of the Second World War / Larry D. Rose.

Includes bibliographical references and index.
Issued in print and electronic formats.
ISBN 978-1-4597-3828-7 (softcover).--ISBN 978-1-4597-3829-4 (PDF).-- ISBN 978-1-4597-3830-0 (EPUB)

    1. Military planning--Canada--Decision making--History--20th century. 2. Political leadership--Canada--History--20th century. 3. Decision making--Canada--History--20th century. 4. World War, 1939-1945--Canada. I. Title.

D768.15.R67 2017   940.54'1271   C2017-904648-9
                                           C2017-904649-7

1 2 3 4 5   21 20 19 18 17

 Conseil des Arts   Canada Council
du Canada   for the Arts

We acknowledge the support of the **Canada Council for the Arts**, which last year invested $153 million to bring the arts to Canadians throughout the country, and the **Ontario Arts Council** for our publishing program. We also acknowledge the financial support of the **Government of Ontario**, through the **Ontario Book Publishing Tax Credit** and the **Ontario Media Development Corporation**, and the **Government of Canada**.

Nous remercions le **Conseil des arts du Canada** de son soutien. L'an dernier, le Conseil a investi 153 millions de dollars pour mettre de l'art dans la vie des Canadiennes et des Canadiens de tout le pays.

Care has been taken to trace the ownership of copyright material used in this book. The author and the publisher welcome any information enabling them to rectify any references or credits in subsequent editions.
— *J. Kirk Howard, President*

The publisher is not responsible for websites or their content unless they are owned by the publisher.

Printed and bound in Canada.

VISIT US AT

 dundurn.com | @dundurnpress | dundurnpress | dundurnpress

Dundurn
3 Church Street, Suite 500
Toronto, Ontario, Canada
M5E 1M2

In memory of
Gladys M. Rose

CONTENTS

Acknowledgements		9
Timeline		11
Canada in 1939:	On the Edge of War	15
Decision One:	To Go to War	21
Decision Two:	The Unloved Corvette	42
Decision Three:	Canada's Air Training Colossus	65
Decision Four:	Putting "Canadian" in "Royal Canadian Air Force"	87
Decision Five:	Appointment of the Minister of Everything	111
Decision Six:	The Ogdensburg Agreement — Canada Turns to America	132
Decision Seven:	Dieppe	151
Decision Eight:	Simonds Appointed to Command II Canadian Corps	175
Decision Nine:	The Greatest Political Crisis of the War	206
Decision Ten:	From War to Peace	235
Conclusion:	The New Canada	256
Notes		263
Image Credits		290
Index		291

ACKNOWLEDGEMENTS

Many people and organizations have assisted in the preparation of this book. Thanks to Dr. J.L. Granatstein, who has offered, as he did with my earlier work, *Mobilize!*, encouragement and advice over several years. For reading part or all of a manuscript thanks to Major-General (Ret'd) Fraser Holman, Brigadier-General (Ret'd) Garry Thomson, who also contributed two Dieppe photographs, Lieutenant-Commander (Ret'd) Ed Sparling, Sergeant Peter Moon, Dennis McIntosh, and Alain Rivet.

Thanks to Robin Rowland, Colonel (Ret'd) Allan Methven, Captain Steven Dieter, Penny Lippman, Librarian at the Royal Canadian Military Institute, the Toronto Reference Library, the City of Toronto Archives, the Laurier Centre for Military Strategic and Disarmament Studies for making files available, and Jerry Michaels for assistance with photos. For assistance with maps, thanks to Dr. Stephen Harris of the Directorate of History and Heritage and to Mike Bechthold.

Thanks to Lenore Wagner Floyd, formerly of Teeterville, Ontario, for information about and photos of her three uncles who were killed in northwest Europe in 1944 and 1945. Also to Gert Penwill and the Penwill family for making available letters written by Flying Officer Robert English, a British Commonwealth Air Training Plan graduate who died on operations in Italy in 1945. Thanks to Pilot Officer (Ret'd) Bill Milne for information about his RCAF service in Bomber Command and for his continued support.

Thanks to Professor Howard Hisdal, Chair of the Department of History at Okanagan College, for assistance in making available his thesis "Lieutenant-General Guy Simonds and the Battle of the Scheldt: A Study in Generalship." Thanks to Dr. Aaron Plamondon of Mount Royal University for making available his Royal Military College of Canada master's thesis titled "Canada and the Oghdensburg Agreement: the Historial Analysis of a Logical Progression." Thank you to Stephen Hayter, of the Commonwealth Air Training Plan Museum in Brandon, Manitoba, for assistance with photos. Thanks to Team Dundurn and to editor Kate Unrau.

And most of all, thanks to my ever-supportive partner, Michael Kevin Brennan.

Any errors are my own.

TIMELINE

The Ten Decisions are in boldface.

1939

August 2	The Einstein-Szilárd letter is delivered to U.S. president Franklin D. Roosevelt advising of the potential use of uranium to construct an atomic bomb.
September 1	Germany attacks Poland, beginning the Second World War.
September 3	Britain, France, New Zealand, Australia, and India (by its Viceroy) declare war on Nazi Germany. Battle of the Atlantic begins.
September 10	**Canada declares war on Germany (Decision One).**
September 17	The Soviet Union invades Poland and occupies eastern Polish territories.
December 13	The German pocket battleship *Admiral Graf Spee* is scuttled off Uruguay.
December 17	**British Commonwealth Air Training Plan Agreement signed in Ottawa (Decision Three).**

1940

February 7	**Canadian government orders sixty-four corvettes (Decision Two).**
March 26	Liberals re-elected in federal election.
April 9	**C.D. Howe appointed minister of munitions and supply (Decision Five).**
May–June	German blitzkrieg overwhelms Belgium, Holland, and France.
May 10	Winston Churchill becomes prime minister of Britain.
May 26–June 4	British Expeditionary Force evacuated from Dunkirk.
June 10	Italian dictator Benito Mussolini declares war on the Allies.
August 17	**Ogdensburg Agreement reached between Canada and the United States (Decision Six).**
September	British victory in Battle of Britain forces Hitler to postpone invasion plans.
November 11–12	British naval fleet uses aerial attack to defeat Italians at Battle of Taranto.

1941

June 22	Hitler begins Operation Barbarossa, the invasion of Russia.
December 7	Japan attacks Pearl Harbor, and the U.S. enters the war. Japan attacks Hong Kong and defeats a British-led force that includes a Canadian brigade. Hundreds of Canadians become prisoners of war.

1942

February 15	Singapore falls to the Japanese.
May 5	The U.S. bastion at Corregidor, the Philippines, falls to the Japanese.
June 4–7	American victory at Battle of Midway marks turning point in Pacific War.
June	Mass murder of Jewish people underway at Auschwitz.
August 19	**The Dieppe raid (Decision Seven).**
October 23–November 11	British victory at Battle of El Alamein.
October 25	**Formation of No. 6 Group, RCAF (Decision Four).**

1943

February 2	German surrender at Stalingrad.
July 5	Beginning of the Battle of Kursk, the biggest land battle of the war.
August 9–10	Invasion of Sicily includes Canadian division and armoured brigade.
September 8	Italy surrenders, but Germany takes over the battle.

1944

January 2	Allies land at Anzio and bomb monastery at Monte Cassino.
January 30	**Lieutenant-General Guy Simonds appointed commander of II Canadian Corps (Decision Eight).**

June 6	D-Day. Allied invasion of France. Third Canadian Division is part of invasion force.
July 20	Bomb plot against Hitler narrowly fails.
August 8–13	Operation Totalize led by II Canadian Corps, near Falaise.
August 10	Guam liberated by the U.S.
August 25	Paris liberated.
November 22	**Second conscription crisis in Ottawa (Decision Nine).**
December 16	Beginning of the Battle of the Bulge, last major German offensive of the war.

1945

January 19	U.S. Marines attack Iwo Jima, their bloodiest battle of the war.
January 27	Auschwitz liberated by Soviet troops.
February 20	**The first "Baby Bonus" cheques mailed — part of Canada's postwar planning (Decision Ten).**
April 12	U.S. president Roosevelt dies. Harry S. Truman succeeds him as president.
April 30	Hitler commits suicide.
May 8	VE-Day. German surrender.
June 11	Liberals re-elected with minority government in Ottawa.
August 14	VJ-Day. After atomic bombs are dropped on Hiroshima and Nagasaki, Japan surrenders.

CANADA IN 1939

On the Edge of War

In 1939 Canada was unprepared for war and totally unprepared for total war. That was obvious in many ways but most of all in the state of its army, navy, and air force. There were only 4,169 officers and men in Canada's regular army at the start of the Second World War.[1] The uniforms the soldiers wore looked just like those from 1918 because, in fact, they *were* those from 1918. The army was not able to buy new uniforms or much new equipment until the months before the war broke out. There were about twenty-five thousand men in the army reserves and most were untrained. In pre-war years some summer artillery exercises had to be cancelled because artillery shells were too valuable to actually be fired. The biggest training exercise of the decade was held in 1938 and it was a shambles. Most senior army officers were too old or too sick to be effective, and drinking was a serious problem. As memorably described by John English in *The Canadian Army and the Normandy Campaign*, the army shamefully neglected the study of war in those years.[2] Top officers instead spent most of their time running relief camps or on ceremonies and parades.

The Royal Canadian Navy had six serviceable destroyers and four minesweepers, but those ships had to cover two long coasts. Before the war the Canadian destroyers trained alongside the big ships of the Royal Navy. The British believed the principal threat they faced would be from German surface ships while submarines were a menace that could be managed. On the outbreak of war there were 1,189 officers and men in the regular RCN. There were three reserve formations: the Royal Canadian Navy Reserve (RCNR), made up mostly of officers and sailors in the merchant marine; the Royal Canadian Navy Volunteer Reserve (RCNVR), mostly weekend sailors and yachtsmen; and the very small Fishermen's Reserve. Together the three made up another 1,900 officers and ratings. So when the war broke out the navy had a grand total of about three thousand men.

There were 275 aircraft in the Royal Canadian Air Force. With the exception of a few new Hurricane fighters, most of the planes appeared to have been stolen from a museum. One squadron operated the Armstrong Whitworth Atlas, an army co-operation biplane that first flew in 1925. On the outbreak of war the air force was supposed to have fifteen squadrons, but it had to scrape together everything that flew just to muster twelve. There were about 4,100 officers and men in the regular air force and air force reserve combined.

In 1939 there were eleven million people in Canada. In many ways the country was British. No maple-leaf flag flew on any flagpole, but instead the Canadian Ensign, or more commonly, the Union Jack. There were pictures of the young king, George VI, in every school, including, presumably, King George School in Moose Jaw, Saskatchewan, King George School in Saskatoon, and King George VI School in Kenora, Ontario.[3] And all those British products — Lipton tea, Royal Doulton china, and, from the tiny village of Port Sunlight, near Liverpool, Sunlight soap — lined Canadian store shelves.

Canadians in most parts of the country were proud to be part of one of the great empires of history, the British Empire. For the true Empire boosters the biggest moment of their lives was the Royal Tour of May and June 1939. King George and Queen Elizabeth had been invited to Canada after their coronation in 1936, but no one could have imagined the trip would take place on the very edge of war. The Royal Tour was a sensation and helped rally the nation to the Empire in a time of dire need. Even in Quebec most people welcomed the King and Queen with uncommon warmth. In most other respects, however, the three and a half million people who made up French Canada, were the "great exception" in the nation. The differences were fundamental and historic. Most important in 1939 was the French-Canadian view of possible war in Europe. Francophone Canada was determined that it would not be part of any new "Imperial" war. Through most of the Second World War this French–English divide would command the political agenda again and again.

In the pre-war years multiculturalism was unheard of. There were people from Germany in Kitchener, Ontario, people from Iceland in Gimli, Manitoba, and minorities from other countries scattered across Canada, but they were often shut out of the mainstream. Some minorities remained at the bottom of the social ladder. When conscription became an issue later in the war, recent immigrants simply wanted to be left to their farms and workbenches. Most were barely scratching out a living, anyway, only trying to survive.

At the beginning of the war Canada was an economic weakling. It was a wounded country, still in the grip of the Great Depression. Factories had produced steel, durable goods, and clothing in earlier years, but hundreds of those plants had shut their doors. In the 1920s Canada had been the second largest auto producer in the world, but by 1939 only a handful of plants remained open. Between 1929 and 1939 the Gross Domestic Product (GDP), the total of goods and services the country produced, dropped 40 percent.[4] World wheat prices were dramatically lower than they had been a few years before. Parts of the prairies were dust bowls, having suffered years of drought. In tiny Minton, Saskatchewan, most of the population of 890 depended on government relief or charity; even the chickens in the town depended on relief feed.

Because of the economic problems, because some Canadians did not want to be part another war under any circumstance, and because of the French-Canadian aversion to any new "Imperial" conflicts, Canadians chose to ignore the events in Europe year after year. As journalist Bruce Hutchison memorably commented, in the face of a growing crisis, "Canadians turned out the lights and hid under the bed."[5]

During the war a most unlikely warlord led Canada. Prime Minister William Lyon Mackenzie King could never get military ranks straight, and the military culture was completely foreign to him. Today he is probably remembered mostly for his odd personal life, which included séances with his dead mother. King was a devious but very sharp political leader. It was said that in Parliament he knew the answer to anything before the opposition could think of the question. Most of King's speeches were droning affairs. When presented with a draft speech, King, with his trademark stubby pencil in hand, would sniff suspiciously, cross out, amend, and rewrite in the margins to the point of impenetrability and oblivion.

Mackenzie King had been around Ottawa since before the First World War and had been prime minister during the 1920s. At the start of the Second World War he was a tubby, balding sixty-four-year-old. He was respected but not loved by his party, at least not in the way Liberals had loved Sir Wilfrid Laurier. But it would be a huge mistake to underestimate King. He was, apart from dominating Parliament, a good picker of men. Some have described the wartime cabinet as one of the strongest Canada ever had.[6] Ordinary Canadians recognized that while he might not have been a spectacular figure, he was, in a way, very Canadian: solid and reliable. He was the comfortable sweater of Canadian politics. A bit tattered and worn. You would have thought there would be better sweaters around, but this was the one everyone had grown used to. Not much of a sweater to look at, really — not very inspiring, but there it was.

For most of his career and certainly through the Second World War, King's great challenge was the division between French and English Canada. He understood the most fundamental political principle of Canadian history: in a nation that has a significant minority, the government cannot simply rely on majority rule to decide questions that divide the two groups.[7] When the war began, King had support from across the country and about one-third of his MPs were from Quebec. His alliance with French Canada cut two ways. The Francophones had a lot of clout in Ottawa because King was often forced to take account of his Quebec caucus. But that meant that French Canada also had a big stake in King. If they did not support him, someone worse might come along. King's greatest achievement during the war was that, in partnership with his influential Quebec lieutenant, Ernest Lapointe, he kept French and English Canada together.

Lapointe was the key to it all.[8] A dynamic and gifted speaker, Lapointe was a lawyer originally from Rivière-du-Loup. He was first elected in 1904 at the age of twenty-seven and became a protegé of Laurier. He was a vehement opponent of the Union government that brought in conscription in 1917, and he opposed conscription until the end of his career. He and King were not close personally, but they went back a long way. Lapointe had played a pivotal role in King's election as Liberal leader in 1919. Lapointe was literally the King-maker, throwing his influence and support to King just in time to bring him victory.

Lapointe, the long-time justice minister, was a hard man to miss in Ottawa. He towered over most of his colleagues and was once described as "the most gigantic man in politics in the British Empire." The Anglo-Quebecker Chubby Power said, "It was to Lapointe that we looked for leadership, for generalship, and for anything relating to either policy or tactics in Quebec political life."[9] When Lapointe died in 1941, it was an enormous setback for King, for Quebec, and for Canada.

It is almost unimaginable to think today how small the government was in 1939. The federal government's expenditures in that year were a puny $680 million. King ran a big slice of the government out of his hip pocket. He was both prime minister and secretary of state for foreign affairs. The cabinet war committee, a sub-committee of cabinet, made most crucial decisions about the war. It was initially called the cabinet sub-committee on defence, but its title and membership changed over time. Basically, it was made up of all the heavy hitters in cabinet, including Lapointe and, after Lapointe's death, Louis St. Laurent. For most of the war the defence trio were Defence Minister James Ralston, Chubby Power, who was the air minister, and Angus Macdonald, who ran naval services. When C.D. Howe became minister of munitions and supplies, he joined the sub-committee. While the cabinet war committee made most of the important decisions, King could be very crafty. If he felt he would get more support from the whole cabinet, as he did in the worst of the conscription crisis, he would raise the issue there.

This book examines the best, the worst, and the most far-reaching Canadian decisions in the Second World War. Some of the decisions selected may be surprising. Some were political, some military, and some a mix of both while one was diplomatic. The problems Canada faced in the Second World War may have been similar to those in the United States or Britain, including building new ships, creating a war-winning economy, and training thousands of airmen. But in at least one respect Canada's problems were unique. In no other nation did conscription have the potential to break up the country.

Among the ten decisions there are undoubted omissions as there would be with any short list. The Canadian military disaster at Hong Kong is little mentioned even though it was a horrifying episode. There is no chapter on Rear-Admiral L.W. Murray, the only Canadian theatre commander in the Second World War. There is not much detail about the breadth of the Battle of the Atlantic as such, nor indeed the entire Normandy and Italian campaigns for the army. The role of women, which changed dramatically during the war, is briefly covered.

Despite these omissions, each of the ten decisions selected has a powerful resonance. For good or ill they captured headlines, triggered public debate and political storms, caused outrage or praise in the press, and provided controversies for journalists and historians for decades afterward. Some of the controversies continue still.

DECISION ONE

To Go to War

When Britain declared war on Germany on September 3, 1939, did that mean that Canada was at war, too? The *Free Press* in London, Ontario, thought so. Its headline that day read "CANADA IS NOW AT WAR. FRANCE JUMPS IN TOO." Many Canadians assumed that since Britain had declared war, Canada was automatically at war. At the start of the First World War that is what had happened.

But things had changed. In 1931 the British passed the Statute of Westminster, which transferred control of Canadian foreign affairs, including the right to declare war, to Ottawa. Still, in 1939 some foreign policy experts and many in Parliament were not exactly sure what the law meant. The British high commissioner in Ottawa believed that Canada *would* go to war, but he was not 100 percent certain it *had* gone to war. Despite it all, it was clear enough to Prime Minister King — Canada was not at war. He told questioning reporters that only the Canadian Parliament could declare war, and it had not met yet.

Parliament was in recess, so King announced that a special parliamentary session would begin on September 7. When Parliament did finally meet, the governor general, Lord Tweedsmuir* delivered the Speech

---

* Tweedsmuir was a remarkable figure. He was famous as John Buchan, author of the thriller *The Thirty-Nine Steps*. He also wrote historical novels, a twenty-four volume

from the Throne. He noted "the extreme gravity of this hour" and called for an immediate declaration of war. The debate that followed was emotional and heartfelt. Nearly all English-Canadian members of Parliament supported going to war.[1] First World War veteran Henry Hamilton from Algoma West in Ontario addressed Parliament, suggesting Hitler threatened more than just Europe. "This is Canada's war. The effective defence of Canada consists in the utilization of the organized and united power and strength of this Dominion … wherever and whenever it can best be used to defeat Germany's armed forces."[2]

The near total agreement among English-Canadian MPs, and English Canadians generally, was in contrast to the situation a year or two earlier when opinion about going to war if Britain were attacked had been much divided.

One of the most closely watched speeches was that of Justice Minister Lapointe. Many French Canadians were adamantly opposed to Canada declaring war because it would likely mean conscription. Still, the passionate and emotional Lapointe appealed to all MPs, English and French alike, to *support* the declaration. He said it was for "Canada's soul, Canada's dignity, Canada's honour."[3] The comments were not entirely new, but they were exceptional in their strength and clarity and they were being delivered at a crucial moment. There it was. Lapointe, the Quebec titan, supported the war declaration. The speech shocked — even outraged — many in Quebec, but in the end most Quebec MPs followed Lapointe's lead. The war declaration passed without even a formal vote. As of September 10, 1939, Canada was at war.

The next day the *Globe and Mail* commented that there had been fears of a French-Canadian revolt on the issue, but those fears had vanished. The many speeches, Lapointe's most of all, had shown that French and English Canada had reached an understanding, a way forward. It was a stark contrast to the divisive French–English debates in Parliament during the First World War and the riots and fury that followed. At times they verged on civil war.

---

history of war, and biographies. In addition, he was a successful publisher and member of the British parliament. The governor general's speech was, of course, written by Prime Minister King.

Today Canadians likely view the nation's war declaration in 1939 without much thought. As a non-event. A given. Expected. But that was far from the case. In reality, Prime Minister King had engineered it despite maddening divisions, challenges, setbacks, and, in some cases, his own mistakes. Earlier on there had been divisions among English Canadians, and then as war neared the French–English divide persisted. In reality, the war declaration was one of the most far-reaching and significant Canadian decisions of the Second World War. That was so not only because it marked the start of the conflict — although that certainly was historic — but also because Canada began the war without fatal divisions. Historian Desmond Morton said, "In all Mackenzie King's long political career perhaps no achievement was as remarkable or as improbable as bringing Canada united into the Second World War."[4] September 10, 1939, was one of the greatest days of King's career, if not *the* greatest.

King was helped by the significant contribution of Lapointe in the last years before the war and by some support from newspapers. Most notable among them was the *Winnipeg Free Press*, at the time one of the most influential newspapers in the country. King was also aided to a great extent by developments in Europe. Each of Hitler's outrageous new demands or land grabs served to drive Canadians together. Still, it was King's quiet but relentless campaign that was the critical factor in determining Parliament's decisive actions in September 1939.

For many in French Canada the 1939 Commons debate recalled some of the searing events of the First World War. In 1917, with bloody fighting in France showing no let-up, the Canadian army had run out of volunteers. The only real choice the government had to keep up the strength of front line divisions was to enact conscription — to draft thousands of men into the army. But most French Canadians considered the conflict to be a British Imperial war. They would be drafted not to protect Canada but to be just another part of Britain's Imperial army. Prime Minister Robert Borden's conscription announcement touched off two days of rage and violence in Montreal that left one demonstrator dead and others injured. More than one hundred police officers had to be called in to disperse the crowd.

On January 1, 1918, the government began to enforce the Military Service Act. In March a new round of violent opposition erupted, this time in Quebec City. Over a period of days several thousand rioters ransacked the government conscription office, two pro-conscription newspapers, and other businesses. Almost eight hundred soldiers had to be deployed, some brought in from Ontario. Four people were killed and dozens injured. English and French Canada had not been so divided since Louis Riel was hanged in 1885.

The conscription crisis left scars that were felt for a generation or more. The Conservative Party, the leading force in the Union government that enacted conscription, was finished in Quebec and would be for a long time to come. Liberals who supported the Union government were similarly blighted, although those who stayed out of the coalition were not. Among the latter was Mackenzie King, whose decision to stay out of the coalition and stand with Wilfrid Laurier in opposing conscription saved his career.

While everyone hoped that the end of the First World War would bring permanent peace to Europe, that did not happen. By the early 1930s, with the arrival of Adolf Hitler in Germany, the turmoil began all over again. Sixty-six thousand young Canadians had died in the mud of France and still, fifteen years later, it appeared Europe had not had enough.

One of the most poignant events of the time, and a reminder of the fearful losses Canada had suffered, was the dedication of the Vimy Memorial in France in 1936. More than six thousand Canadian veterans and family members went to Vimy for the occasion. The pilgrimage included nostalgic reunions, but most of all it was a time for remembrance and reflection about the cost of war. A number of ships were chartered for the trans-Atlantic crossing. On just one of them were more than fifty mothers, each bearing a Silver Cross, marking the sacrifice of their husband or son. Journalist Gregory Clark, himself a decorated veteran, recounted how he was moved at the arrival of so many of these women in France who, to his astonishment, were asked to line up in four lines in a military-style formation. "Elderly mothers, women of sixty and seventy wearing berets on their head ... [were] marching in fours to the waiting trains on the quay. These, the mothers of the men who died twenty years ago, marching in fours. If I wept, I was not the only one."[5]

In their speeches, the honoured guests, including the new King Edward VIII, echoed the common phrase, "never again." The timing of the event was ironic. Only a few months before, Germany had sent troops into the previously demilitarized Rhineland territory, a direct violation of the 1919 Treaty of Versailles signed after the First World War. As *Maclean's* magazine put it, the dedication was taking place even at a time when Europe was "hovering on the brink of another mad orgy of slaughter."[6]

In these years Canadian public opinion was sharply divided on what to do about the growing crisis in Europe. Most English Canadians supported Britain and the Empire. If the worst happened, they wanted Canada to stand with Britain as it had done in 1914. Many Canadians were British born or had relatives in Britain and always thought of Canada as a British Dominion. There were many patriotic groups among them, including the Canadian Legion, the Imperial Order Daughters of the Empire, and the protestant Loyal Orange Order, with its emphatic allegiance to the Crown. The prime minister between 1930 and 1935, Richard Bedford Bennett, was a great champion of the Empire. Canadians continued to view the imperial connection with pride, determined that no shadow would ever be placed over the Union Jack.

Despite that, some Canadians were isolationists or pacifists. The isolationists did not oppose war as such; they just did not want to be dragged into yet another European squabble. Isolationism was also a powerful political force in the United States. The word "pacifists" may sound odd to our ear today; the equivalent now might be "anti-war activists." They may have been in the minority, but they were vocal and their feelings heartfelt. The Vimy dedication had been a reminder to them of the cost of war.

Disarmament was a big international issue. The Washington Naval Treaty of 1922 attempted to put limits on building new battleship fleets. A World Disarmament Conference in Geneva started in 1932 and provided a forum for major arms cutbacks; however, in the end the conference was crippled by Germany's withdrawal in 1933.

There were many organizations and individuals in Canada opposed to any new military involvement in Europe. Anti-war sentiment became so loud that one book on the period is titled *Decades of Discord*.[7] The

United Church, in particular, was very active. In late 1932 the Church Council declared that "armed warfare between nations was contrary to the spirit and teachings of Christ." Articles in the Church's magazine said that capitalism, the Versailles Treaty, and original sin were all threats to world peace. In Britain the 1937 Oxford Conference of Churches decried war as "a particular demonstration of the power of sin in the world."

There were numerous prominent church figures who spoke out, including J.S. Woodsworth, who later opposed the war declaration in Parliament in 1939. Woodsworth had studied at Oxford and become an ordained Methodist minister in 1896. He became well known in the Winnipeg General Strike in 1919 and was elected a member of Parliament in 1921. In January 1937 Parliament debated a motion from the left-wing Co-operative Commonwealth Federation (CCF) calling for Canadian neutrality in the event of any war, regardless of the belligerents.

The universities, although much more conservative than today, still contained pockets of isolationist and anti-war sentiment. A survey in the 1920s at the University of Alberta showed that as many as 20 percent of students would refuse war service of any kind. One of the most controversial Canadian commentators in the interwar period was Frank Underhill. His relentless criticism of the British Empire and British foreign policy put him at odds with the University of Toronto administration and almost cost him his job. In 1938 a University of Saskatchewan professor, Carlyle King, criticized both British imperialism and the policies of Prime Minister Chamberlain while calling for international disarmament. Professor King was attacked by newspaper editorialists, four separate branches of the Canadian Legion, the Sons of England Benefit Society, and the English Speaking League of Saskatchewan.

Outspoken critic Frank Scott of Montreal worried that Canadians might again become the "cannon fodder of imperialism." Participation in a new European war, he felt, would bring with it conscription which would tear the country apart. Among his most widely quoted comments about a possible new European war was that "elderly sadists of the last war are emerging from their obscurity to join the war dance again, their eyes glistening and their mouths watering as they think of the young men whom they will send to the slaughter."[8]

Father Charles Coughlin, the Canadian-born host of a U.S. radio show, became a household name in both the United States and Canada with his insistent demands for everyone to stay out of European troubles. It was the same with many newspaper writers and ordinary citizens. In one letter to the editor, N.T. Carey of Winnipeg asked, "Have Canadians no higher aspirations than to be a reservoir of men and supplies to be sacrificed in Britain's imperial wars?"[9]

Loudest of all against joining any war in Europe was French Canada. War and the threat of conscription would hang over every turn in European events and every hint at Canadian rearmament. The Roman Catholic Church, far and away the most powerful institution in Quebec, opposed rearmament and conscription. In Quebec Hitler was not necessarily admired, but Mussolini was a different matter. He had settled the Lateran Treaty in 1929, which finally solved the territorial disputes between Italy and the Vatican. But above all, the communists, not the fascists, were considered the greater threat. Many recalled that in the Spanish Civil War General Franco said he was making a stand against "Marxist savagery."[10] A Montreal commentator writing in the *Financial Post* in 1937 was outraged at the return to Canada of Dr. Norman Bethune, who had been working with communists in China.[11]

One of the most significant events in the interwar years in Quebec was the 1936 election of that bon viveur Maurice Duplessis. To the horror of Mackenzie King, Duplessis defeated a long-time Liberal provincial government, replacing it with his coalition of conservatives and nationalists. Perhaps the clearest demonstration that the communists were seen as the greater enemy in Quebec was the "Padlock Law" of 1937. It was intended to prevent the printing or distribution of communist propaganda. The law made it illegal to use any house or building to print or distribute any such written material. A violation of the act permitted the property to be closed — "padlocked" — for up to one year. Those responsible could be arrested. The law was vague, did not define communism or Bolshevism, and denied the presumption of innocence to those arrested. It was used both against left-wing groups and Duplessis's political opponents.

In short, it was clear that in this period Canadian opinion on any new European conflict was fractured. There were supporters of the Empire, and there were isolationists such as Frank Scott and pacifists such as J.S. Woodsworth. Isolationists and pacifists were not merely cranks on the political fringe; they were in the mainstream of political debate. French Canadian opinion was anti-communist and strenuously, one might even say explosively, isolationist.

On top of all this came the Great Depression, a catastrophe for so many countries, economically, politically, and socially. It served to underline Canada's isolationism. Everyone was focused on mere survival. With Canada's unemployment rate soaring to 20 percent and higher, keeping bread on the table was much more important than dealing with upheavals in faraway lands. With one family in five on welfare — at least such welfare as there was — how could a country afford new weapons or a bigger army? Every cent was needed for more urgent things.

The Great Depression also rattled Canada politically. On the left, the Co-operative Commonwealth Federation was founded in 1932 while a right-wing Social Credit government was elected in Alberta in 1935, even though it was completely new and did not have a party leader. Taking financial control away from the evil banks, which had been the ruin of so many farmers, was a big issue with Social Credit. For the first time, in the federal election on October 14, 1935, an array of new political parties entered the battle. They might bring with them a radical, near-revolutionary shift in politics. Certainly that had happened in Germany. In the Canadian election it seemed that there were as many parties as candidates. On the ballots were Liberals, Conservatives, CCF, Social Credit, Liberal Progressive, Reconstruction, United Farmers of Ontario, Communist, Labour, and a half-dozen more. The total number of candidates reached a staggering 894.

It might be surprising with this political smorgasbord spilling everywhere that one party, let alone a traditional one, would win a majority government, but the Liberals did. The party defeated the Conservative government of R.B. Bennett. Mackenzie King won 172 of 245 seats including fifty-five of sixty-five in Quebec. The Liberal leader ran on the slogan "King or Chaos." It has been said that since King won less than

"King or Chaos" — Mackenzie King fought the 1935 election amid the upheaval of the Great Depression. The Liberals claimed there would be "chaos" if voters chose R.B. Bennett's Conservatives or any one of several new and untried parties. King won a majority government.

50 percent of the popular vote, more people voted for chaos than for King. But the outcome was a clear victory for the political centre and a repudiation of revolutionary change, even though King was aided by a much-divided opposition and the first-past-the-post electoral system.

The election was critical for the years ahead in many ways. It is true that social welfare issues would not get the priority that the CCF or Labour might have wished, but at a time of growing crisis the prime minister who assumed office was committed, above all, to preserving national unity. The Liberal government had representation from both English and French Canada and from across the country — the only party that did. A Conservative government, for example, would have been without representation from French Canada, with potentially disastrous results.

Even as the new government took office there was a demonstration of how strong isolationist sentiment in Canada was at the League of Nations in Geneva. The League had been one of the shining hopes for peace after the First World War. For the first time in history it provided a way to resolve international disputes peacefully. However, the weaknesses of the organization quickly became apparent. For some years Germany and Russia were not allowed to join. U.S. president Woodrow Wilson had been a great promoter of the League, but the U.S. Senate refused to allow America to join.[12] So, to begin with, key players were not in the organization.

The decisive event came in 1935 when Benito Mussolini invaded Ethiopia in an attempt to reprise the glory days of European colonialism. The League imposed some half-hearted sanctions, Italy ignored them, and that was, effectively, the end of it as a credible institution. Mackenzie King's actions were unheroic to say the least. There was talk of sanctions, including an oil embargo, but in the end Canada mostly sat on its hands. The reason was that most Canadians would not support anything that might challenge Mussolini, which in turn might bring a war closer. This was perhaps the best example of the policy that King pursued immediately after his election in 1935: avoidance. Avoid all problems in the hope that they would solve themselves or just go away.

King's avoidance policy was also evident in the summer of 1937 when he was in London for George VI's coronation and, at the same time, an Imperial Conference. By this time Germany was rearming and had remilitarized the Rhineland while Adolf Hitler was musing aloud about uniting Austria with Germany. The British were counting on Canada and other dominions for help. The British wanted a commitment to Imperial defence and a commitment to join any war if Britain were attacked.

In brief, Canada's response was: no and no. There would be no commitments. King's defence minister, Ian Mackenzie, argued that the Canadian public would not support contributing to Empire defence. Neither would Canada allow any kind of limitation on its decision making on war and peace. There was no consensus at all in English Canada for that kind of decision, and French Canada was adamantly opposed. King would not be sandbagged by commitments on a purely hypothetical situation. No blank cheques. When the time comes, said King in a phrase he used over and over again in the months ahead, "Parliament will decide." Of course, he had control of Parliament, but it sounded good.

The British were infuriated by King's answers, but two things should be stressed. First, the Canadian leader did not say Canada would *not* participate in any coming war; he only said that when the time came, Parliament would decide. Second, King actually felt that when the time came, public opinion would likely support Canada standing with Britain, but that was something he could not say publicly. Privately, he told the new British prime minister, Neville Chamberlain, what he thought.

When King was in Britain at the suggestion of the British foreign office, he made a side trip to Berlin. On June 29 he met Hitler, hoping to nudge him toward peace. The interview was supposed to last thirty minutes but stretched to an hour and a half. King, usually a hard-nosed politician, was completely bamboozled by Hitler's flattery and left with the entirely erroneous view that Hitler presented no real danger. However, King did at least make clear that in the event of war the Commonwealth would join Britain's side.

VIP in Berlin — *In his student days, Mackenzie King lived for a time in Berlin. He returned in 1937 and was given VIP treatment, including escorted tours around the city. Later he met Adolf Hitler, who told King, "You need have no fear of war."*

With the conviction that Hitler was not a menace, and a policy of avoidance already in place in Ottawa, it is hardly a surprise that after the 1935 election King was a supporter of appeasement. He hoped that somehow there could be a deal between Hitler on the one hand, and France and Britain on the other. Appeasement, like the League of Nations, represented trying to resolve international disputes without killing another twenty-five million people. Appeasement offered the hope that international boundaries could be moved without a war. *Appeasement* is a dirty word today, and it destroyed Chamberlain, but the alternative was war. At the time most Britons and many Canadians supported it. It is clear in hindsight that King held on to appeasement far too long; the result was that serious rearmament in Canada began very late. It was only in the 1937 budget that Canada modestly increased its defence spending, although that increase did not take effect until 1938.

The next European upheaval came on March 12, 1938, with the German annexation of Austria. Without a shot fired, the German Reich dramatically expanded its borders while Hitler defied Britain and France. Then, in September 1938, came the worst moment of the pre-war period — the Munich Crisis. Hitler demanded the German-speaking areas of Czechoslovakia be incorporated into Greater Germany. Hysteria gripped Britain. Slit trenches were dug in English parks, gas masks were distributed, and the fleet was put on standby. A senior official at the British Foreign Office, Sir Robert Vansittart, kept suicide pills and burned his private papers. The tension was palpable even among Canadians. Historian C.P. Stacey recalled being in Toronto at the time and that "one actually sensed a fear of war in the air ... I have never had such another experience before or since."[13]

The immediate issue was the fate of German-speaking citizens in Czechoslovak border areas. The German government and local Nazi thugs organized strikes and protests demanding the area be annexed to Germany. That would have been a catastrophe for Czechoslovakia. Within the so-called Sudetenland lay all the vast Czech military fortifications. Removing the areas to German control would also sever Czechoslovakia's entire system of road, rail, and telephone and telegraph communications and eliminate 70 percent of its electrical power. The

Czech army was formidable, so substantially reducing it would bring a significant shift in the balance of power in Europe. For Hitler it would free up another fifteen or twenty divisions to face France.

In Ottawa, in the midst of the crisis, Prime Minister King sounded out his cabinet about what to do. He favoured sending a note to Chamberlain saying that if the British prime minister's efforts failed and war came, Canada would stand on Britain's side. King noted that there was general agreement among cabinet members, but Justice Minister Lapointe was in Europe at the time. When King sent a message to him asking for his opinion, the result exposed a clear cabinet rift. Lapointe's sharp reply insisted that the government must stick to the message of "Parliament will decide." No letter was sent.

Chamberlain made two unsuccessful trips to Germany in an effort to avoid war. Even after them, as he addressed the House of Commons to say how desperate the situation was, he received word that Hitler had agreed to a third meeting. Chamberlain's final session with the German Fuhrer in Munich on September 29 ended with a deal, even if a grim one — Czechoslovakia would be carved up. This was Hitler's final demand. Chamberlain returned to London for his triumphant "peace for our time" moment. There were delirious celebrations. For Mackenzie King the Munich deal came "like a reprieve to a condemned man."[14] King sent Chamberlain a telegram saying, "The heart of Canada is rejoicing." Immediate newspaper coverage both in Britain and Canada was positive, but that did not last long. Munich was soon called "peace by surrender."[15] Winston Churchill commented, "We have sustained a defeat without a war," and described Munich as "a disaster of the first magnitude."

This was the moment at which the *Winnipeg Free Press* published what remains, even today, probably the most famous newspaper editorial ever written in Canada. On September 30 J.W. Dafoe, editor of the paper, wrote "What's the Cheering For?" He said in part, "The doctrine that Germany can intervene for racial reasons for the 'protection' of Germans on such grounds as she thinks proper in any country in the world which she is in a position to coerce ... has now not only been asserted but made good; and it has been approved ... by the governments of Great Britain and France."[16]

The editorial was enormously controversial because of its criticism of Britain and France. However, it and similar comments were a contributing factor in pushing many Canadians toward the view that appeasement had failed.

If war had broken out in September 1938, apart from everything else, it would have been a political and military calamity for Canada. The state of the army, navy, and air force was dreadful, but attempts at rearmament had been greeted by outrage in Quebec. The cry was that you only need to rearm if you intend to go to war. One headline in *Le Devoir* asked, "WHY DOES CANADA NEED TO BUY WARPLANES?"[17] In a 1937 debate on defence estimates, sixteen French-Canadian backbenchers spoke out against increased military spending. An outbreak of war would have exposed jagged French–English divisions in the cabinet, in Parliament, and in the country. In this state, commented Desmond Morton, "It seemed inconceivable in 1938 that Canada would go to war at all."[18]

Munich marked a turning point for Britain, but, importantly, it was also a turning point for Mackenzie King personally. King biographer Blair Neatby described it as a "personal crisis" for him because he realized he could "avoid" no longer.[19] Avoidance had failed; appeasement had failed. Since war was likely, the issue for King became trying to shape a consensus among Canadians.

One indication of a rapid change in the prime minister's thinking was his determination that a way had to be found to begin rearmament. It had been "wholly inadequate and ineffective" in the past, he said, and simply must be done.[20] His solution was astute. He declared that the spending would be for home defence only, not for overseas adventures. And to underline that, most of the money was spent on the air force and the navy but almost none on the army. It would be clear that the government was not building up the army for overseas service. In December 1938 the cabinet decided to nearly double the military budget.

King now focused on finding a workable political formula for unity.[21] His approach might be described as "muddling through," dealing with smaller problems one at a time. The prime minister, as a member of heroism's second team, shuffled toward a solution. To start with, it would have to be something that he, himself, believed in. King was a complicated man. He was a nationalist but also the product of late Victorian times, and he was often a romantic about Canada's Imperial heritage. In this case, he strongly believed that it was in Canada's interest to stand with the Empire. It was the best policy for Canada. The prime minister's closest adviser, the nationalist Oscar Skelton, said, "We are the safest country in the world — as long as we mind our own business." King emphatically did not agree.[22] As the world edged closer to war, Skelton became much more outspoken in calling for Canada to stay out of the European mess. King more and more turned away from Skelton's advice. The prime minister emphasized that if Britain and France fell, Canada would not be left as some tranquil, untouched idyll. The shift in world power would be catastrophic for Europe but also for Canada. In any event Germany would make no distinction between Britain and Commonwealth countries in any war.

In January 1939 King thought the situation in Europe was getting more and more desperate by the moment. He wrote in his diary, "I fear a year of frightful uncertainty, month by month."[23]

He received a series of secret warnings from London that war could break out at any moment.* They turned out to be false alarms but still left everyone on edge. One of his first moves to galvanize public opinion was less than a success. In a speech to Parliament in mid-January, King ended up quoting Laurier's famous dictum, "If England is at war, we are at war and liable to attack," but, he said, it would be up to Parliament to decide the extent of participation. Lapointe hated the speech, and prime ministerial aide Jack Pickersgill thought it was appalling. King said he felt he must "prepare people for the worst" regardless of what his Quebec colleagues thought.[24]

King would have to have a united cabinet first if he was to have any hope of uniting Parliament and the country. One of the key events in his campaign was a testy cabinet meeting on January 27. He wanted cabinet to discuss the issue of a war declaration. What were the differences around the table? What would French-Canadian ministers accept and

---

* Between December 1938 and mid-April 1939 there were at least twenty warnings from British intelligence about possible German military action. One of the sources was a "German staff officer."

what would they not? Was there common ground? It began with the prime minister saying he was unhappy with the reaction to his speech. There had been general agreement in cabinet earlier that any aggressor would regard Canada as simply part of the British Empire, and it would be subject to attack.

Lapointe disagreed, saying the government should to stick to its "no commitments" policy until a crisis developed. Once the actual situation was clear and public sentiment had been measured, he said, then the cabinet could decide. In what must have been an unsettling development, the justice minister dropped heavy hints of resignation. Some French-Canadian ministers, he said, might have to consider if they could do a better job outside cabinet than in. King replied that the greatest service anyone could do would be to keep the cabinet together. Anything else would bring about a situation similar to 1917 with a new version of the Unionist or "National" Government. King recalled, "I then pointed out ... that a break in the cabinet would mean an inevitable demand for National Government. That National Government would lead to anything, conscription and all the rest. That if they wished to avoid a situation of that kind, it would be for all of us to stay together."[25]

Debate continued for two rancorous hours, but in the end the discussion cleared the air. There was no final agreement, but there was the shape of a consensus, which one writer described as a "watershed."[26] The formula that broke the deadlock was not made public at that point, but it was summed up later by the phrase "no neutrality, no conscription." This was the crucial blue print, but as important as it was, not everything was solved. Lapointe knew that one way or another English Canada was going to demand that the country go to war if Britain were attacked, but after the meeting he said the decision might only be acceptable if the government declared that no expeditionary forces would be sent overseas. That way it would be clear there would be no conscription. In any event, he had still not made a final decision about what to do.

On March 14 and 15 Hitler sent troops into Prague and the rest of Czechoslovakia, tearing up the Munich agreement in the process. For the first time, he offered no claim that his actions were meant to unify Germans or German territory. In fact, there was no justification offered at all. If there had been any doubts before about Hitler's intentions — and there had not been many — now there were none. The move led Chamberlain to deliver a speech in Birmingham that has since been called the greatest foreign policy reversal in modern British history. Even for him the time for appeasement was over. He said that from that point on any attack on Poland, Romania, Greece, Turkey, or other countries would be tantamount to war.

Opposition in Britain to German actions had been building for some time, but at this point public opinion changed dramatically. Churchill said, "a veritable revolution in feeling and opinion has occurred in Britain and reverberates through the self-governing Dominions."[27] There had been the Rhineland, the Austria grab, the Sudetenland, not to mention Kristallnacht and the German and Italian intervention in Spain. Finally, the attack on what was left of Czechoslovakia brought it all to a boil.

Canadians had been waiting until they were forced to make a choice about what to do. It looked like the time had come. There were no polls in Canada at the time, but it is clear that events were shifting public opinion. Although the fervent isolationism of French Canada was unchanged, and opinion among a great number of non-English residents was little changed, the attitude among English Canadians was dramatically changed. The protestant churches sharply altered their views as the moral issues became more and more obvious. They could see that Hitler had smashed democracy, attacked the Christian church and demonized Jews. As political alternatives, pacifism and isolationism were becoming less and less realistic.

Typical of younger Canadians whose views were evolving was Hampton Gray from Nelson, British Columbia. He had enrolled at the University of Alberta in 1936 and later attended the University of British Columbia.[28] Gray had been a supporter of the Student Peace Movement, but as the political situation in Europe worsened, he had second thoughts. After the war broke out he enlisted in the Royal Canadian Navy and later became a fighter pilot on an aircraft carrier in the Pacific. He died in August 1945 after an attack on Japanese destroyer and was awarded the Victoria Cross for heroism.

Hopes Shattered — Hampton Gray, VC, was typical of many idealistic young Canadians in 1939. He had originally been a peace activist, but once the war began, his ideas changed completely and he enlisted in the Royal Canadian Navy Volunteer Reserve. He was awarded the Victoria Cross posthumously in 1945.

With the cabinet edging toward a consensus, King again turned his attention to the country. He addressed Parliament on March 20, saying it was necessary to make clear Canada's determination "to stand with other democracies in opposing aggression and attempt at domination of the world by force." He said, "If there were a prospect of an aggressor launching an attack on Britain, with bombers raining death on London, I have no doubt what the decision of the Canadian people and Parliament would be. We would regard it as an act of aggression, menacing freedom in all parts of the British Commonwealth."

King said he was willing to sacrifice nearly everything for peace, but not liberty.[29]

On March 30, with the House of Commons packed and the galleries overflowing, there was a seismic moment. This day and the next marked the climax, the turning point of King's campaign. Biographer Bruce Hutchison said, "Parliament beheld that day a little man, pale, wracked and uncertain, no hero when the times cried out for heroism," but, despite it all, he rose to the occasion.[30] The prime minister spoke for two hours, beginning with an outline of what a new conflict would bring. It might be even more devastating than the horrors of the First World War. He defended Munich, saying emphatically that Neville Chamberlain had made the right choice, because if he had not made that third trip to Germany and war had broken out, people would have always said that an opportunity to avoid the dreadful carnage had been missed. King said that war could break out at any moment and that English Canadians should be assured that, if it did, Canada would stand beside Britain. Then came the definitive and decisive statement. He said that French Canada would have a guarantee of no conscription. "The present government believes that conscription of men for overseas service would not be an effective or a necessary step. Let me say that so long as this government may be in power, no such measure will be enacted." King could make the statement with the additional assurance that Conservative leader Robert Manion had announced earlier that he would also oppose conscription.

The following day it was Lapointe's turn. At this moment it became clear that Lapointe's stand had changed since the cabinet meeting of January 27. The justice minister began by giving no quarter to isolationists, saying that standing apart from any conflict could not be done without a civil war in Canada. "The ostrich policy of refusing to face dangers will not keep them away. Indeed, a deliberate policy of drift may involve a greater risk." But, any declaration of war came with a clear understanding that he would never support conscription. He appealed to all members of Parliament to hear French Canada. His speech and the one given in September, together, marked the highlight of Lapointe's career.

When it was over, some English-language papers thought King had still not gone far enough although Lapointe's speech was better received. The *Globe and Mail* said the leader of French Canada "placed Canada side by side with Britain" in comments that were "more British than anything Prime Minister Mackenzie King has said on Canadian foreign policy."[31] King thought the two speeches had, side by side, brought a powerful message. "I feel that between us, we have built a substantial structure for Canadian unity." To go further would only have antagonized one side or the other. "Together, our speeches constitute a sort of trestle sustaining the structure which would serve to unite divergent parts of Canada, thereby making for a united country."[32]

Author Gordon Case said the two speeches represented "the pinnacle" of King's efforts.[33] His words settled the issue for most people. The whole subject was not raised in Parliament again until the outbreak of war. There was no reason that it should have because there was little opposition to what King and Lapointe had said. It was clear that this decisive action matched the temper of the Canadian people.

Of course King's "no conscription" commitment lit a long fuse that later exploded in his face (Decision Nine). The formula did not settle the conscription issue for the entire war even though it was an effective short-term solution. Did King regret making the bargain? Bruce Hutchison said he never regretted it. "Without it, he believed until his dying day, he could never have led the nation into war, except as two weak and quarreling fragments."[34]

For King a fortunate turn of events was the Royal Tour of May and June 1939, the first ever by a reigning monarch. The prime minister had invited the royal couple to Canada in 1937, but he had no idea they would arrive on the eve of war. The young king and his sparkling consort were welcomed everywhere they went. The visit served to reinforce and celebrate the British connection in a way nothing else could. Even in French Canada the two were acclaimed. *La Presse* shouted, "Québec Vit Des Heures Historiques."

One of the most remarkable events came on June 3 in Melville, Saskatchewan, a town of perhaps four thousand people. The king and queen were supposed to stop for ten minutes in the late evening. They appeared, but ten minutes stretched into half an hour and still the crowd would not move. Some estimates said as many as sixty thousand people came from all points of the compass to pack themselves — somehow — into every corner of the town. Two chartered trains carried three thousand people from Kamsack and Yorktown to Melville.

There were almost a million people at events in Vancouver, while Mackenzie King said that, without question, Victoria was "a crowning gem." The throngs in Canada, and later others in the United States, especially enjoyed Queen Elizabeth and her beaming personality. The British magazine *Sphere* said the Queen's smile had "charmed a continent."

When the war finally did come with the German invasion of Poland on September 1, the reaction in Quebec was muted. Chubby Power was surprised, saying Quebec opinion was "much less antagonistic" than he thought it would be. Even Cardinal Jean-Marie-Rodrigue Villeneuve, an outspoken nationalist and ultra conservative, said Quebeckers could not limit their horizon to this continent.

A recurring question is why Canada went to war at all in 1939. The United States did not. In what is perhaps the most widely quoted comment ever made about the question, J.L. Granatstein said Canada went to war "because Britain went to war. Not for Democracy, not to stop Hitler. Not to save Poland."[35] Canada in 1939 was still a British colony, emotionally. Today, many Canadians may have warm feelings for the Commonwealth and for Queen, but it is not a part of our national DNA in the way it was on the brink of the Second World War.

In some ways Mackenzie King's policies before the Second World War were shameful, but what he achieved in the end was monumental. A few years before the war J.W. Dafoe of the *Free Press* had predicted that any new conflict would bring with it "profound disunion and national disintegration."[36] He was wrong. On September 12, 1939, King told his caucus that the country had been brought into the conflict "with quietude and peace … that we had kept down all passion and faction, and now were a united country in the greatest effort that a nation could put forward."[37] He was right.

DECISION TWO

The Unloved Corvette

When the corvette *Hepatica* sailed into port in Scotland in January 1941 there may well have been tittering and pointing from those on shore. The ship's main gun had a noticeable droop at the end of the barrel. Anyone who saw it, even the Royal Canadian Navy crewmen on board, might have thought of anatomical comparisons. Some might have wondered how such a gun could have been fired. The answer was — it couldn't. It was not a real gun at all but a wooden dummy. *Hepatica* crew members had gathered some bits and pieces of wood, strapped them together and wrapped them in canvas. Crew member Ernie Adams thought the result was convincing and that it would "hopefully frighten the enemy to death."[1]

Hepatica had left Halifax on December 18, 1940, on a frozen, nightmarish Atlantic crossing, armed with only a half-dozen depth charges, a few rifles, and, of course, the frightening fake gun. But that was not all. Another anxiety was that, except for the captain, almost all the crew were on their first trip. Said Manitoba native Lionel Kennedy, "The rest of us had never seen anything bigger than York Lake or the Assiniboine River."[2]

In all, six corvettes sailed for Britain in late 1940 with guns made from wooden packing crates, flagpoles, or whatever else came to hand. Most of them had novice crews just like those with a death grip on the railings aboard *Hepatica*. It is a wonder that these ships could be dispatched across the Atlantic, dodging a screen of U-boats, in this situation.

The reason for the fake guns was simple: there were none for new ships like *Hepatica* anywhere in Canada. The basic corvettes had been built in Canadian yards, but there were no guns and no equipment to outfit them. Most everything had to be added in Britain. As for the novice crew, that was the way it was and would be for the next two years, when most corvettes were commissioned.

But beyond the gun and the novice crew, what about the ship itself, the corvette? How did a ship that was barely big enough, that was not really a warship at all, and that was largely unwanted by the brass hats in Ottawa — how did it end up in the thick of the Battle of the Atlantic? How did it, in time, move past the perils and defeats of the war at sea and become a symbol of the ultimate victory in the Battle? How did it become the *legendary* corvette? To explain how that happened, it is necessary to go back to the beginning of the war and earlier to look at the broader picture and the problems the Royal Canadian Navy faced.

When the war began, the Royal Canadian Navy began escorting convoys from Halifax to Britain although they only had enough ships to escort each for a day or two before the escorts had to turn back for home. The convoys went most of the way to Britain unescorted, until just off the Irish coast. While saying the navy had six destroyers and four small coal-powered minesweepers gives an idea of the problems the RCN faced at the beginning of the war, it still does not capture the real breadth of the navy's crisis. Here is a small example of the deeper problem: In 1936 several hundred young men applied to be officer candidates in the RCN, but only eight were selected. The next year the number was six. In the entire navy, in two years there were only fourteen new officers.

It was nearly impossible for the navy to expand quickly when the war began. The destroyers aside, in almost every other respect the navy had no ability to expand its numbers, bases, or infrastructure. With the outbreak of war, the navy desperately needed new sailors. There were thousands of volunteers, but they had to be turned away. The RCN first had to train the trainers for all those recruits, and before that it had to build the buildings to put the trainers in, and before even that, it had to buy the property to put the buildings on. The Royal Canadian Navy had none of these. In April 1940 fewer than half the 1,394 naval personnel in Halifax could be housed in navy buildings. The RCN had to take over glorified cattle barns on the Nova Scotia Exhibition grounds for use as barracks. In short, according to Tony German, a wartime navy commander and later historian, "The RCN lacked the essential base for a self-sufficient navy."[3]

This desperate situation continued long after the war began. Lieutenant Owen Robertson recounted that as late as 1941 he was standing on a dock when Captain G.C. "Jetty" Jones drove by and, seeing Robertson, whom he knew, ordered him to report to his — Jones's — office.

Robertson reported, "I went to his office in fear and trembling, because old Jetty had quite a temper, and I figured I'd done something wrong again. When he heard what I was doing, he said, 'Forget that. Go and start a Naval College.' I asked "Where, sir?" He yelled at me, 'If I knew where, I'd do it myself.' I asked, 'For how many, sir?' He yelled at me, 'If I knew that, I'd do it myself!' So I went off to start a Naval College."[4]

There were other glaring weaknesses. Contrary to expectations it was the U-boat that became the centre of the most stupendous sea battle in history (or, more accurately, the most stupendous "maritime campaign in history"). Ralph Hennessy, at this time a junior officer but after the war a vice-admiral, said both the Royal Navy and the Royal Canadian Navy were "basically prepared for the wrong war."[5]

There were just two anti-submarine officers in the RCN because everyone knew that an anti-submarine specialist was headed for a career dead end. The gunnery officers were the ones with the gold braid. One of the two anti-submarine experts was Lieutenant-Commander Arthur Pressey, whose specialty was so obscure that because his personnel file noted "A/S," it was assumed that he was trained in "Airships." Earlier in his career he had been mistakenly sent to Montreal to help land an airship after its trans-Atlantic crossing. There were no Canadian submarines for training, and in exercises with the Royal Navy the few submarines available were stood down after dark. Neither had the Royal Navy given much thought to anti-submarine aircraft, which turned out to be a crucial weapon against the U-boats.

In the first months of the war Britain and Canada were fortunate because, remarkably, Hitler's Kriegsmarine was almost as unprepared as the Allies for a U-boat war. When the war broke out, Germany only had twenty-two ocean-going submarines and they had to reach the Atlantic by a circuitous route around Scotland. On the first day of the war there was a U-boat attack on the passenger ship *Athenia*. The liner was carrying 1,100 people, mostly Americans and Canadians, when it was torpedoed and sunk by U-30 off the Irish coast. It was a mistake. Hitler had ordered German submarines *not* to attack liners, but U-30's captain thought, in the failing evening light, that the ship was an armed merchant cruiser, not a passenger liner.

The Germans had chronic problems with their torpedoes, a significant number of which failed to explode on contact. In September 1939, a torpedo failure in an attack by U-39 very likely saved the aircraft carrier *Ark Royal*. The next month U-56 had three torpedo hits on the battleship *Nelson*, none of which exploded. Meantime, the German building program provided only two or three new boats a month. The Germans did have one enormous asset, however, in their U-boat commander, Admiral Karl Donitz, once described as "one of the most able, daring and versatile flag officers on either side in the entire war."[6]

To its credit, the RN did make a couple of important preparations in the face of the submarine threat — its plan for merchant ship convoys and establishing a submarine tracking room. Intercepting radio transmissions from German submarines for the tracking room gave the Royal Navy at least some idea of their location.

To go back a bit, the Royal Canadian Navy, in building up its small flotilla before the war, had wanted, first and foremost, destroyers because they were the only blue-water warships a small navy like the RCN could operate. The argument about having destroyers was that only they, acting as a group and using torpedoes, could take on a surface raider. But, of course, pride had something to do with it. Being the captain of a destroyer was a mark of a real sailor, especially when Canadians were rubbing shoulders with the British navy.

Before the war, when it finally did decide on a measure of rearmament, the government had supported the RCN's push for more destroyers because they fit in with Mackenzie King's own priority, home defence. Destroyers would defend Canadian ports, Canadian coasts, and Canadian merchant ships. Of course, this was simply a fig leaf because if a destroyer could defend Canadian ports, coasts, and shipping, it could also be used on the other side of the Atlantic to defend British ports, coasts, and shipping, or French ports. Prime Minister King just ignored that, saying that if war should come, "a large navy would keep Canada out of trouble."[7]

As for small coastal ships — the navy tried in every way to avoid them. The worst nightmare of Rear-Admiral Percy Nelles, the diminutive chief of the naval staff and a fervent anglophile, was that the RCN would be turned into a two-bit fisheries patrol navy. So Nelles pined for destroyers. But he didn't want just any old destroyers; he wanted the latest in gleaming shipcraft, the Tribal-class destroyer. The Tribals, all teeth and speed, were described at the time as being so large they were halfway to being cruisers. They were sometimes called "pocket cruisers," a play on the German "pocket battleship." The Tribals were about 1,800 tons, could make an incredible thirty-six knots, and were armed with eight 4.7-inch guns and torpedoes. They were impressive ships. In his budget proposals of January 1939, Admiral Nelles did want some smaller ships, but most of all he put on a big push for Tribals. He hoped to have twelve new destroyers within a year or two, and as many of them as possible would be Tribals.

Apart from all the other navy problems — too few men, no trainers, no bases, and all the rest — there were daunting handicaps when it came to expanding the fleet, the most conspicuous being that Canada had almost no shipbuilding industry in 1939. The only navy ships the industry had built were the four minesweepers. (The destroyers were British built.) The Great Depression had wiped out most Canadian shipyards, which had never been impressive in any event. Davie Shipbuilding of Lauzon, Quebec, for example, was in dire circumstances. Founded in 1887, Davie commissioned three vessels in 1938, a small ferry, a mixed passenger/cargo ship, and the RCMP patrol boat *French*, but before that there was only one ship commissioned in 1934 and none in 1935, 1936, or 1937. Collingwood Shipyard on the Great Lakes built a naval minesweeper in 1938, along with a small cargo ship, but those were the only significant orders it had received since 1932. Nelles wanted Tribals, but getting Tribals built in Canada was impossible.[8]

On top of all this, there was yet one more problem. No Canadian shipyard could build a Tribal, but at this point in the war British shipyards were jammed with Royal Navy orders. The RN had been on a huge rebuilding program since 1936, and every one of the major British yards was booked up for years. The only way the RCN was going to get a new Tribal was to go begging to the Royal Navy. As historian Marc Milner has said, "Not being able to pull a fleet from a hat when you needed it was clearly one of the perils" of a country that had ignored its armed forces for two decades.[9]

It might be thought that the RCN could have bought ships in the United States, but that was not a realistic option. The RCN had never used American ships and, anyway, they would have been far too expensive.* Once the shooting started, neutrality laws forbade the U.S. from supplying warships to combatants. It was only later, when the Battle of the Atlantic reached a crisis, that the British and Canadians held their noses and took on fifty aged United States destroyers.

Despite its loathing of small ships, the navy knew it would ultimately have to have some ships for inshore coastal patrol, minesweeping, and harbour protection. And there was, indeed, a plan for them — although not a very good one. The idea was to take up about forty or more civilian craft — luxury yachts, ex-government fisheries ships, and whatever else came to hand — and put a gun or two on them. When the war started, the plan was put into effect and the result was a bizarre little fleet. There was HMCS *Ambler*, a 273-ton vessel with a top speed of nine knots, armed with three machine guns. There were *Cariboo* and *Husky*, both private yachts armed with one small gun each while *Acadia* and *Cartier* were two hydrographic survey ships that dated back to the Edwardian era. There were no spare parts for any of them, most were usually found tied up to a dock, and one, HMCS *Bras d'Or*, simply disappeared at sea without a trace.

In any event, the Royal Navy agreed to add one more used-but-usable destroyer to the Canadian flotilla, but that would be all. The RCN knew its plan to use auxiliary yachts was a temporary fix at best, that there had to be a better long-term solution, and that it would have to obtain a large

---

* The British suggested that Canada get shipbuilding assistance from the United States, which was a good idea but was never taken up.

Weathered Veteran — *The corvette HMCS* Battleford, *built at Collingwood, Ontario, was commissioned in 1941 and was part of the force that destroyed U-356 in December 1943.* Battleford *served in the Battle of the Atlantic until the end of the war.*

number of coastal patrol ships for escort and minesweeping. The ship the navy wanted was the eight-hundred-ton Halcyon-class minesweeper, which was, despite its small size, a real navy ship. But there was no chance that any Canadian shipyard could build any in time or in any numbers. Even the Halcyons were too much for Canadian shipyards. And it might be added that it is extraordinary that the Royal Canadian Navy seems not to have known that before the war and made plans accordingly.

There was really only one solution, and it was an ugly one for the navy brass. It had to get a small ship built to commercial rather than naval standards. Forget the special steel, the watertight compartments, and the redundant electrical systems that any warship has as a matter of course. In its extremity, the RCN would have to take something for the here and now. Maybe a scrappy patrol vessel, pretty small, with a gun or two on it. Pile on some depth charges or minesweeping gear. Never mind speed, and as for the engine, the simpler the better. Cheap is good. Don't make it good; make it Tuesday.

The above is, of course, a rough description of the corvette.

The beauty of the corvette was that, however un-navy-like it might be, it could be built quickly by almost any company that could bend metal and was accessible to either coast. Fortunately, the Admiralty in London had been mulling over the same problem that the Royal Canadian Navy faced. It had been sifting around, looking at various possibilities for a small patrol vessel. It settled on a vessel first designed in 1895, the most recent incarnation of which was the whaling ship *Southern Pride*. The RN decided to start with it, calling it blandly, the "patrol vessel whaler type."

Members of Canada's National Research Council happened to be in Britain in the late summer of 1939. They heard about the whaling ship, got hold of a set of plans, and brought them back to Ottawa. At first the RCN regarded them as a superstitious sailor might view bananas — a bad omen. However, at Naval Service Headquarters in Ottawa, Captain Leonard Murray, the head of operations and training, began to promote the corvette. In a comment years later, he said his campaign to build the ship received an unexpected boost with the sinking of the liner *Athenia*. The sinking resulted in sensational front-page newspaper coverage. Murray was able to point out to the government that the sinking showed that patrol ships were urgently needed.[10] The blueprints had arrived in Ottawa at precisely the right moment.

In the end, the corvette was "ruefully adopted."[11] While the corvette was a ship Admiral Nelles really did not want, he was ultimately convinced that at least it could be a stepping stone toward a deep-sea fleet. The corvette could be used for now and discarded at the end of the war. So, in this rather miraculous way, the navy was able to submit its first shipbuilding and fleet-expansion program to the government on September 18, only eight days after the declaration of war. The navy wanted destroyers to deal with surface raiders and a small ship for coastal patrol and escort. The government approved the proposals. Captain Murray later recalled that the navy was given carte blanche for its expansion plans over the next three to five years, especially because building the smaller ships would stimulate the shipbuilding industry and create jobs.[12] This new expansion program marked a turning point for the corvette. The government still had to decide the size and scope of the program, but preliminary work could begin.

The corvette was something of a gamble. When the war started only one of them had actually been built in Britain and no one knew if it would be up to the job, but it was not long before the Royal Navy was convinced. The ship took on a new name to become the "Flower-class corvette." One story suggests that Winston Churchill thought naming the ships after flowers would be a huge joke on the Germans. Imagine a menacing submarine being sunk by a ship named HMS *Buttercup*.

In one of his more inspired moments, Admiral Nelles decided to have the RCN corvettes named not for flowers but for small Canadian cities and towns. Nelles observed that women in dozens of communities across the country knitted mittens. And so, in time many Canadian ships would receive all kinds of assistance from the communities their ships were named after, including lots of mittens.

As it was designed, the corvette was barely adequate even as a coastal patrol or minesweeping ship. It was 205 feet long, thirty-three feet at the beam, and it displaced about 950 tons. It had a top speed of sixteen knots, which, some joked, was reached only going downhill with a following wind. It had a range of about 3,500 miles at twelve knots. The original establishment was four officers and forty-eight men; although, much later in the war as many as one hundred officers and sailors impossibly squeezed themselves into every conceivable cranny of the ship.

The corvette was divided in three: the forward section housed crew quarters, a mess deck, and modest officer quarters; midships held the boilers and machinery; and the stern included the engine room, another small mess deck, and some storage. It was powered by a steam reciprocating engine of antique design that anyone who had ever worked in a railway shop could handle. A four-cylinder, triple-expansion engine produced 2,750 horsepower and turned just one screw. The engine was so robust that one corvette, HMCS *Sackville*, ran with the same set-up for forty years.

There were glaring weaknesses. First, and most perilous for the crew, there were virtually no watertight compartments. When it came to sinking a corvette, one torpedo would usually do. In 1944 HMCS *Alberni* was torpedoed by U-480, and within twenty seconds only the bow remained above the surface. One can hardly imagine working in a corvette's engine room knowing that if a torpedo struck, there was almost no hope.

The corvette was always wet, and the sailors aboard it stayed wet until it reached port, which could be anything up to three weeks. The short forecastle — the raised deck at the bow, forward of the bridge — allowed almost any wave to slosh over it. "It was a diabolical arrangement if ever there was one," said J.E. Schumacher of HMCS *Amherst*. "Nothing could have been conceived to have made a seaman's life more miserable."[13] A sailor had to put up with near intolerable conditions. "[Water] permeated his clothes, his food, his possessions and even his sleep.... The main deck was wet even on calm days."[14]

Although the ship could survive Atlantic gales climbing one mighty wave after another, it bobbed up and down like a cork and became infamous for rolling in any kind of sea. The motion, sometimes compared to that of a runaway elevator, left the crew weak-kneed and retching. Howard Cousins of *Algoma* said, "A corvette on the crest of a wave could have one-third of the forward portion clear of the water. As the ship rolled and roped down into the trough, it was almost a free fall. The poor blokes in the forecastle felt virtually weightless; anything on the lockers, shelves and tables, including your meal, frequently floated off. When the ship smashed into the back of the next wave, it felt as if the ship had been dropped on concrete."[15]

The corvette bridge was too small. Temporary bridge wings had to be added almost immediately. Another crippling problem was a lack of a gyrocompass. Along with many pieces of equipment, gyrocompasses were in short supply, so instead, the first corvettes were equipped with old-time magnetic compasses — adequate for catching whales, but hardly useful in modern war. The compass needle swayed with every movement of the ship, and using it in any battle against U-boats meant that the bearings for most depth-charge attacks were just educated guesses. The magnetic compass used a different power system so that, later on, it made the Canadian corvettes difficult to modify when new sonar systems came into use.[16] By contrast, the British corvettes did have gyrocompasses, electronically controlled and stabilized, and connected to repeaters throughout the ship. No matter how much the ship pitched and yawed, it gave true readings. Another weakness was that early plans for Canadian corvettes did not include any kind of radar.

The Mark IX four-inch main gun, besides being unavailable early on in Canada, was pretty much useless for actually hitting anything. The First World War–era gun was itself accurate enough, but there was no fire-control system and the principal method of gunnery was guesswork. The gun did turn out to be useful because firing it generally caused any U-boat to dive, giving the corvette an opportunity to track the submarine and start firing depth charges. On the after-deck, in what was usually called the "band box," the corvette could also carry a high-angle forty-millimetre anti-aircraft gun. This weapon had limited use. For one thing, it required fifty-one revolutions of the traversing hand wheel to turn a complete circle. While some might have suggested that the most important weapon aboard the corvette was the ship's bow, used to ram U-boats — and that did actually happen — in reality the depth charges were the most important threat to U-boats. Initially, a corvette carried about forty of them, but later on there were as many as one hundred. Each was packed with about four hundred pounds of explosives.

One of the principal tools of British and Canadian warships to track U-boats was "asdic," or as it became known later, sonar. It sent a "ping" sound wave out from the ship and, if it hit a U-boat, another "ping" would come back. While early versions could be effective in the hands of an experienced operator, the system could be fooled by differing water temperatures, so many depth-charge attacks targeted whales, icebergs, shipwrecks, or nothing at all. Sonar could track submerged submarines, but most U-boat attacks were conducted not when the submarine was submerged but rather on the surface at night.

In any event, some officers did not have the faintest clue about sonar and were not well trained in its use. While corvette officers may have struggled with it, officers in destroyers tended to be even worse. Robert Welland, one of the leading anti-sub specialists in the RCN, said Canadian destroyers would have been much more effective in the North Atlantic if the commanding officers had understood sonar better. "Captains of ships didn't understand what the instrument was capable of doing and didn't know how to use the damn thing. So a lot of gung-ho guys in destroyers felt the world revolved around guns and torpedoes, when actually the most important thing on board was the asdic [sonar]. None of them had ever been trained on it — none."[17]

Among other corvette drawbacks were the messing arrangements, which required sailors to deliver food across the open deck and a long way from the galley. Then there were the toilets. "The final indignity of the first corvettes was the straight pipe that ran from the ships' heads to the sea. "Timing," said one sailor, "was everything."[18]

The corvette had one unexpected and often overlooked asset. It had the tightest turning circle of all Allied warships, most importantly, tighter than that of a submerged U-boat. In any submarine confrontation, the corvette was the manoeuvring master.

Good and bad — add everything together and the 1895 model whale catcher–cum–corvette became a man o' war. It would be adequate for short jaunts up and down the coast, poking around harbours, and a bit of minesweeping before returning to home port after a week. In the beginning no one ever, in the remotest way, imagined the Canadian corvette as a mid-Atlantic convoy escort ship.

It was only on December 9, 1939, that the naval staff was able to complete the specifications of the corvette so that, if the plan gained cabinet approval, it could be put out to tender.[19] Rear-Admiral Nelles dreamed up a scheme to have at least twenty extra ships built so that they could be traded to the Royal Navy in exchange for British-built Tribals. Then, for reasons that are not clear, there was a cabinet delay of several weeks. One factor may have been the mounting cost of the conflict. At this point Canada was fighting a "limited liability" war. It was not yet a world war and the King government wanted to limit the stupendous cost. The air force had had to scale back its expansion plans after howls of outrage from the finance minister. How could Canada, with its limited financial resources, afford all this without going bankrupt? In time, the staggering money problems were solved with a variety of measures including income taxes and the sale of millions of dollars in government bonds, but at this point in the war, the mounting costs were unprecedented and unimaginable.

Finally, on January 29, 1940, an exasperated Prime Minister King lectured his foot-dragging ministers, saying it was time for a decision. He noted in his diary,

> We might find ourselves where our coasts might be attacked on the Atlantic, and I thought quite possibly before the year was out, on the Pacific, and our own position such that we could not get munitions from Britain ... the last thing the people would forgive would be any shortage at a time of need. I have also stressed the necessity of shipbuilding time and again, but have met with opposition on that score. That we cannot do more, etc. While I have been the one that has been pressing these matters strongly and unable to make headway because of the argument and colleagues. I am the one whom our opponents are blaming as holding my colleague back and responsible for not having done more.[20]

On February 7, 1940, came one of the best and most far-reaching Canadian decisions of the war. Captain Murray and the deputy minister of national defence met with the finance committee of cabinet. By this time the navy had realized that it would need a much bigger fleet than it originally thought, so the program to build corvettes became a huge undertaking. Then, with Admiral Nelles's plan to swap ships for Tribals, it became even larger. Would the government agree to such an expansion? Could Canada afford it? The committee went through everything in what Murray called a "fine-tooth comb" examination.[21] The committee and then the full cabinet gave approval for contracts valued at $49,250,000, the largest naval program in Canadian history. The decision called for building an astonishing sixty-four corvettes and twenty-four smaller Bangor minesweepers. Forty corvettes would be for Canadian service, with the rest, and about half the Bangors, headed to Britain.*

The contracts went to builders on the Great Lakes, in British Columbia, and on the upper St. Lawrence, while East Coast yards were mostly considered too busy with ship repair work. Davie Shipbuilding

---

* Strictly speaking, the first order was for fifty-four corvettes, but ten more were added before the end of the month. Another six corvettes and ten Bangors were ordered in August.

got the biggest order — ten corvettes. Others winning large orders included Canadian Vickers, Montreal (8); Collingwood Shipbuilding, Ontario (8); Marine Industries Limited, Sorel, Quebec (7); Port Arthur Shipbuilding, Ontario (7); and Burrard, Vancouver (4).

Politics likely played a role in some of the decisions. Marine Industries, owned by one of the wealthiest and most powerful clans in Quebec, the Simards, did well. Only a few years earlier, members of the family were at the top of the Liberal patronage lists, and the Simards were later awarded one of Canada's largest and most profitable federal armament contracts.

There were nowhere near enough trained shipbuilders, so hundreds of workers had to be hired off the street and trained from scratch. As a result the building program soon fell behind schedule. Here again Canada paid a price — having even a limited number of shipyard workers trained before the war would have meant big dividends. On average it ended up taking about ten months to complete a corvette. When it is recalled that later in the war a Canadian-built Park ship, similar to the U.S. *Liberty* ship, was built in thirty-eight days, it is clear how primitive and desperate the shipbuilding situation was early in the war.[22]

With the Bangor minesweeper contracts, the government tried to encourage start-up companies, including Dufferin Shipbuilding of Toronto, which laid its first keel in the summer of 1940. Unfortunately, three weeks earlier the RCMP had arrested the company owner, James Franceschini, who was among six hundred Italian Canadians interned as possible security risks.[23] Franceschini was born in Italy in 1890, came to Canada in 1904, married an English-Canadian woman, and became a British subject in 1916. According to writer James Pritchard, he became "a victim of war hysteria." Although Franceschini was released before long, the government took control of his company and never offered compensation, ruining the former owner in the process.

The shipbuilders' work was nicely underway when suddenly the German blitzkrieg of May 1940 was unleashed. Within weeks of the Germans overrunning France, it was able to reposition U-boats in French ports, including Brest, Lorient, and Saint-Nazaire, giving them much easier access to the mid-Atlantic. The first U-boat left Lorient on

August 7, 1940, after which the sinking of convoy ships increased dramatically until, later on, they were sinking faster than the British could turn them out — a truly frightening turn of events. The English Channel was unsafe because of U-boat and air attack. Also in August came the first of the "wolf pack" operations. By this time the German U-boat–building program was also in full operation, such that Admiral Donitz expected to have 250 boats by the end of 1940.

The British responded by extending their escort fleet farther and farther out into the mid-Atlantic. And here was the big change for the corvette. In this desperate emergency the British began using the corvette not only as coastal escort but also as deep-sea convoy escort. This marked the most significant development in the operational history of the corvette. Its role would be completely changed from this point in the war. Despite the British extension and the use of corvettes, the Germans simply moved further out to the middle of the Atlantic where there was no air cover and, at this time, no convoy escort either.

By late 1940 the submarine menace had changed the nature of the war at sea. The very survival of Britain was at stake. It is easy to forget today that the greatest danger to the Allies during the Second World War was the precarious state of the Atlantic Ocean lifeline between North America and Britain. As British Admiral Dudley Pound warned, "If we lose the war at sea, we lose the war."

At this point it might be well to recall the earlier comments about how small the navy was at the start of the war and how difficult it would be for the RCN to expand. It is here that the real significance of those comments comes into focus.

A great liability of the early corvettes was not just the ship's armament, the skimpy bridge, or the fact that it rolled and pitched virtually every moment at sea, but rather the lack of a trained crew. In the spring of 1940 there were at least thirty-two RCN corvettes under construction plus the Bangor minesweepers, but there were few sailors ready to go aboard any of them. All the regular navy officers and sailors were needed for the seven RCN destroyers and six four-stack destroyers the Royal Navy foisted on the RCN in the destroyers-for-bases deal with the U.S. Starting in 1941 the RCN also commissioned three converted passenger ships, *Prince Robert*, *Prince David*, and *Prince Henry*, as armed merchant cruisers, all of which had to be crewed. That left nothing, or very little, for the corvettes.

The scope of the crisis was breathtaking. In late 1940 the director of naval personnel, Captain Harold Grant, informed the top brass that he would need three hundred Royal Canadian Navy Volunteer Reserve officers by the following spring, when a huge batch of corvettes would be ready for commissioning. None of those officers had yet enlisted, and about ten times that number of seamen would be required. These sailors would become famous as the "Wavy Navy," so-called because the stripes on officers' arms were not straight as they were in the RCN, but wavy. Nearly all signed up only for the duration of the war.

The first corvettes were not yet finished when they were rushed down the Great Lakes for completion in Halifax to beat the winter freeze up. At Davie Shipyard in Quebec, HMS *Windflower* was launched on August 8 and given a "flower" name because it was intended for the Royal Navy. On October 20 it was the first Canadian-built corvette to be commissioned and was among those sent to Halifax, arriving on October 31. It was after sea trials that *Windflower*, with a skeleton crew, started out on its perilous maiden voyage to Britain, among the ten that had to use fake guns for the crossing.

Those ten early corvettes were supposed to be turned over to the Royal Navy and have a British crew put aboard once they arrived in Scotland. In the end, the Royal Navy did provide guns and other equipment for them, but such was its desperation at that time, the Admiralty decided not to provide crews. "Much to the RCN's dismay," said Marc Milner, "the Royal Navy simply kept these corvettes in commission with their delivery crews and assigned them to operations — and then complained about how poorly manned and inefficient they were."[24]

By 1941 many officers and 80 percent of the sailors in the corvettes were new to the sea. "The transition from a prairie wheat field to the deck of a sea-going ship had sometimes to be made within a period of ninety days. Years had to be telescoped into months."[25] Bill Perry of Victoria went to sea on HMCS *Alberni* with a completely green crew, and the result, he said, was a "comedy of ineptitude."[26] HMCS *Kamsack* crewman

Frank Curry said one sailor from Trois-Rivières became seasick before the ship had completely left port.²⁷

In many ships only the captain himself was capable of basic navigation, to the point that the safety of everyone depended on his ability to stay awake for days at a time.²⁸ Lieutenant-Commander Alan Easton, who had been in the merchant marine for ten years before the war, enlisted in 1939. Since he was an experienced officer, he was appointed to command HMCS *Baddeck*, which was commissioned in May 1941. Easton later said of his shipmates, "Of the three [other] officers only the navigator had been in a ship before. He had been twenty-five years at sea in all sorts of small vessels.... Of the fifty men, about five had been professional seamen or fishermen and, below, no more than six were experienced with engines and boilers. So with more than three-quarters of the complement as fresh to the sea as the ship itself, it was hard to perform our simple task; hard to keep steam up, avoid the shoals or even to steer a straight course. Had anything warlike occurred, there would have been a shambles."²⁹

One of the officers aboard HMCS *Spikenard*, Sub-Lieutenant Joe Marston, said his captain, H.G. Shadforth, had a near impossible job. "He was expected to go out and kill U-boats and for this purpose he was provided with a slow ship — useful but slow — with obsolete weapons and instruments, and a crew of novices with a light sprinkling of trained seamen who had limited military training.... In addition, the captains were sent off with other ships with which they had never worked and in many cases they did not know the captain of the other escorts, nor indeed had ever met them."³⁰

All too often after a few Atlantic crossings on one ship, when the crew had finally settled down, learned to work as a team, and become at least moderately effective, the return to Halifax for refit brought the reassignment of most crew members to other ships. That meant a breaking in a new crew, likely with a new captain. In 1941 and 1942 HMCS *Chambly* had 259 officers and men on its books, nearly five times the original complement.

As the corvettes were assigned to convoy escort duty in 1941, they faced a rough indoctrination. A prime example was the fate of convoy SC 42, which left Sydney, Nova Scotia, en route to Liverpool on August 30.[31] It became one of the most besieged convoys of the war. The escorts were the RCN destroyer *Skeena,* along with three corvettes, *Orillia, Alberni,* and *Kenogami,* which was on its first crossing. The four had to defend sixty-four merchant ships spread out over thirty square miles.

The convoy was intercepted near Greenland by a wolf pack of fourteen U-boats. The escorts chased contacts in all directions but with little effect. At one point *Skeena,* speeding between the rows of merchant ships in response to a call for help, passed a U-boat going the opposite direction, but it was so close that the destroyer's guns could not be depressed low enough to fire. A torpedo barely missed *Alberni's* stern. After two or three sinkings *Orillia* stopped to pick up survivors, but soon there were so many of them on board, hardly anyone on the ship could move, let alone fight a battle. In any event, *Orillia* ended up assisting a damaged tanker seven hundred miles to safety. While that was a remarkable rescue operation, it meant that the corvette was out of the rest of the battle.

The only good news was that HMCS *Chambly* and its monocled, larger-than-life captain, Chummy Prentice, came to the rescue along with HMCS *Moose Jaw.* Commander Prentice, a Canadian who had formerly served in the RN, became one of the best and most celebrated captains in the Battle of the Atlantic. He had been conducting training nearby when he heard of the attacks and approached the convoy at night "up moon," meaning the convoy and one U-boat were silhouetted for him. His tiny flotilla was able to catch and sink U-501, the first RCN victory of the war.

Still, the overall result was a slaughter. At least sixteen ships were sunk or damaged, one-quarter of the convoy. It was clear that at sea level "these early corvettes were not much of a threat to a skilled submariner," as authors Ken Macpherson and Marc Milner have argued.[32] There was a long and painful list of issues: there were not enough escorts for a convoy that size; communication was poor between the corvettes and the senior escort officer, and better crew training was urgently needed. It was also obvious that most of the corvette captains knew precious little of the basic principles of convoys — a terrible indictment of the rush to get someone — anyone — to command all the new ships. On top of everything, at this stage of the war there was still no air cover in the mid-Atlantic.

Also highlighted was the urgent need to rebuild the original corvette for its new role. It required a longer forecastle for better seagoing, a better bridge, and radar to detect U-boats on the surface at night. The new Hedgehog weapon was being introduced in Britain. It threw twenty-four small bombs ahead of the ship. The bombs detonated only when they hit a hull or similar surface. With that direct contact their explosion was much more deadly than the shock waves of a depth charge.*

The RCN was well behind in adopting the Hedgehog. The Canadian built radar, the SW1C (Surface Warning 1st Canadian), turned out to be near useless. On a sunny day in iceberg territory, it might detect a tiny berg at long range but at midnight give no hint of an oncoming monster. It would be a long time before the RCN could cope with the onslaught of fourteen U-boats in one encounter.

Not every crossing was a disaster, but neither was SC 42 entirely an exception. There were many examples of ineptitude or mischance. On convoy SC 48, HMCS *Shediac* somehow missed an emergency convoy turn at night and lost its convoy for five days. Also its radio, for unexplained reasons, was not properly tuned, and it did not know the rendezvous points. Not long after that in November 1941, convoy SC 52 was driven back to port. It was intercepted shortly after it set out, not far off Newfoundland, and four ships were sunk. With U-boats in contact so early in the voyage, it was likely they would have maintained contact all the way across with unending attacks. It was one of the few times in the war a convoy was ordered back to port. The decision proved to be a good one because when it did sail a short time later, it was able to evade detection.

The U-boats were by no means the only challenges the escorts faced. In one of the stranger episodes of the war, crewman Frank Curry said

---

* The fact that the Hedgehog was thrown ahead of the ship overcame a serious problem with the depth charge. To fire depth charges, the ship had to be over or close to the submarine. That meant that there was a "blind spot" for the asdic because the range was then too short. With the Hedgehog there was no blind spot, and the ship could keep track of any last-minute submarine manoeuvres.

Kamsack escorted a convoy for eight solid days in a fog that never lifted. In that entire time no one on his ship even once caught a glimpse of the thirty ships they were escorting. *Kamsack* turned them over to another escort and picked up twenty other ships, but for eight days, *they* were completely invisible. Curry said, "The ships were there, with their crews, a stone's throw away but nary a sight of ship nor man. Sixteen days in all, with some fifty ships, and never a glimpse of our flock."[33]

As a replacement for the corvettes in the heart of the mid-Atlantic battleground, Canada ordered thirty-three new, larger, and better-equipped ships in October 1941. Originally called "twin-screw corvettes," but later dubbed "frigates," the ships were faster and had double the range of the corvette. In addition, crew accommodation was much better. As the design was too big for the shipyards on the Great Lakes, all the frigates built in Canada were constructed on the West Coast or on the St. Lawrence.

Until the new ships could be delivered, the corvettes ploughed on. One particularly bad encounter came in the last week of 1942. Twenty U-boats fastened onto convoy ONS 154 outbound from Britain to North America. Over three days Canadian destroyer *St. Laurent* and corvettes *Battleford*, *Chilliwack*, *Kenogami*, *Napanee*, and *Shediac* did what they could, but in time, fourteen of fifty merchant ships were lost. The outcome was described by Marc Milner as "a disaster of the first order."[34] Those losses brought the total merchant ship losses that year to more than six million tons.

One dramatic moment in the Battle of the Atlantic came on August 28, 1943, as U.S. warships, along with the Canadian corvettes *Oakville*, *Halifax*, and *Snowberry* were escorting a convoy east of Cuba.[35] The submarine U-94 was about to attack the convoy when it was spotted and attacked by an American aircraft. *Oakville* then sped to the scene, by which time the sub had surfaced. *Oakville* fired several shells that hit both the conning tower and boat's deck gun. The corvette attempted to ram twice, failed, and then let go a depth charge that exploded under the sub's hull. Right after this, *Oakville* was finally able to ram, a risky business which could easily end in more damage to the corvette than to the submarine. But at that point the U-boat captain ordered his crew to abandon ship.

A boarding party was dispatched to seize the boat and recover, if possible, any secret code books or communications gear. Sub-Lieutenant Hal Lawrence and Petty Officer A.J. Powell, armed only with pistols, leapt onto the deck of U-94 and rushed toward the conning tower. After clearing away dead bodies covering the hatch, the two headed below, only to be surprised by two German sailors dashing toward them. The Canadians opened fire and that ended resistance. Lawrence searched for secret documents, but they had apparently been tossed overboard. Powell then escaped and Lawrence was just able to leap into the water before the boat began its final plunge to the bottom. The boarding crew and nineteen German survivors were recovered by *Oakville* and the destroyer USS *Lea*.

Incredibly, the Royal Canadian Navy expanded to more than fifty times its original size during the war — to ninety-six thousand men and

Drama at Sea — In 1942, in one of the most dramatic episodes of the war at sea, Sub-Lieutenant Hal Lawrence (left) and Petty Officer Art Powell (right) from HMCS Oakville *boarded the submarine U-94. Lawrence was barely able to escape the sub as it sank.*

women. By comparison the Royal Navy increased eight times in size, the U.S. Navy, twenty times. No wonder the RCN had such growing pains. The most important measure of the RCN's success — which included both the work of corvettes and other ships — was the safe passage of more than twenty-five thousand merchant ships under its escort. In the course of these operations the navy sank or shared in the destruction of thirty-one enemy submarines. The RCN lost fourteen warships to U-boat attacks and another eight to collisions and other accidents in the North Atlantic.

The corvette was the mainstay of the U-boat war until 1943. To the RCN's enormous surprise, the corvette — rolling and pitching its soggy way to 'Derry and back for the umpteenth time, with its crazy, spinning compass, its cramped-beyond-endurance quarters, its pop gun on the bow, and rust all over, and with mid-winter green monsters crashing down on its decks — became a beloved icon. It was a ship that came, more than any other, to symbolize trials and final triumph in the Battle of the Atlantic.

After it was all over, each corvette crewmen was left with his own vivid memories, but it was sometimes not the scope of the twentieth century's most titanic struggle they recalled but the little details, the smallest things. Morley Barnes of *Kincardine* commented, "After three days at sea anything that was breakable was broken."[36] Food was a problem and within days of leaving port any bread remaining was mouldy. "However," noted Doug May, also a *Kincardine* sailor, "extra jam covered the mouldy spots and down it went."[37]

The navy's top commanders didn't love the corvette any more at the end of the war than they did at the beginning. From 1939 the RCN expansion plans focused on a single purpose and that was to have, in the postwar years, a major fleet, a real navy, a deep-sea navy. The corvette never did fit that grand design. By 1945 all the early corvettes were both battle-weary and outdated anyway, so the navy was quite happy to see the last of them the moment the war ended. The North Atlantic battle proved to be, as Marc Milner said, "the defining moment in the navy's history, although, paradoxically, it was not the kind of war nor the type of fleet, the RCN wanted."[38]

When you think of the great naval ships of history you tend to think of battleships or vast aircraft carriers, so it is hard to imagine a ship being both small and great at the same time. But this one was. Former seaman Ray Burwash called it "probably the most rugged and seaworthy ship ever built, for any navy."[39]

The corvette was great for the simplest of reasons: it was there. It was there when nothing else was. The ship allowed the convoy system to be extended from shore to shore across the North Atlantic and bought time for the RCN to become a really effective anti-submarine force. With the corvette, "The line of the Atlantic was held somehow; until, out of a gallant chaos of early effort, there emerged a force of ships and seamen capable of holding up its head in any naval company."[40] And Joseph Schull was surely right when he said the campaign against the U-boats was won by a "precariously narrow margin."[41]

There is a kind of mystique about the corvettes. There's the ship, of course, but also the sailors. Their achievement, too, is imperishable. The corvettes were not crewed by the professionals of the Royal Canadian Navy but almost entirely by young men, just amateurs there for the duration. Decked out in their turtleneck sweaters and toques and whatever else had arrived in a package from home, the citizen sailors of the RCNVR were Canada itself. In 1941 sonar operator Frank Curry, aboard *Kamsack*, described his crew as including "veteran fishermen, merchant seamen, landlubbers from the offices of Montreal and Toronto, prairie farmers, west coast lumbermen, bakers [and] even a Maori merchant seaman from New Zealand who had left his ship in Montreal and joined the Canadian navy."[42]

Among them, said Curry, was also a fifteen-year-old boy, the acknowledged master of the very worst profanity on the ship, and the worst in the naval lexicon.

DECISION THREE

Canada's Air Training Colossus

The most astonishing thing about Canada's air training plan in the Second World War was the sheer size of it. It has been said that it was a bigger project than hammering together the mighty Canadian Pacific Railway itself. The numbers tell the tale. Over five years the British Commonwealth Air Training Plan (BCATP) turned out 131,553 graduates.[1] It operated on more than seventy airfields, many of which had to be built from scratch. As many as 8,300 new hangars, barracks, administration, recreation, and medical buildings had to be built. The BCATP needed a fleet of 3,540 aircraft, which included 1,368 Anson twin-engine trainers, 702 Tiger Moth basic trainers, 720 North American Harvards, and many others besides. So many Ansons and Harvards were needed that new production lines had to be set up to build them in Canada.

But even all that was not the end of it. Each school had to have instructors, administrators, ground crew, security staff, radio operators, supply and weapons specialists, doctors, and dozens of others. When it got going, many communities that had been obliterated by the Great Depression sprang back to new life. Sometimes Canada is a "just get through the winter" kind of nation. It might seem at times that the national motto is "we're doing the best we can," but the scale of this leviathan says something entirely different.

It actually began in 1939, but attempts were made to start a training plan long before that. In the late 1930s the British proposed three different versions of a scheme to be set up in Canada, but they all came with political baggage. The British wanted to run the operations and have the graduates end up in the Royal Air Force. The idea looked too colonial to Mackenzie King, and so — no deal.

The outbreak of war changed everything. Thousands of pilots, navigators, air gunners, and radio operators would be needed, but the skies over Britain were far too crowded for that kind of training. Canada, on the other hand, had wide-open spaces. In London, Canadian high commissioner Vincent Massey eagerly promoted a big scheme being set up in Canada. The original idea was to train British and Canadian aircrew, but Massey and Australian High Commissioner Stanley Bruce hatched the idea of also training Australian, New Zealand, and other Commonwealth airmen.[2]

On September 26, only three weeks after the war began, British prime minister Neville Chamberlain sent a "special, personal" telegram to Mackenzie King saying that a large-scale training program "might be decisive" in the outcome of the war. King seized on the idea partly because it would represent a hefty contribution to the war effort and might be an excuse to avoid sending Canadian ground troops to Europe. As King put it, "with concentration of Canadian energies on air training and air power there would be less risk of agitation for conscription."[3]

King wanted a letter from Chamberlain declaring that an air training program would be the "greatest service Canada could perform in the war." The idea was that King could wave it in front of anyone who criticized him for not sending troops. Chamberlain then sent a letter saying that while the air scheme would be a top priority, sending troops would also be welcome. For public consumption King simply edited it to suit his purposes.*

On October 16 a British delegation headed by industrialist Lord Riverdale arrived in Ottawa to work out the fine print. The British wanted

---

* Despite the letter, the Canadian cabinet decided to send the 1st Canadian Division to Britain, starting in December 1939.

to run the operation and stream most of the graduates into the Royal Air Force. That idea said a great deal about the relationship between the two countries in 1939 and about the way much of official Britain saw Canada throughout the war. The British thought the Royal Canadian Air Force could never organize and control a scheme of this magnitude and that they — the Brits — would have to do so.

Riverdale, arriving with a grandee's air of condescension, assumed that reaching an agreement would be a trifling formality. He would simply tell the people in Ottawa what had to be done. To his dismay, his plans were greeted by Mackenzie King with the stony contempt of an Easter Island statue. King wrote that it was "amazing how these people have come out from the Old Country and seem to think that all they have to do is tell us what is to be done."[4] The Australians and New Zealanders said they simply could not afford the original plan, and discussion grew so acrimonious their delegations gave up and went home. After much hammering away, and many changes, it finally looked like an agreement with the British would be reached in the late evening of December 16, 1939. However, Mackenzie King dawdled until just after midnight, so the signing would be on December 17, which just happened to be his sixty-fifth birthday. After brief birthday greetings, the deal was signed. Despite the acrimony and despite reduction in size and cost, in the end the agreement to start the British Commonwealth Air Training Plan was one of the best and most far-reaching decisions for Canada in the Second World War. The BCATP became far bigger and more successful than anyone could have imagined in 1939.

In its final form the overall cost of the plan was cut to $607.3 million with Canada paying $353 million. The four principal countries would pool resources, each sending trainees and contributing money according to the number of candidates enrolled and the money it had. Britain would supply most of the planes and some instructors; Canada would supply additional instructors and administrators and build dozens of training bases. Everyone would use Royal Air Force training methods and the RAF syllabus. The program would run until March 1943, by which time everyone assumed the war would be over. Canada would have overall administrative control, but "some" British officers would be brought in.

Even though the scheme was pared back, the British still wanted to produce, at the peak, thirty-nine thousand aircrew a year. In an understatement worthy of the drollest Briton, Air Commodore E.W. Stedman of the RCAF said everyone was "quite taken aback" by the whole idea.[5] Elementary flying training schools would be established in Canada, Australia, and New Zealand, but most advanced training, including pilot, air observer, and radio operator/air gunner training, would be done in Canada. Canada would have twelve elementary training schools, twenty-five advanced pilot schools, fifteen for air observers, fifteen for bombing and gunnery, one large radio training school, and three for air navigation. Fifty-four thousand men and women would have to be found — somehow, somewhere — to run them all.

Another key point was that the British agreed to pay for salaries, uniforms, and equipment for RCAF airmen in Britain. King felt Canada was contributing enough without having to pay more for Canadians overseas. Later on, that became an enormous controversy because, of course, if you were paying the airmen, you would expect that you would have control of where they served, their discipline, and their promotions.

At this point it might be well to briefly include something that is more extensively covered in Decision Four on the "Canadianization of the RCAF." There was a time bomb written into the original BCATP agreement. While the King government deserves great credit for the BCATP, and while the RCAF and many civilians deserve even more credit for making it a success, the original BCATP agreement included one section that turned it into what has been called a "colonial document."[6] That was Article Fifteen, which dealt with what would happen to aircrew when they graduated. It is not clear whether King simply did not understand the significance of it, felt he had pressed the British as far as he could, or understood it but was too cheap to do anything about it. King wanted the Canadian graduates to go into RCAF squadrons. The British chose an entirely different interpretation, concluding everyone would go into RAF squadrons that might be distinguished in some vague way as "Canadian," "Australian," or "New Zealand." There is a vast difference between the two.

The British emphatically did not want a separate Royal Canadian Air Force in England. They only wanted a few token RCAF squadrons with none of them formed into "groups" (made up of a number of squadrons). They just wanted more airmen for the RAF. A separate air force would have its own agenda and priorities, its own operational ideas, and, besides, would need its own huge administrative set-up. Until 1943 the British argued that a second air force would be an operational disaster — sort of two pilots fighting over control of the same airplane. However, the result was that thousands of Canadian BCATP graduates ended up serving not in RCAF squadrons but in British squadrons with British commanders.*

The deal was finally signed. In a radio broadcast marking the historic event, King commented it was an undertaking that would "establish Canada as one of the greatest air training centres of the world."[7] That was breathtaking. However, at almost the next moment there were a thousand questions. Where to build the airfields? Where to find the instructors? But first of all, where to begin?

At least a few pieces of the puzzle were at hand. The RCAF did have several bases, including Dartmouth, Nova Scotia, and Trenton, Ontario, which could be expanded. The Department of Transport also had twenty-four airports it controlled which needed only some extra buildings to be transformed into operational training bases. Fifteen "intermediate" landing fields would require more modification but were, at least, available. Existing private or public buildings outside the bases could be converted for initial training, which did not involve flying but only ground instruction. Earlier in 1939 the government had taken over the private Eglinton Hunt Club in Toronto, which had spacious grounds. Coincidentally, it was also being used as a top secret research centre where scientists, including the celebrated Sir Frederick Banting, were working.** Before many months the researchers would have to shuffle over into the corner and make room for the RCAF's No. 1

---

*   Later in the war, when American bomber units began arriving in England, the British tried to put them under RAF operational command. The Americans absolutely refused.

** The scientists, including Wilbur Franks, were developing pressure suits, sometimes called "anti-g suits." The important research was aimed at helping pilots cope with extreme manoeuvring, which could lead to unconsciousness.

Initial Training School. Perhaps the most unusual acquisition was the Ontario Psychiatric Hospital complex in St. Thomas, Ontario. It became the No. 1 Technical Training School, an enormous set-up that could train up to two thousand students at a time. The students would become aircraft electricians, aero-engineers, airframe and instrument mechanics, and sheet metal workers. There were few trained technicians in any of those fields in Canada before the war, so those skills were absolutely critical. The RCAF moved quickly to scoop up many commercial pilots and commission them as RCAF officers. Several dozen had received letters in the summer of 1939 inviting them to join the air force. Among them was nineteen-year-old Russ Bannock of Edmonton, who had just earned his commercial licence.[8] He applied to join up, and after further flight training and an officer's training course, he was awarded his air force wings. As with many early pilots Bannock was shattered to find that he would not be allowed to go overseas because he was too valuable as a BCATP instructor. It was not until 1944 that he managed to get out of Canada.

Eight flying clubs — many with licensed pilots, their own aircraft and even airfields — had been doing elementary training for the air force since June 1939. They and fourteen more were given contracts on the outbreak of the war. The pilots became civilian BCATP instructors. Commercial airlines also got involved, eventually employing eighteen thousand people to do engine repair and aircraft maintenance.

Seven hundred Americans were delighted to become flight instructors in Canada. At the time, the United States Army Air Corps would not enlist any pilot under twenty years of age or over twenty-six, those who were married, or those who lacked two years of college education. So Americans who might have been excellent pilots but who did not fit those strict requirements, rushed north.

A further boost came in January 1940 when eighty-five Royal Air Force officers and other ranks arrived in Halifax, among them logistics and armaments specialists who went on to make an invaluable contribution to the organization. Most outstanding among the arrivals was the formidable Air Commodore Robert Leckie. He later switched from the RAF to the RCAF and then in 1944 became chief of the air staff.

Leckie came with a bristling personality and a spectacular history. He had been born in Glasgow, Scotland, but came to Canada as a teenager. He took civilian pilot training in Canada and then returned to Britain to become a Royal Naval Air Service pilot in 1915. Leckie gained fame as the only airman credited with downing two giant Zeppelin airships in the war. The Germans had begun airship attacks on Britain in May 1915. In 1917 Leckie attacked Zeppelin L-22, which had been sent up to observe Royal Navy ship movements in the North Sea. At one point, using special incendiary ammunition, he fired away from the near suicidal range of twenty feet.[9] The Zeppelin caught fire and, as Leckie sped to safety, one million cubic feet of gas exploded in a fireball. His second attack occurred in August 1918 after a Zeppelin force was spotted approaching the English coast. There was a wild scramble to get fighter aircraft into the air. Leckie jumped into the gunner's seat of a DH-4 aircraft while Egbert Cadbury, a member of the famed chocolate family, hurried into the pilot's seat. The two were able to gain enough altitude to attack one of the intruders from underneath. In the late evening light Leckie fired eighty rounds of incendiary bullets into the ship and destroyed it. Both Cadbury and Leckie were awarded the Distinguished Flying Cross.

After the First World War Leckie's military service included flying from two of Britain's early aircraft carriers, HMS *Hermes* and HMS *Courageous*. Returning to Canada in 1940 he was put in an awkward spot. He was brought in to run the BCATP because no RCAF officer was considered experienced enough to do so. However, the RCAF twice tried to stop him from coming because he was senior to everyone in Canada except the chief of the air staff. Leckie never made an issue of it and the controversy quickly died down.

All planning focused on "Zero Day" — April 29, 1940 — the day the BCATP training would actually begin. Before then there was a mind-numbing list of things that had to be done. An early step was to set up the RCAF's own Directorate of Works and Buildings to design all structures, a job which one official, Group Captain E.C. Luke, described as turning into "the everlasting pursuit of the impossible."[10] Survey crews and other specialists were dispatched to find airfield locations even before the BCATP agreement was signed. They had to rule out sites closer than five miles from the United States border and swampy areas or other bad terrain, and they had to find out where the nearest electricity or roads were. Drinking water, especially on the prairies, turned out to be a chronic problem. In the case of the school at Moose Jaw, a seven-mile-long pipeline had to be built. Each base had to have room for the main runways and a couple of additional rough runways nearby as practice fields. The bombing and gunnery schools required a huge area to avoid damage to life or property.

The first contracts were let at the end of 1939. Even in the winter some work was done, levelling the ground and clearing fields. Construction of the buildings — mostly wood because steel was in short supply — began in the spring. In a marvel of the time, most structures were pre-fabricated and standardized. Local crews were hired (seventy-five cents an hour for a carpenter, forty-five cents for a labourer), and before long a hangar could be put together in a matter of hours. Pre-cut components were bolted together, ready-made doors were attached, and shingles put on the roof. To the dismay of airmen long afterward, turnbuckles bracing the buildings were forever having to be adjusted because so much green wood had been used. Still, Group Captain Luke recalled that in one instance, the keys to a finished school were handed over to an RCAF advance party only six weeks after the first truck had driven onto a farmer's field.

Training had to start with whatever aircraft could be scraped up. The RCAF's own uninspiring collection was not much help, although a fortunate exception was the British-built Tiger Moth, which the RCAF had been using as a basic trainer since 1938. Plans were in hand to build them at de Havilland Aircraft in Toronto, with the first prototype flown in March 1940. It was a simple aircraft, and production quickly ramped up. One roadblock, however, was that during the entire war Canada never made aircraft engines, so they had to be imported from Britain or the U.S.

One plane that became a BCATP stalwart was the twin-engine Avro Anson, used as a navigation and radio communications trainer. "Faithful Annie" was obsolete as a front-line light bomber but much admired in its new role. However, it was the North American Harvard that became the iconic aircraft of the program. About the same size as front-line fighters of the day, it was rugged and reliable. It was not really new, first introduced in the United States in 1937. The original fuselage was fabric covered, but it had an all metal, stressed-skin wing with flush riveting. Its single Wright radial engine gave it a cruising speed of 145 miles per hour (233 kilometres per hour). Like modern fighter planes, it had a retractable landing gear. Numerous improvements were made to it in the course of production, and eventually the RAF and RCAF took on 1,173 Harvards.

Both the Harvard and the BCATP got a star turn in the Hollywood movie *Captains of the Clouds*, a wartime propaganda film starring two-fisted actor James Cagney. Much of the movie was shot at Uplands Airport in Ottawa and at northern Ontario logging camps. One scene showed a massive flypast of RCAF aircraft at a "wings parade," the graduation ceremony for pilot trainers.

The Harvard was not the easiest aircraft to fly. One student pilot, Robert English from St. Catharines, Ontario, flew it and declared, "What a ship! But it's no toy."[11] Student pilot Andy MacKenzie of Montreal said that after the Tiger Moth, the Harvard "scared the daylights" out of him.[12] A production line for Harvards was set up at Noorduyn Aircraft in Montreal and later at Canadian Car and Foundry in Fort William, Ontario.

From the first day of the war the RCAF was overwhelmed with young men hoping to be transformed into heroic fighter aces. However, by November it had stopped accepting new applicants because there was nowhere to train them. Nevertheless, in the spring of 1940, with furious construction still underway, the first BCATP recruits were called to report for duty. At this point the RCAF had expanded to twice its size in seven months.

All air careers began in the cheerless manning depots, where thousands of bunks were crammed into every available corner. There were endless lineups for paper work, only interrupted by those for food, medical shots, or pay. It was often commented that the uniforms came in two sizes — too big and too small. There was no privacy whatever, which led to some unpleasant encounters. Ken Fulton, later a navigator in No. 426 Squadron, told of one man who never showered. He was grabbed by a number of other recruits and tossed into the stalls. Later arrivals at manning depots were greeted with the universal welcome "You'll be sorry."

Iconic Aircraft — The North American Harvard came to symbolize the British Commonwealth Air Training Plan. As many as twenty thousand of the advanced trainers were built.

Movie Fame — Even Hollywood celebrated the wartime role of the British Commonwealth Air Training Program. This movie starred James Cagney, who in real life hated flying. Legendary pilot Billy Bishop played himself in a few scenes.

Everyone soon learned not to volunteer for anything. "Any of you chaps like music," asked the sergeant? "Well, then move that piano."[13]

The first actual training operation to open was No.1 Initial Training School, at the former Hunt Club site in Toronto, mentioned earlier. It had the comparative luxury of a bowling alley and swimming pool, if anyone had the time to use them. The first group of 221 trainees arrived for a four-week basic training course, which was later extended to ten weeks. All recruits were classified as Aircraftman Second Class, usually known as "acey duceys," the lowest form of life on the planet. The pay was $1.70 a day.

There were the expected deep knee bends, marching, and boot polishing, but also cram courses on algebra and trigonometry. Each candidate spent time in the Link Trainer, a forerunner of today's flight simulator. Seventeen of the men in the first course washed out, but the rest went on to become aircrew. The big question for those who survived basic training was whether they would become pilots, radio operators, or something else, a huge decision that affected the rest of their careers. Those who failed to master the finicky Link, and who were sent to the next phase of training as observers and not pilots, were furious that they had never really had a chance to show what they could do in the skies. Sometimes there was not much choice anyway. Howard Hewer, from Toronto, reported that, to the enormous disappointment of his entire class, everyone was assigned to be radio operator/air gunners because of a shortage in that specialty.[14]

Word among trainees soon got out that if you wanted to be a pilot, it was best not to get top marks in math. Do well but not too well because as J.R. Wood, an air observer trained in 1940, said, "The smart boys in math were tagged to be observers" even though many wanted to be pilots. The observers did navigation.[15] Some careers were brief. Andy MacKenzie passed his course despite being intimidated by the Harvard but said it was disconcerting to see fellow students "wash out." They simply packed their bags and got out as quickly as possible, which MacKenzie described as, a "slight and very sad affair."[16] Many went on to volunteer for the army.

In addition to the large number of American civilian instructors in the BCATP, there were eventually about 8,800 U.S. students enrolled. Among the first of them was John Gillespie Magee Junior, whose missionary family was from Pittsburgh but who was actually born in China. In 1940 he won a scholarship to Yale University but chose instead to join the RCAF. Magee gained imperishable fame for his poem *High Flight*, which begins, "Oh! I have slipped the surly bonds of Earth / And danced the skies on laughter-silvered wings." Sadly, he was killed in a midair collision in Britain in 1941.

The first months of the Second World War were usually known as the "Phony War" because nothing much happened on the ground in Europe, but that all changed with the German attack west in the spring of 1940. The first BCATP class had hardly begun training when it happened. With the fall of France, should the entire program be cancelled and all available resources sent to Britain? The British — with great resolve — urged that the program continue. However, the RCAF's chief of the air staff announced that the expansion planned for the coming two years would have to be crammed into one. It also became apparent that with Britain fighting for its very life, it could no longer supply Ansons or other aircraft. That put another near-impossible wrench into the program. The decision was made to build Ansons in Canada, but it was more than a year before the first one could be produced. In the meantime, the BCATP turned to the U.S. for Cessna Cranes, an aircraft order that saved the company from bankruptcy.

The RCAF had fifty-nine Ansons by the end of May, enough to equip only one school. However, the Harvards were beginning to arrive, later ramping up to a rate of twenty a month. There was one bit of relief in the form of 110 Yale training aircraft, a cousin to the Harvard. They had been ordered by the French government, but with the Nazi takeover the planes wound up in the hands of the BCATP. The Yales were even trickier to operate than the Harvards because the French had ordered them with throttle levers that operated in the opposite direction and all gauges in metric.

There was a critical change in the King government in the spring of 1940. Quebecker Charles Gavin Power, mentioned earlier as an admirer of Ernest Lapointe, was sworn in as the minister of national defence for air and took on responsibility for running the BCATP.[17] Chubby Power was a bon vivant, a boozy but formidable career politician, born near

Quebec City in 1888. A soldier in the First World War, he had been seriously wounded, awarded the Military Cross for gallantry, and invalided out of the army. He was first elected a member of Parliament in 1917. On a few occasions Power was found meandering the corridors of the Parliament Buildings completely plastered. Mackenzie King drank only occasionally and hated drinkers, but he recognized Power's enormous ability.

The first pilots received their wings at Camp Borden, Ontario, on September 30, 1940, months ahead of schedule. Proud to be proclaimed the first graduating class, the new pilots expected to be quickly dispatched overseas. Like Edmonton's Russ Bannock, however, they were crushed to learn that they would be needed at home as flying instructors and staff pilots. It was the same for the next three classes — nearly all of the pilots were ploughed back into the training scheme.

There were a few exceptions, including a class of thirty-seven observers sent overseas after they received their wings in October 1940. There were few massive flypasts at most wings parades, or for that matter, sometimes not even much of a wings parade at all. Pilot Andy MacKenzie described it: "We got our wings in navigation class. The school commander came in and in his British accent said, 'Well, chaps, you've made the grade and passed your wings check.' He had a cardboard box filled with wings insignia and said, 'Come up here, and if you've got twenty-two cents in your pocket, that's what they want from stores; twenty-two cents to pay for the wings. Each of you can take a set, and my congratulations chaps. You've all done well.'"[18]

Each training school was under great pressure to get on with training no matter what, and in every kind of weather. There were grass runways at Camp Borden, but when winter arrived, rollers tamped down the snow and the planes kept flying. By December 1940 a total of 358 pilots and 115 navigators had graduated.

The intake of students was so immense that by March 1941 the RCAF had erased its backlog of applicants. There was a sudden shortage of enlistees because not just the air force but the army, navy, and industry were all scrambling for a share of the same manpower pool. The RCAF required twenty-five thousand recruits for 1942, but with the backlog gone there were simply not enough young men turning eighteen to meet requirements. Standards had to be lowered. Would-be pilots were allowed to enlist at seventeen-and-a-half years of age with parental permission. The maximum age for pilots was raised from twenty-eight to thirty-one and then thirty-three, while the maximum age for air gunners was bumped up to thirty-nine. Strict medical standards were eased, and promising candidates who did not have high school diplomas were given the courses they needed to graduate, then sent to flight training.

By 1942 the program was in full operation — seventy-three schools in all. By that time aircrew were finally being dispatched to Britain in large numbers. That turned out to be significant because that was the same time that Air Chief Marshal "Bomber" Harris took over Bomber Command. He vastly expanded the air campaign against Germany, something that would have been impossible without the BCATP.

The training programs changed dramatically over time. At the beginning of the war the front-line aircraft used were rudimentary including such stalwarts as the RAF's Gloster Gauntlet, but with the introduction of higher performance aircraft such as the Spitfire and Typhoon, more advanced training was required. It was the same for bombers as relics, such as the Handley Page Heyford, were discarded in favour of the Wellingtons and Lancasters.

Later on flight engineers were given some pilot training since most RAF bombers operated with only one pilot. The bomb aimer was added as a new specialization in 1942. There was a constant stream of new developments, including the navigation aids "Oboe" and "Gee." Oboe, first employed in January 1943, used radio transmitters on the ground to locate the position of an aircraft. It could only be used by one aircraft at a time, and the British chose the speedy Mosquito fighter-bomber to act as a pathfinder aircraft. The result was more accurate bombing even when targets were covered by cloud. Gee worked on similar lines but was smaller and could be used by as many as eighty aircraft at a time.

A dramatic change came when the air force formed the RCAF Women's Division. First recruits were enlisted in October 1941. Initially, there was great resistance to women enlisting, but the vast majority of the WD members turned out to be highly effective. They enjoyed the situation on most bases, where young men outnumbered them nine to one. At first women were limited to being clerks, hospital assistants, drivers, and telephone operators, but in time their roles were much expanded.

In a massive air training program it was inevitable that there would be air crashes and casualties. In the very first pilot's class in 1940, two students died. From the beginning of 1942 to the end of 1944, there were, on average, five fatalities a week. Through the entire length of the BCATP's existence, 856 students died during air training in Canada, 469 of them members of the RCAF.[19] Newspapers all too frequently carried headlines like the one in the *Courier* in St. Stephen, New Brunswick, in December 1943: "FOUR AIRMEN KILLED IN CRASH OF BOMBING PLANE AT MCADAM." The RCAF crewmen from the nearby Pennfield training base had been killed when their aircraft hit a twenty-foot pole above a water tank. In 1941 alone forty accidents were blamed on low flying and aerobatics. Far too many student pilots ended up in plane crashes after trying to show off to girlfriends or family members. Robert English, the young man from St. Catharines, wrote home saying that a pilot at his training base near Hamilton, Ontario, was killed apparently in a stunt and "the C.O. gave us quite a talking to."[20]

Most crashes involved a single aircraft, but Charley Fox, from Guelph, Ontario, miraculously survived a midair collision at a BCATP operational training squadron. When his Harvard collided with a Hurricane fighter, Fox was forced to bail out but was not seriously hurt. He soon returned to flying. Fox went on to be one of the outstanding Canadian pilots of the war, credited by many with carrying out the strafing attack in 1944 that seriously wounded Field Marshal Erwin Rommel. Some accidents were even more dramatic and tragic than Fox's. In May 1942 a student pilot stalled an aircraft at a school in Portage la Prairie, Manitoba, and crashed into a hangar filled with a dozen fully fuelled Anson aircraft. The entire building and everything in it was engulfed in flames.[21]

Of course, not all crashes were fatal or even involved injury. Later Wing Commander Ralph Manning said one of his most vivid memories was seeing an aircraft land, wheels up, at Camp Borden, Ontario. Sirens blew and a hush fell over the station as all three top officers on the base, including Wing Commander "Bull" Riddell, pounded across the field toward the perpetrator. "Tension was relieved and noses were removed from hangar windows," said Manning, "only when it became evident that the culprit would not be hanged on the spot but would be permitted to live to fly another day."[22]

It didn't help that some aircraft were known to be particularly unforgiving. The wooden and fabric-covered Airspeed Oxford, used in a variety of roles, was notorious for its training mishaps. The Fleet Fort, the only aircraft completely designed and built in Canada, was a fire hazard and disaster that had to be discarded.

Dozens of training bases were located on the prairies. Most towns and villages went out of their way to provide hospitality, including Dafoe, 150 kilometres north of Regina. It was home to No. 5 Bombing and Gunnery School. (Motto: "We Aim to Teach and We Teach to Aim.") The school officially opened on May 22, 1941, with forty-three officers and 486 airmen on hand. The base eventually accommodated up to 366 trainees at a time, flying day and night. Farmers, businesses, and tradesmen

Everyday Experience — *Sometimes it was the weather, sometimes it was inexperience or mechanical failure, and sometimes it was sheer recklessness. Among the BCATP planes involved in crashes was this Bolingbroke aircraft. From 1942 to 1944 there were on average five fatal crashes a week.*

in the area supplied many services along with such products as milk, butter, and meat. Theatres, curling rinks, golf courses, and dance halls in a wide area surrounding Dafoe were actively patronized. Some married men in the air force wanted to live off the station, which brought about the sudden appearance of "Boomtown." It was a grubby assortment of trailers, shacks, and improvised houses that sprang up just outside the base even though there was no tap water or electricity. In Dafoe and elsewhere there were romances, weddings, and the departure of some young women to far-flung destinations.

For many young airmen from overseas the Canadian prairies provided an eye-opening experience. Bob Stanford, age eighteen, had never been outside Britain. After a twelve-day crossing of the Atlantic and a 1,500-mile rail journey, the young RAF airman finally arrived in Moose Jaw, Saskatchewan. A perhaps somewhat embellished version of his arrival said, "Stanford couldn't believe his eyes when he got off the train. The vista could have come straight out of the old movie at his local cinema on Saturday mornings. There were duckboards on either side of a rough main street, a station hotel, two or three shops, a few wooden shacks, the odd horse and cart, and a few battered old farmers' trucks."[23]

It may have taken time to adjust to everything, including beer that was too cold, but students like Stanford at least welcomed ample supplies of fresh bread on the breakfast table, instead of the doubtful ingredients of the "National Loaf," a grey and unpopular staple of wartime Britain. Pilots liked flying on the prairies, where visibility was fifty miles or more. If a pilot got lost, most grain elevators displayed the town's name on the side, while the railway, the "iron compass," went east and west, a navigational godsend.

Not surprisingly, there were some occasions when mayhem gripped various towns. Fights broke out in some communities over the attentions of local young women. There were also linguistic confrontations in a few Quebec communities, notably Victoriaville, where there were fights between residents and servicemen.

By 1943 victory was still a long way off, but Britain and the Commonwealth countries, including Canada, had built up both industrial and military forces to unheard of levels. The United States was increasing its military and industrial strength by the day. The BCATP reached its high water mark in 1943 when there were seven million hours of flying training and 39,178 students graduated. The number one Technical Training School in St. Thomas, Ontario, was well on the way to turning out its total of fifty thousand ground crew technicians.

In England casualties in Bomber Command continued at frightening rates, but to that point at least, there was no shortage of pilots. Robert English, the young man from St. Catharines, was sent to Britain only to find a backlog such that he spent weeks sightseeing in London waiting for an assignment. He was finally sent to Egypt and then Italy to fly Spitfires in ground attack missions.[24]

Long before the original BCATP agreement expired in March 1943, there was a conference in Ottawa to set out the plan for the rest of the war. In a significant decision, the conference renewed the BCATP agreement to March 1945 and confirmed Canadian control of the entire operation. That was a loud endorsement of Canada's administration of the program, especially in light of earlier doubts. From that point on Canada would

Eager Pilot — Robert English from St. Catharines, Ontario, was among thousands of young Canadian men who dreamed of being a fighter pilot. After his first flight in a Harvard, he wrote "What a ship! But it's no toy."

absorb half the cost and provide half the trainees. At the same time a total of fourteen schools run by the Royal Air Force, operating in Canada but separately from the BCATP, would be brought under its administrative control. In one of Canada's most generous acts of the war — and one that was quickly forgotten afterward — hundreds of millions of dollars the British owed the program was simply erased from the books.

Even after the prodigious graduation numbers for 1943, another thirty thousand aircrew marched in wings parades in 1944. The growing backlog of pilots meant that the program had simply been too successful. In February 1944, after consulting with the British, Air Minister Power decided that the entire operation would be cut in half within one year. Thirteen schools closed only a few weeks later. When the brakes were jammed on there were still thousands of recruits in various stages of training. Courses that had just begun were cancelled and trainees given the choice of transferring to another category of aircrew or taking a discharge. Forty-two hundred pre-entry aircrew candidates were released and urged to enlist in the army.

Among those caught up in the numbers game was pilot trainee Paul Hellyer from the Brantford, Ontario, area. Hellyer was dismayed to find that he would not be allowed to finish his pilot training but equally dismayed that, when he enlisted in the army, he had to repeat his basic training and receive new medical shots.[25] He later wrote that he "abhorred" the fact that, when the army was desperately short of reinforcements, "grown men indulged in silly games." Much later, of course, Hellyer became one of the most controversial defence ministers in Canadian history when he imposed unification on the armed forces. The experience in 1944 likely had some influence on his later actions. For his part, student pilot Bill Milne of Barrie, Ontario, talked with two of his pals about what to do. Milne decided to become an air gunner because they were still much needed. After training he went overseas to see combat missions with No. 419 (Moose) Squadron, while his two friends stayed in pilot training and never got overseas.[26]

Many instructors finally found reason to rejoice; freed from their training duties, they were given priority in overseas postings. The Bombing and Gunnery School in Dafoe, Saskatchewan, shuttered its doors on January 11, 1945, and "Boomtown" went bust. The last of the Brits had graduated, and they went back to their warm beer and National Loaf.

It is breathtaking to recall the transformation in the BCATP from its first days to its last. The aircraft, the training. The bases springing up across the country. The flood of new airmen going overseas. The BCATP ended on March 31, 1945, only weeks before the war in Europe itself. The plan turned out to be more of a war winner than any visionary could have imagined. It was a triumph, a *Canadian* triumph. The bombing campaign over Germany could not have continued without the graduates of the BCATP, among them 72,835 Canadians.

Over its life the BCATP trained not only Commonwealth airmen but those from a number of other countries as well. Almost nine thousand Americans served in the RCAF during the Second World War, many of them joining the BCATP.[27] There were also two thousand French citizens, nine hundred Czechoslovaks, and smaller numbers of Poles, Belgians, and others. There was a great affection for the Norwegians. Their pilots were warmly welcomed, setting up their own operation at "Little Norway" at what is today Billy Bishop Airport on Toronto's waterfront. Little Norway opened in August 1940, while many students went on from there to receive advanced training with the BCATP in Moose Jaw. In total, more than two thousand Norwegian airmen were trained in Canada.

The program overwhelmed Axis forces in terms of sheer numbers. Those numbers "played a significant part in establishing Allied air superiority at a time when *Festung* Europe seemed impregnable to ground attack," said the RCAF's official history.[28] However, in the end, the quality of the graduates themselves and the standard of their training were equal to, or even more important than, the numbers. From the start Air Marshal Leckie demanded the training schools be canvassed for frank criticism. They were, and that was only the start of ironing out the kinks and improving the entire plan over time. Senior British officers examined the program carefully and were quick to point out failings. There was not enough instrument training for pilots, and in 1943 navigation standards were described as "low."[29] One senior British officer, Air Marshal A.G.R. Garrod, rated the general instruction in the plan as "good" and the morale of the pilot graduates, high.[30] In broad terms, the British (and Canadians) were happy with the training.

In addition to its other challenges, the BCATP also had to overcome doubters and skeptics among the Canadian public. In the early going Air Minister Power said that what was happening was not generally understood and that it was "looked upon with more or less skeptical derision" by many Canadians.[31] It took time. In the end the BCATP was a great tribute to those who planned and ran the program and especially the instructors. But the later success of the Canadian and other aircrews who fought and — too often — died is also a reflection of the determination, patriotism, and just plain guts of the airmen. Some of the greatest tributes have come from airmen who really knew what it meant to face, night after fearful night, the prospect of death in the sky. RAF pilot and instructor Denis Miller-William commented after the war that he was filled with admiration for those who, with little experience, flew four-engine bombers at night to Berlin and back. "That, for me, is the real tribute to the excellence of the training."[32]

FINAL TOTAL OF THE BRITISH COMMONWEALTH
AIR TRAINING PLAN GRADUATES BY NATIONAL AIR FORCE

RCAF	72,835
RAF (and allies)	42,110
RAAF	9,606
RNZAF	7,002
TOTAL	131,553

TOTAL RCAF GRADUATES[33]

Pilots	25,747
Navigators	12,855
Air Bombers	6,659
Wireless/Air Gunners	12,744
Air Gunners	12,917
Flight Engineer	1,913
TOTAL	72,835

It is hard to think of those terrible years without remembering the sacrifice of so many young men. Of the 204 aircrew who graduated from the very first BCATP class in 1940, 93 were killed in action. Robert English, the same pilot who had declared the Harvard was "no toy," was shot down in Italy just two weeks before the war ended. He survived initially but was killed on the ground, likely murdered by retreating German troops.

Despite the terrible casualty numbers, many airmen did somehow survive. Charley Fox of Guelph went on from his midair collision to his rendezvous with Field Marshal Rommel later in the war. Fox came home with 222 operational missions to his credit along with two Distinguished Flying Crosses. By April 1945 early flight instructor Russ Bannock had destroyed eleven enemy aircraft, damaged four, and destroyed nineteen V-1 flying bombs (today's "cruise missiles"). Another of the graduates was the remarkable James "Stocky" Edwards, who, in October 1940, had hitchhiked one hundred miles across Saskatchewan to enlist in the RCAF. He later flew Kittyhawk fighters and became a high-scoring ace in the North African campaign, with nineteen kills. By the end of the war, at age twenty-four, he was a wing commander.

Even after the war, the BCATP sent lives careening off in unexpected directions. Royal Air Force corporal George Barter, from Farnsworth, England, had been sent to do ground crew training at the BCATP School in Pennfield, New Brunswick, in the middle of the war. When he was released from RAF service in 1945, he returned to Canada to marry his Canadian sweetheart and live in St. Andrews, New Brunswick, and later Montreal. Their two children were born in St. Stephen, New Brunswick.

DECISION FOUR

Putting "Canadian" in "Royal Canadian Air Force"

The shattering attacks on the German city of Duisburg and the industrial Ruhr on October 14 and 15, 1944, were dubbed Operation Hurricane. Never mind the thousand-bomber raids of 1942; this time there would be *two thousand* British, Canadian, and American bombers in the skies. It was a double attack: two raids on the same target within twenty-four hours. When it was over, by one account, Duisburg was toppled "as if a tornado had struck."[1]

One of the key formations in the operation was No. 6 Group, Royal Canadian Air Force.* The Duisburg raids were history-making for the Group — "the greatest day's effort in its existence," with 239 Halifax and Lancaster bombers taking off from bases in Yorkshire.[2]

The double raids were a planning challenge. Still, the two operations went ahead all the same, and in the end only five aircraft were lost. A number of other bombers were damaged, one of them by a one-thousand-pound bomb that came loose and dropped right through the closed bomb doors without going off.

---

*   Various documents use different versions of the group's title, including "No. 6 (Canadian) Group" and simply "6 Group."

The operations that No. 6 Group were involved in, including the Duisburg raids, were remarkable in many ways, but it is remarkable in itself that the Group even existed, set up only after years of dispute and acrimony. The establishment of No. 6 Group marked one of the best and most far-reaching achievements of the RCAF during the war. In effect, it put the "Canadian" in "Royal Canadian Air Force."

The process has been called "Canadianization," which sounds complicated but is really not. It simply meant that RCAF airmen overseas would serve together. They would be in RCAF and not British squadrons, under RCAF and not British command, and their promotions and postings would be decided by Canadian and not British officers. That is the way it was in the Canadian Army. At its peak, No. 6 Group consisted of fourteen Lancaster and Halifax bomber squadrons, each with about eighteen aircraft. Each squadron had about 660 airmen and ground crew (and later, some airwomen). The total strength of No. 6 Group was about twelve thousand members.

In Canada the RCAF was run almost entirely by Canadians, but it was completely different for the RCAF overseas. While the idea of having

Legendary Lancaster — By late 1944 thirteen squadrons in No. 6 Group, RCAF, were flying the Lancaster, the most famous Allied bomber of the war. The aircraft shown honours Andrew Mynarski, VC, who died during a bombing mission in 1944.

Canadians under Canadian command may seem simple enough, putting that concept into effect was an enormous undertaking. Senior British officers hated Canadianization, and people in Canada and in the air force were divided about it for a long time. Newspapers lambasted it, and the Mackenzie King government fumbled putting it into effect.

"Bomber" Harris, more formally known as Air Chief Marshal Sir Arthur Harris, air officer commanding-in-chief of Bomber Command, Royal Air Force, was not pleased with the whole idea of forming a Canadian Group. He wanted mixed crews — British, Canadians, and New Zealanders — all together in one squadron, or even in one aircraft. He deplored the idea that Canadians would "huddle into a corner by themselves."[3] The bomber chief sometimes referred to airmen from Commonwealth and Empire countries as "coloured troops" — a semi-jocular term that has not aged well. Incidentally, while he grudgingly praised Commonwealth air and ground crews in his 1947 memoir, it is quite clear he believed British airmen made up the real heart of Bomber Command. Harris, one of the most choleric and controversial Allied commanders of the entire war, only briefly mentions the formation of No. 6 Group in the book and entirely skips over his vehement opposition.[4] Despite years of acrimony, and despite the detours and delays, No. 6 Group finally began operations on January 1, 1943 — a landmark in the march toward a Canadian national identity.

During the First World War things had been different. There was no Canadian air force similar to the army's famed Canadian Corps. Canadian airmen had to go to Britain and serve under British command. In the interwar years the Canadian government opted for a Royal Canadian Air Force on the cheap, which meant the fledgling service was almost totally reliant on the Royal Air Force for planes, equipment, and training. The Mackenzie King government had said if war came, Canadians should fight the air war in separate Canadian formations, but King did not spend the money necessary to make that happen. One result of this was that dozens of Canadians took up short-term commissions in the Royal Air Force in Britain. It was much easier for aspiring Canadian pilots to join the RAF than it was for them to join the RCAF in Canada. About nine hundred of them did so, among them Johnny Kent from Winnipeg, considered one of the best squadron leaders of the war. He gained fame during the Battle of Britain as commanding officer of No. 303 Squadron, which was made up mostly of Polish pilots. He became a much-admired group captain later on.

In the first weeks of the Second World War, a telegram arrived from London that revealed what the British really wanted from Commonwealth countries. The telegram requested that Canada "concentrate first on the individual training of pilots, observers, and particularly air gunners and W/T [radio] operators *for service in RAF units*" (emphasis added).[5] It marked the beginning of years of attempts by the Royal Air Force to have Commonwealth flyers incorporated as individuals into RAF squadrons under British control rather than serve in their own air force squadrons under their own national control.

The main "vehicle" for that happening was the British Commonwealth Air Training Plan. The main provision the British used in routing graduates to the Royal Air Force was, as mentioned earlier, Article Fifteen of the BCATP Agreement. That key section read: "The United Kingdom Government undertakes that pupils of Canada, Australia and New Zealand shall, after training is completed, be identified with their respective Dominions, either by the method of organizing Dominion units and formations or in some other way, such methods to be agreed upon with the respective Dominion Governments."[6]

Right from the beginning, Prime Minister King, an ardent nationalist, commented, "It is the desire of this Government that Canadian Air Force units be formed as soon as sufficient trained personnel are available."[7] Canada's intention was also underlined as early as November 23, 1939, in a letter from the chief of the air staff, Air Vice-Marshal George Croil, to Defence Minister Norman Rogers: "It would be detrimental to Canadian prestige as a nation to restrict its official air effort to Home Defence and Training." Croil added, "We have every reason to expect that Canadians will do well in the air. *If they serve in Canadian squadrons they will bring credit to Canada as a nation*" (emphasis added).[8]

Despite the plain black and white statement that Canadians would — in time — serve in Canadian squadrons under RCAF control, the British simply ignored it. While Canada had one idea, "London, however, preferred to think that only some of the [BCATP graduates] would be posted to a limited number of Canadian squadrons," while the rest would simply go to the RAF.[9] RCAF airmen — numbering in the thousands — were channelled by the British into Royal Air Force squadrons and stations. In short, the whole thing ended up looking like a recruiting scheme for the RAF, the very thing King had rejected before the war.

One problem was that King failed to demand specific numbers and deadlines. In the early negotiations he wanted to set up Canadian squadrons, but the negotiations were protracted and difficult and, after a series of compromises, the deadlines and numbers went out the window. That one single failure presaged years of acrimony.

Also, as a brief aside, there is one rather mind-boggling note about the BCATP Agreement. Incredibly, the tiny word *the* was at the centre of a considerable controversy in the negotiations. The final agreement did not say "*the* pupils of Canada, Australia and New Zealand" would be assigned to RCAF, RAAF, or RNZAF squadrons, it only said "*pupils* of Canada, Australia and New Zealand." The difference is that the first version would mean "*all* the pupils" while saying "*pupils* of Canada" could mean some, a few, many, hundreds, or just about anything. The final version of the agreement dropped the word *the*.

In a penetrating examination of what went wrong, one writer emphasized another factor as being perhaps the most critical of all.[10] Leslie Nuttall argues that the most far-reaching failure was that the King government agreed to send Canadian aircrew graduates overseas with the understanding that the British would be paying them once they arrived in Britain. Since the British would foot the bill, it certainly followed that London would have ultimate control over them. Historian Desmond Morton summarized that as "cheapness outweigh[ing] nationalism."[11]

There is plenty of room to blame King, although the situation was not an easy one. The BCATP was a daunting financial undertaking for Canada. The cost was $353 million for three years at a time when the entire Canadian federal budget was $500 million a year. The cost of fifteen RCAF squadrons overseas, meantime, was estimated at $750 million.

* * *

The first trickle of graduates from the BCATP began arriving in Britain in November 1940, but the RCAF also sent a few formed squadrons. The first was No.10 Squadron (later 400 Squadron), an army co-operation unit set up on February 25, 1940, and equipped with Lysander aircraft. That made RCAF history — the first Canadian squadron on the front lines of an air war. However, No.10 Squadron turned out to be useless in France because by the time pilots were fully trained, the Battle of France was over. The first Canadian fighter squadron, No. 1 Squadron RCAF (later No. 401 Squadron) arrived in time to take part in the late stages of the Battle of Britain in 1940.

As noted earlier, in the spring of 1940 Prime Minister King appointed Chubby Power as Minister of National Defence for Air.[12] Power was guilty of missteps, but he became a champion of Canadianization.[13] He gave orders in no uncertain terms to "put the RCAF on the map" and played a critical part in turning it into a credible, modern, and independent military organization. Power could not work with the chief of the air staff, Air Vice-Marshal George Croil, who, while competent, was determined to keep the minister away from important decisions. Croil was soon gone. His replacement, the bluff and hearty Air Vice-Marshal Lloyd Breadner, initially thought Canada could set up as many as seventy-seven squadrons in Britain by the end of 1942. Given the BCATP, that was an impossible order.

Power and Breadner stumbled badly in the early going. Breadner sent instructions that the newly established RCAF headquarters in London was to be simply a liaison office and would not directly command Canadians in Britain. Power told the cabinet that the intention was to have RCAF personnel in Britain integrated into RAF squadrons. The prime minister was flabbergasted to hear that neither Power nor Breadner knew that the setting up of Canadian squadrons was a government priority. King then bypassed the air minister and instead dispatched Defence Minister Layton Ralston for upcoming talks in London to argue for more Canadian squadrons and a bigger role for the Canadian headquarters there.

Britain's minister for air, Archibald Sinclair, pushed the British view that having too many Canadian squadrons or a separate Canadian headquarters would create severe operational problems. Canadian proposals threatened to make the system of assignments, promotions, and transfers unmanageable, he said. Ground crews were another complication. Most fighter squadrons had fifteen or so pilots but more than one hundred ground crew. Having Canadian squadrons with British ground crews would effectively mean hundreds of Britons would be serving in the RCAF. All this would become a familiar theme. Time and again the British opposed Canadianization because it would cause severe operational problems and would "tend to destroy the essential mobility and elasticity in the Royal Air Force."[14] Actually, it did cause operational problems later on, but most of them were overcome.

On January 7, 1941, after the talks ended, the two sides signed what became known as the Ralston-Sinclair Agreement. Ralston accepted that it was impractical for the RCAF to send up to seventy-seven squadrons to Britain. The British made only one significant concession, agreeing to increase the number of Canadian squadrons from fifteen to twenty-five by early 1942. Britain would pay for them.

The RCAF official history calls Ralston-Sinclair "an enormous compromise."[15] If the BCATP deal had failed to put Canadianization on the road to reality, this agreement kept it on the bumpy back alleys even longer. Yes, there would be a few more RCAF squadrons, but the British were determined to keep control of the entire air campaign overseas, and they did. It's clear that Ralston simply had not grasped the numbers involved in the air training plan. As many as 2,900 Canadian aircrew would be available within a few months, while twenty-five Canadian squadrons would need only about one thousand of them, perhaps as few as six hundred. Under Ralston-Sinclair, Canadians surplus to those needs would simply be scattered among RAF squadrons. Also the new agreement stated that RAF officers would continue to hold senior appointments in RCAF squadrons, air bases, and headquarters, at least in the short term.

Still, there was some progress as the first Canadian bomber squadrons were formed in the spring of 1941. At that time the air war in Europe had been raging for twenty-one months and Allied formations were at their lowest ebb. On April 23, 1941, No. 405 Squadron was set up at Driffield,

Yorkshire, while No. 408 Squadron was set up on June 24 at Lindholme, also in Yorkshire. Both were equipped with near-useless Handley Page Hampden medium bombers. The No. 408 commanding officer was Wing Commander Nelles Timmerman, from Kingston, Ontario, one of those who had made their way to Britain in the 1930s to join the RAF. The appointment of Timmerman and that of Wing Commander John "Moose" Fulton from Kamloops, B.C., as commanding officer of No. 419 Squadron, showed that at least a few outstanding Canadian officers were available. Later, when Fulton was lost on an operation, the squadron was renamed No. 419 (Moose) Squadron in his honour, the only RCAF squadron named for an individual.

Despite the new Canadian aircrew pouring into Britain, incredibly, even months after the Ralston-Sinclair Agreement, the twenty-five Canadian squadrons had still not been fully staffed. In any event, some of the "Canadian" squadrons were really a mixture of several nationalities while, memorably, one "Australian" squadron had only one Australian in it.

It might be asked why bomber crews were not formed in Canada and sent over to Britain complete to prevent the RAF from assigning airmen as individuals. That would have made the establishment of Canadian squadrons, and later a Canadian group, much easier. The answer is that it was simply not practical. The Canadians arriving in Britain were not necessarily what Bomber Command needed — too many pilots perhaps, but not enough flight engineers or radio operators. Pilots required open space for training, so many of them were trained in Canada but flight engineers and radio operators were often trained in Britain. To the end of the war, many Canadian bombers flew with British flight engineers. An operational squadron may have needed a replacement pilot but not an entire crew.

In the summer of 1941 Chubby Power began a new effort to energize the stalled Canadianization program, writing to Prime Minister King that the issue required "urgent attention." In his letter, Power cited examples of Canadian airmen being reported missing on operations but the RCAF unable to provide families with any information about them because they were serving in RAF squadrons. At one point information got back to Canada that a flying boat had crashed off Portugal with six

Canadians on board, but the RCAF did not know who they were or why they were there.

Meeting the next day, the cabinet resolved to send Power to Britain to try again to get more control over personnel postings and promotions. Power, along with Air Vice-Marshal Breadner and others, arrived in London on July 1. Canadian estimates showed that by January 1943 the number of RCAF airmen in Britain would reach forty-five thousand. In meetings with the British, Power argued that the Canadian public would not accept RCAF personnel being handed over to the British "like mercenaries."

One chronic problem in forming Canadian squadrons was a shortage of Canadian ground crews. The Canadian government then agreed to send one thousand ground crew members to support at least some of the Canadian squadrons.

The tug of war between operational necessity and a Canadian national identity continued, with the British saying they were "troubled" by Power's message. Britain's Harold Balfour said postings and promotions had to be "treated as a whole," while another British official said it was "undesirable that there should be watertight compartments." A grating issue was the commissioning of BCATP graduates. The British practice was that some top graduates would be offered commissions at the rank of pilot officer while the remainder would become sergeant pilots. The Canadians felt that was part of the "old school tie" mentality, in which only candidates with ritzy family backgrounds would be commissioned. Canadians wanted all graduating aircrew to become pilot officers as a reflection of the much more egalitarian atmosphere in the RCAF.

The British accepted some of the points Power raised and agreed to have the RCAF better informed about its airmen in RAF squadrons. The official RCAF history calls the result of the meetings a "moderate first step."[16] Then the British finally conceded, for the first time, that it would be feasible to form a Canadian bomber group. Considering how Ralston had been stiff-armed only months before, this was a remarkable turnaround. Power noted, "The principle of a Canadian bomber group was accepted and would be a definite objective although delayed."[17] The bomber group would require the formation of new Canadian squadrons first.

One legitimate problem in setting up a Canadian group was a shortage of aircraft. Factories in the U.K. were going all out to produce three new heavy bombers, but some of them had to be sent to the U.S.S.R. The British hoped to get new American planes, but in the end the Americans decided to keep most of them for their own crews. With all that, a Bomber Command plan to expand to four thousand aircraft had to be pared down to 2,500 aircraft. The shortage had another direct effect on Canada. On September 18, 1941, Ottawa decided it would build the Lancaster bomber in Canada. This was an immense undertaking because the Lancaster was one of the most sophisticated aircraft of the time. As many as fifty-five thousand major parts went into building one, not including the engines or turrets. As with the earlier Anson project, there were monumental delays in production.

There was a significant change in November 1941, when newly promoted Air Vice-Marshal Gus Edwards took up his post as RCAF senior officer in London (later, air officer-in-chief, RCAF Overseas). Edwards was a bulldog, "the most forceful man in the RCAF," according to later Air Marshal Wilf Curtis.[18] As memorably described by Vincent Rigby, Edwards's temper sometimes "broke loose from its fragile casing."[19] If the air force wanted a heavyweight to go toe-to-toe with the RAF, the spiky, tempestuous Edwards was just the man. He became this country's greatest promoter of Canadianization, to a point that bordered on obsession.

Edwards's was an inspiring story. He was born in England but raised among the coal mines of Cape Breton. He went to work in the mines at fourteen but still studied night and day to get a formal education. His rise through the air force ranks was a tribute to remarkable determination and ability. Unfortunately, his effectiveness was undermined by a debilitating heart condition that shortened his career and led to his death not long after the war.

Edwards arrived in Britain to find Canadians dispersed over "hell's half acre," while the RCAF headquarters in London looked to him "as dead as a doornail."[20] The headquarters was uncertain of the location of more than six thousand Canadian airmen. Edwards could not find the whereabouts of his own nephew. In a letter to Ottawa, he said that if something drastic were not done, "I do think that sometime in the future the people of Canada will make the discovery that they have not got an air force at all."[21]

For some time the RAF had been sending Canadian pilots to reinforce depleted RAF squadrons in the Middle East. On January 29, 1942, Edwards issued instructions that no further Canadians were to be posted out of England or to any RAF squadron without his authority. Meantime, a letter to the RAF asked why no Canadian squadron leaders were appointed to three Canadian night fighter squadrons. The reply was that Canadians would be promoted to squadron command but only through normal wastage, which, as one Canadian officer commented, "at the present rate of casualties means approximately never."[22]

There were pockets of progress. No. 419 Squadron was 83.7 percent Canadian by February 1942.

The "Battle for Canadianization" reached its most fateful moments in May 1942. Those moments included a War Cabinet Committee meeting on May 22 and a series of meetings in Ottawa with British representatives shortly afterward. Together, they constituted the turning point in the battle.

At the cabinet committee meeting, Power told his colleagues that Canadianization was bogged down. He said that the government should press forward to get a commitment on a definite number of new Canadian squadrons to be formed and a strengthened Canadian headquarters to take control over RCAF personnel. The committee gave him the green light.[23]

At the first meeting with the British representatives, Power laid out a series of goals: that more Canadians would receive commissions, that a Canadian headquarters with broad control over Canadian airmen would be set up, and that Edwards would be delegated more authority. It also wanted a definite timetable for the establishment of more Canadian squadrons and for the formation of a Canadian bomber group.

The negotiations went on for several days, and in the end the British were willing to give ground on some issues. There would be changes in the way Canadian BCATP grads were promoted (more officers, but not all officers), and a Canadian personnel reception centre for arriving Canadians would be set up in Bournemouth to look after the welfare of Canadian airmen. A British telegram back to the Air Ministry in London during the talks said, "Canadians are firm that there must be a Canadian group."

Now there was a program of concrete action. Among RCAF bomber formations, Nos. 405, 408, 419, and 420 squadrons would be moved closer to one another so that it would be easier to set up a new group. Stations where the Canadian squadrons were based would be commanded by Canadian officers as soon as they were available. Canadian officers would gradually take over station headquarters staff. Any newly formed Canadian bomber squadron would be assigned to the group to which other Canadian squadrons already belonged. Power was assured that a bomber group would be set up as soon as there were enough aircraft and air bases available. New bomber squadrons would come on strength by the end of 1942, enough for the creation of a Canadian bomber group in early 1943. Canadianization received a further bump forward in June 1942 when a fifth heavy bomber squadron — No. 425 Squadron — was set up, the first French-Canadian formation in the RCAF. In the months ahead, four other squadrons were also set up, and more the following spring.

It was true that Canadianization was a burden (the British would have said "nightmare") from an operational standpoint. Nevertheless, it had become patently obvious that the RAF was simply stonewalling Canadianization.[24] First among the opponents, of course, was "Bomber" Harris. Another fierce opponent was Air Marshal Trafford Leigh-Mallory of 11 (Fighter) Group. "You couldn't talk to him," said Wilfred Curtis. In June 1942 Edwards was promoted from air vice-marshal to air marshal to deal with the RAF on a more equal footing.

It was all symptomatic of a larger truth that there were huge cultural differences between the RCAF and the RAF — and between Canadians and Britons generally. Of course, there were ordinary Britons by the thousands who welcomed Canadians with open arms and treated them as family. Scots, for some reason, were especially welcoming. In a blizzard of letters sent home (all examined carefully by censors) Canadians spoke warmly of British hospitality and kindness, not to mention the many romantic relationships that sprang up. Many Canadians, like Robert Collins, a ground crew member of No. 6 Group, had family in Britain. "My father's family was here … the King and Winston Churchill were here. And here were the valiant people we admired and cheered on through the darkest years of war."[25]

Nevertheless, some of the experiences of Canadians with the RAF were downright noxious. Author David Bashow said RCAF newcomers to Britain "frequently railed against the heavy hand of British authority and classism."[26] In one infamous incident, a senior warrant officer at RAF Station Cranwell in Lincolnshire, in his first lecture, called Canadians "a bunch of rotten colonials."

Canadians strongly disliked the spit-and-polish mindset apparent on many British bases. RAF administrative officers, usually referred to as "wingless wonders," could be particularly exasperating. Some of the Canadian complaints were simply wartime grouching. Nevertheless, more than a few Britons considered Canadians to be loud, childish show-offs, both brash and quarrelsome. One RAF report described Canadians as "a pretty unsophisticated lot, who come over with a chip on their shoulder … [and] do not know how to hold their drinks." In a wry comment, one writer said at least Canadians could take comfort in one thing: "Americans did their part in improving the image of Canadian airmen."[27]

Meantime, Edwards continued to run into opposition not only from the British, but — perhaps more surprisingly — from senior Canadian officers. During a meeting in May 1942, he was chagrined to find Air Commodore Archibald Campbell, the first Canadian to command an RAF station, was hostile to the idea. Campbell returned to Canada to take up a new posting, only to publicly criticize the policy, saying, "The best squadrons are mixed squadrons.… Canadians are well looked after by the RAF."[28] His outburst went right to the war cabinet, but, extraordinarily, he was not disciplined. Even more extraordinary, his promotion to air vice-marshal went ahead as planned. Much earlier, Air Vice-Marshal Leigh Stevenson had expressed his opposition to forming a group, saying that anything larger than RCAF squadrons would be "most difficult."[29]

Many RCAF members and Canadians alike were genuinely torn about Canadianization because of their emotional ties with Britain. William Carr, a wartime Spitfire reconnaissance pilot and later Canadian Forces lieutenant-general, said most Canadians grew up thinking of themselves as part of the British Empire. He was happy to serve in an

RAF squadron.³⁰ J.K. Chapman of No. 415 Squadron, although proud of his country, was "prouder still of belonging to something greater: the British Empire."³¹ Even so, a 1942 survey of Canadian airmen serving on thirty RAF and RCAF bases concluded that there was considerable support for Canadianization so as long as it did not mean breaking up established crews.³² Les Morrison, who enlisted in the RCAF in 1942, took "enormous pride" in his uniform, the coveted wings and shoulder patches emblazoned with the word *Canada*.³³ Part of it was that some Canadians genuinely felt they were different from their British colleagues, considering themselves to be "a unique breed of tough northern warriors."³⁴ Another change was that, in contrast to the situation in the First World War, the vast majority of Canadian service personnel were Canadian-born.

At home Canadianization became an issue in newspapers and in the House of Commons. Toronto Conservative member of Parliament Tommy Church, for one, said it was nonsense to have Canadian squadrons at all. Church's pro-Empire views were frequently supported by some newspapers, including the influential *Toronto Telegram*. In a later debate the opposition Conservatives challenged the policy, saying it threatened the unity of command. There was a lot of comment that Canadianization was simply political. One airman said it was "purely a political move … and cannot add one bomb to the air offensive."³⁵ A *Globe and Mail* editorial on May 15, 1942, noted, "[The *Globe*] must take strong issue with [Mr. Power] for his professed determination to persevere with an attempt to secure an independent organization for the personnel of the Royal Canadian Air Force serving overseas. For such a move, it is difficult to discern any practical justification such as the promotion of greater fighting efficiency … and none have been advanced. It is a plan of disintegration … the suspicion cannot be dismissed that political motives have deliberately brought it into the limelight."³⁶

At a news conference in England later, Edwards touched off a storm when he made what he thought was an off the record comment to two newspaper reporters about critical newspaper comment. "Some people are talking a lot of bloody nonsense about splitting the Empire. If Canadians who see it from that point of view want to be mugs all their lives, that's their business. I can see no reason against Canadianization."[37] After that had got back to Canada, the *Montreal Gazette* ran a scathing article under the headline "Air Marshal Edwards Is Wrong." The *Ottawa Journal* said, "Air Marshal Edwards should keep his mouth shut."

Other papers supported Canadianization. On September 5, 1942, the *Ottawa Citizen* wrote, "The move to form Canadian groups completely manned, officered, and administrated by men of the RCAF is to be commended.... Canadian airmen have well won the right for Canada to be so distinctively represented." The *Kitchener Record* noted that if grouped solidly together, "our boys will be happier and will fight with that team spirit that is so necessary in winning victories."[38]

In August 1942 Power and Breadner headed to London once more. Told that Air Chief Marshal Harris was "sticky" on further Canadianization, Power said he was "fed up with going around asking favours and would ask no more." However, a meeting with Harris on August 19 went smoothly, with the air chief marshal brazenly claiming he was one of the RCAF's most ardent boosters. While some meetings went well, it was obvious that many in the Air Ministry still regarded the Canadian Headquarters as a downright nuisance.

However, in spite of unforeseen problems the British went a long way to honouring commitments made in Ottawa earlier that year. The Air Ministry had said that Canadian squadrons would be added to Bomber Command when new squadrons were formed, but it turned out that there would not be many new squadrons because of a shortage of new aircraft and high casualty rates. The idea of forming new Canadian squadrons did not go down well with Harris. He thought there were just too many new Commonwealth squadrons altogether. He complained that it bolstered the comment made by the Germans in North Africa that Britain was fighting to the last Australian.

In January 1943 a crisis erupted that has since been referred to as "the Edwards controversy."[39] It began with the latest in a long series of demands and complaints lobbed from Ottawa onto Edwards's desk in London. The messages prompted the air marshal on January 22, 1943, to send a blistering rocket to the Air Ministry. He accused the RAF of deliberately resisting Canadianization, saying, "I do not think the co-operation we requested has been given." He said the phrase "operational necessity" used by the British was a convenient catch-all for doing nothing. He pointed out that 585 aircrew were still needed to complete Canadianization in RCAF squadrons but that there were more than twelve thousand RCAF members in the U.K. at that point. Edwards might have gotten away with most of that, but then, reaching far beyond his authority, he threatened to abrogate all existing agreements with the British that dealt with RCAF members overseas.

The threat was bad enough, but the timing was also unfortunate. Unknown to Edwards, Canada had finally agreed to pay for all RCAF members overseas — a dramatic and long-overdue step. Pay was the issue that had been backstopping practically every argument about who had control of Canadian airmen overseas, so the decision on money fundamentally changed the equation. Now, at long last, Britain would be giving up control because Canada would pay the bill.

Having seen Edwards's letter, Breadner volleyed back, accusing Edwards of going "off the deep end." There was all kinds of fallout from the affair, not the least of which was that, although Edwards could not be fired or recalled without a public row, his authority was sharply curtailed. Breadner made a hurried trip to London to meet with Air Chief Marshal Charles Portal, the RAF chief. While Edwards's outburst initially appeared to damage the Canadian cause, and while it damaged his career, it may actually have been a catalyst for long-term change.

Finally, a history-making moment: No. 6 Group, RCAF, was formed on October 25, 1942, with nine squadrons. It was Canada's largest air formation ever. Among the first tasks was to find a permanent headquarters, and after some searching, a rambling seventy-five-room Yorkshire castle was selected. The owner, Lord Mowbray, turned out to be a chronic whiner, while his bleak Victorian pile became known among Canadians as "Dismal Castle."

The Canadian Bomber Group began operations without ceremony. Squadrons that had formerly operated under No. 4 Group RAF simply began to take their orders from the new Group Headquarters at one minute past midnight on January 1, 1943. The squadrons were Nos. 408, 419, 420, 424, 425, 426, 427, and 428, while No. 6 Group also controlled the station at Skipton-on-Swale, which was then still under construction. The Group was also given control of No. 405 Squadron, then serving with Coastal Command. The Group flew its first mission on the night of January 3–4, when six aircraft from No. 427 Squadron were sent to lay mines off the Frisian Islands. It was the start of a momentous year in the war, marked by the German debacles at Stalingrad and Kursk, defeats in North Africa and Sicily, and the tide turning in the North Atlantic.

At the beginning, and for many months following, there were serious problems in No. 6 Group. In the period from January to July 1943, Group losses were the worst in Bomber Command; indeed, they bordered on catastrophic. In the Battle of Berlin, from November 1943 to March 1944, the Group suffered 6 percent casualties, higher than Bomber Command as a whole. Among the worst group operations was the bombing of Magdeburg on January 21–22, 1944, when the casualty rate was a disastrous 12.3 percent.

There were many reasons. Not only the Group but also many of the squadrons were new. Navigators especially were new. Crews were not explicitly following assigned routes, leaving aircraft more vulnerable to night fighters and flak. There was a shortage of capable leaders. A number of key positions still had to be filled by British officers while extensive training was done by the RAF.

The first Group commander was Air Vice-Marshal George Brookes. Born in Yorkshire in 1894 and a later immigrant to Owen Sound, Ontario, Brookes focused too much on renovating his headquarters. He knew little about operational matters. Harris had been critical of Canadian leadership, and, it turned out, he was not entirely wrong in the early days. Much more successful was the next commander, Air Vice-Marshal "Black Mike" McEwen, who had started his career as a fighter pilot in the First World War. McEwan built No. 6 Group into a solid organization and commanded it until the end of the war.

There were daunting problems with the Yorkshire bases. They were so far north that each bombing flight involved an extra half-hour flying time, while the bases themselves had seriously overlapping flight patterns. Also, at the start of operations, three squadrons were equipped with the Halifax heavy bomber. Later Halifax models were much improved, but early versions had a limited payload and an obvious engine exhaust that gave away the bomber's location at night. Defensive armament was inadequate and the plane was tricky to fly. Crews eventually warmed to the Halifax, but "Bomber" Harris never did, offering scathing criticism of the plane to the very end. Other No. 6 Group squadrons flew Wellingtons, which by this point in the war were near obsolete. In time the casualty situation improved. No. 6 Group's numbers were reduced to the point that they were lower than those in the neighbouring No. 4 Group. There is no doubt, though, that early No. 6 Group operations cost a great many Canadian lives.

Prominent among the targets in 1943 were the German submarine pens at Lorient in France, although attacks were mostly a waste of bombs because of heavy concrete construction over the pens. Later came the gruelling Battle of the Ruhr, a five-month campaign against the industrial heart of Germany that included bombing the Nordstern synthetic-oil

Bombing Veteran — The Vickers Wellington medium bomber was flown by at least thirteen RCAF squadrons. Its unique geodesic "cross-hatched" airframe was developed by Barnes Wallis, known for his "bouncing bomb" used in the attack on German dams.

plant and the Rheinmetall-Borsig plant, which made anti-aircraft guns and other weapons in Düsseldorf. As many as four hundred bombers were used to plaster the Krupp armament works at Essen on March 5, 1943. As noted earlier, on October 14, 1944, No. 6 Group supplied aircraft for the attack on Duisburg.

On August 1, 1943, after interminable delays, the first Lancaster bomber came off the Toronto production line. There was a big splash of publicity, but such was the rush to get the plane out the door at Victory Aircraft that it made its first flight from Toronto to Montreal without instruments. The plane, dubbed the *Ruhr Express*, was quietly outfitted in Montreal before heading to Britain to join No. 419 Squadron. Eventually, eleven of fourteen squadrons in the Group were equipped with Lancasters.

The introduction of the Stirling and Halifax strategic bombers had made the bombing campaign vastly more effective, but undoubtedly the Lancaster was the best aircraft of the three. Oddly, the Lancaster was a kind of band-aid solution to problems with the earlier and inadequate Avro Manchester. When the Manchester's two troublesome engines were replaced with four Rolls-Royce Merlins, the aircraft was magically transformed. The "Lanc" was able to carry an eighteen-thousand-pound payload, much more than the American B-17. It could even carry the twenty-two-thousand-pound *Grand Slam* earthquake bomb, the most powerful non-atomic bomb of the war. The Lancaster had a top speed of 277 miles per hour, climbed beyond twenty thousand feet, and had an amazing range of 1,700 miles. Although German night fighters and anti-aircraft fire took a fearsome toll on Allied bombers, airmen loved the Lancaster because it could take punishment and still fly, even on two engines.

Still, all aircraft of that time had built-in hazards. A bombing mission normally began with two thousand gallons of high-octane fuel and ten thousand pounds of high explosive aboard. An engine failure in the first moments of flight in such a heavy and explosive aircraft was usually a death sentence. "Pilot skill was the difference between life and death for a crew at all times … [but] never more so than on takeoff," said author David Bashow.[40]

More Canadians and additional squadrons joined No. 6 Group as time went along. By the end of 1944, Canadians made up 87 percent of the Group's strength. Squadrons in the Group were active almost right up to VE Day, with their final mission undertaken on April 25, 1945.

One of the strangest — if not *the* strangest — tributes to the effectiveness of Canadian bombing during the Second World War came from Nazi propaganda chief Joseph Goebbels. In his diary in early 1943, Goebbels wrote about attacks on the Ruhr industrial region: "The damage is colossal and indeed ghastly.... Nobody can tell how Krupps is to go on.... It drives one mad to think that some Canadian boor, who probably can't even find Europe on the globe, flies here from a country glutted with natural resources which his people don't know how to exploit, to bombard a continent with a crowded population."[41]

In the month of August 1944 No. 6 Group aircraft dropped more bombs than the entire number of bombs dropped on London by the Luftwaffe in the war.

The Allied bombing campaign, of which No. 6 Group was a prominent part, remains contentious to this day. Sir Michael Beetham, a bomber pilot and later RAF air marshal, is among those who have called it "the most controversial campaign of the war."[42] The questions of area bombing and targeting civilians have been particularly disputed in Canada, erupting in a national fury in 1992 with the airing of the CBC program *The Valour and the Horror*. In it, Bomber Command is accused of concealing its plans to deliberately kill or injure six hundred thousand German civilians, mostly old men, women, and children. Controversially, the CBC used actors in the program to portray several key figures, choosing a particularly sinister-looking "Bomber" Harris. Many viewers felt the broadcast did an enormous injustice to the bomber crews, not to mention the forty-two thousand British citizens killed in the Blitz.

It is sometimes overlooked that the casualties in Bomber Command were dreadful: in No. 6 Group alone, 814 planes were lost and casualties amounted to 4,272 dead. The numbers provide a stark reminder of the dangers the crews faced. Roughly speaking, during the course of the war, aircrew in Bomber Command had only a one-in-two chance of survival.

In 1943 and 1944, when Germany still possessed formidable defences, for every one hundred airmen who joined an operational unit, fifty-one were killed in combat operations, nine more in non-operational accidents, twelve became prisoners of war, and three men were wounded or badly enough injured to be removed from operations. Of the original one hundred airmen only twenty-four remained unscathed. A significant number of Bomber Command flyers completed one harrowing tour of thirty missions, only to return later for a second tour. Much beloved Wing Commander "Moose" Fulton of No. 419 Squadron was lost on August 2, 1942, on his second tour after completing more than fifty missions. In a bomber squadron there were twenty crews, but No. 408 Squadron lost twenty in the first three months of 1944 and three commanding officers in less than a year.

While elaborate training, teamwork, and attention to the smallest operational details were crucial to survival, pure luck also played its part. Superstitions abounded: there were charms and mascots, St. Christopher medals, rosaries, favourite photographs, and rabbits' feet. There were all kinds of rituals, among the more common being urinating on the rear wheel of the aircraft before climbing aboard. Group Captain Leonard Cheshire, VC, one of the most fearless and honoured RAF airmen of the Second World War, didn't buy any of it. He famously said, "Either you had luck or you didn't."

If you wanted to survive in a bomber it was best to avoid being a tail gunner because that was the most dangerous job. Most night fighters approached from the rear of the target. If you wanted to survive in No. 425 Squadron, it was best to avoid the bomber "KW-G" because, of the eight aircraft that used that code, two were lost on the first mission and six others were destroyed in fatal crashes.

There were hair-raising and heroic survival stories in profusion. Among the most miraculous was that of bomb aimer John Bailey from Saskatoon.[43] Bailey took over the controls of a heavily damaged Stirling bomber in 1943 after the pilot was badly wounded. Bailey had had some pilot training but had never piloted — let alone landed — a multi-engine bomber limping along on three engines. Showing great coolness, he brought the aircraft to a safe landing at a British airfield and was later awarded the Conspicuous Gallantry Medal. Bailey went back to Canada to take pilot's training but failed the course.

Canada's greatest Second World War bomber pilot was probably the superb John Fauquier. The Bomber Command legend was a tough commander and many airmen found his manner abrasive. The ground crews, however, thought the world of him because he never took them for granted. Born in Ottawa, he was already an experienced bush pilot when he enlisted just after the start of the war. A year later he was posted overseas to No. 405 Squadron, where he flew Wellington and Halifax bombers. After a time at RCAF Overseas Headquarters in London, he was promoted to group captain and posted to No. 6 Group Headquarters. Later he moved to No. 8 Group, the Pathfinders, and began a second tour of thirty-eight missions. He acted as assistant master bomber in attacks against the German V-1 and V-2 facilities at Peenemünde. On one attack he made seventeen passes over the target to make sure following aircraft could pinpoint it. Afterward he was awarded the Distinguished Service Order. However, even with that, he reverted from air commodore to group captain to become commanding officer of the RAF's No. 617 Squadron, the famous "Dam Busters," and fly even more operations.

Among the most extraordinary RCAF airmen of the war was Andrew Mynarski from Winnipeg. Mynarski joined the RCAF in 1941 and graduated as an air gunner. In 1944 he was in a Lancaster bomber that was badly damaged by a night fighter. The crew was ordered to bail out but Mynarski could see that tail gunner Pat Brophy's turret had jammed and he was trapped. Mynarski tried in vain to free his crew mate using a fire axe and even his bare hands. With Mynarski's flight suit and parachute on fire, Brophy eventually waved him away. Mynarski returned to the rear door, where he paused and saluted. He then said, "Good night, sir," and jumped. The bomber crashed and, incredibly, Brophy survived, but Mynarski, with his burned parachute, did not. Brophy's description of what happened led to Mynarski being awarded the Victoria Cross.

By the end of the war, Chubby Power, Air Marshal Edwards, and others did, indeed, "put the RCAF on the map." Nevertheless, full

RCAF Canadianization overseas was never completely achieved.* There never was a Canadian fighter group, while overseas only 40 percent of Canadians served in RCAF squadrons and bases. Meanwhile, Canadian flyers had to listen in fury as BBC news broadcasts regularly reported "Bombers of the Royal Air Force attacked Berlin," while only rarely mentioning the RCAF.

There has been criticism of the King government over Canadianization. The issue of the government's failure in December 1939 to pay for Canadian airmen sent to Britain still nags. As Leslie Nuttall said at that time, the Canadian government "abdicated its responsibility."[44] Nuttall has also alleged that King and Power promoted the setting up of No. 6 Group to avoid a domestic political disaster that was brewing over Canadianization. Why the big push, he asks? "The answer is to be found in politics not war."[45] Nuttall claims that Power knew by 1942 the government was "digging its own political grave" by not recovering control of Canadian airmen overseas, and that no government could allow such a situation to continue. The official RCAF history, for its part, also attributes political motivation to pretty much everything Power did.[46]

It is certainly true that a failure of the government to do anything about Canadianization would have been political suicide. However, while there was sniping in the newspapers, in Parliament, and even the RCAF itself, there was no political crisis similar to, say, the conscription crisis. Politics was most definitely part of the process, and Chubby Power hoped that Canadian control might, among other things, encourage armed forces enlistment in Quebec. However, in Parliament the main opposition was the Conservative Party, whose policies were pro-Empire. It was not demanding faster Canadianization.

Actually, it may be that things were the other way round. Writer Iain Johnston has said, "The political independent-mindedness expressed by Ottawa was moving ahead of, and often driving, the continued growth

---

* In February 1944 negotiations began for the establishment of "Tiger Force," the RCAF's contribution to the final campaign against Japan. Only at that point did the Canadian government insist on retaining full administrative control over the RCAF's planned operations.

of Canadian national identity."[47] The road to Canadianization was not an easy journey. In the end it was a landmark for Canada even though it turned out to be a far messier business than it might have been.

DECISION FIVE

Appointment of the Minister of Everything

He was the commander-in-chief of Canada's industrial army — a mighty legion of more than one million men and women. He controlled the production of ships, aircraft, tanks, guns, steel, automobiles, and a hundred other products at plants sprawled across the nation. He ruled over the production of aluminum, gold, and silver. He set wages for workers and prices for hundreds of products. He built new industrial plants from scratch and, indeed, started whole new industries. At one point Clarence Decatur Howe controlled so many companies that he started to run out of names.*

Howe ("Clarence" to only a few and "C.D." to most) was appointed minister of munitions and supply on April 9, 1940, the same day that Hitler invaded Norway and Denmark. He did not want the job. The Department of Munitions and Supply had a reputation as an unhappy place.[1] If Howe was reluctant, so was Prime Minister King. He knew that appointing Howe

---

* According to Peter C. Newman, Howe's assistants solved the problem by picking names out of the Montreal phone book. At the time many cities used phone numbers with a prefix such as FAirmont or CItadel and then numbers. So the phone number might be FA-1234 or CI-1234. That is how the Fairmont Company (rubber) and Citadel Merchandising (machine tools) got their names.

would reignite a political feud with Ontario's unguided missile of a premier, Mitch Hepburn. The premier wanted one of his cronies appointed to the job, but King decided on Howe, and Hepburn be damned.

Although he had been in politics since 1935, C.D. Howe was not a policy wonk, and not a retail politician. He was an engineer, but even that was not what he did best. His real genius was business. He knew it inside and out and it made him rich. Tough, blunt, a Big Dog, and sometimes called the "Minister of Everything," the living, breathing locomotive was absolutely "the right man to lead the nation's wartime industrial mobilization," according to historian J.L. Granatstein.[2]

Howe's biggest gamble was to bet $50 million on building a Canadian factory to make synthetic rubber, a wager that would be worth perhaps half a billion dollars or more in today's money. The technology to make synthetic rubber was still unproven, and there were no factories producing it anywhere in the country. Losing the bet would have been a calamity of epic proportions.

At the time, natural rubber trees were the only source of almost all rubber products. No synthetic product could duplicate natural rubber's special bounce, flexibility, and versatility. Of course, most vehicles needed rubber tires, but rubber was also widely used in dozens of other products. A Sherman tank used a half-ton of it.[3] Scientists, especially in Germany, had been trying to make synthetic rubber as far back as the nineteenth century. Neoprene, introduced by DuPont in 1931, was used for some things such as electric insulation and auto fan belts but it could not be used for tires.[4]

American companies put enormous resources into research on synthetic rubber, but it turned out the greatest roadblock to development was not science but politics. In 1940 executives from Standard Oil of New Jersey appeared before Congress to call for building new factories to produce one hundred tons of synthetic rubber a day. Nothing came of it. In one of the worst decisions of his long presidency, Franklin Roosevelt turned down a request to invest one hundred million dollars in synthetic rubber factories, saying, "These wealthy rubber companies ought to build their own plants."[5] Robert Solo, a government official, later called that decision "a scandalous, a complete, nearly catastrophic, foul up."[6]

After the attack on Pearl Harbor, rubber supplies were cut off. The Japanese quickly occupied Java, Sumatra, Malaya, and the East Indies, the source of 90 percent of the world's natural rubber. Howe called it a mess of "historic proportions." Fortunately for Canada, a Crown Corporation had stockpiled rubber and had an eighteen-month supply on hand. To conserve it there was widespread rationing of car and truck tires for civilian use and many strange experiments to find substitutes. Garden City Taxi in Halifax tried, unsuccessfully, to use tires made from birch trees.[7]

There was a suggestion that rubber trees should be planted in South America, but it would have taken five years for them to become productive. In Canada scientists, inventors, crackpots, and garage mechanics pummelled the National Research Council with ideas. There *was*, in fact, natural rubber in milkweed, and in 1943 thousands of schoolchildren and volunteer adults helped collect seventy-one thousand pounds of it. Milkweed did not work, though, because large-scale production would have been too expensive.

A big breakthrough came in February 1942 in the U.S. when Standard Oil of New Jersey developed a new refining process that increased the production of aviation gas and at the same time boosted the yield of butylene, a substance that could be turned into synthetic rubber. Howe, as an engineer, well understood the possibilities of what could be done. It was clear the Americans were taking steps to develop large-scale production of synthetic rubber; but actually getting it to work in Canada — and on the first try — was something else. Bugs and design glitches might hold up operations for months, meaning the war could be over before any synthetic rubber could be actually produced.

On January 21, 1942, Howe set up the Polymer Corporation to build and operate a massive synthetic rubber complex near Sarnia, Ontario, close to an oil refinery that would supply the plant with raw materials. Another vital product — benzene — was available from nearby coke ovens at Hamilton steel plants. The St. Clair River was an excellent source of cooling water that was required.

Construction of the plant began in the summer of 1942, involving a complicated mosaic of pipes, conduits, and towers — the first fully integrated synthetic rubber operation in the British Empire. As

Industrial Warrior — C.D. Howe presided over Canada's industrial war, turning out everything from binoculars to bombers, radar to rubber. The nationwide effort was one of the great success stories of the war.

many as 5,579 workers helped build the complex. Construction might have taken five years in peacetime, but Polymer produced its first rubber on September 29, 1943, within nineteen months of the company being incorporated. By the spring of 1944 it was in full production.

The plant produced 3.1 million kilograms of rubber each month, the equivalent of fourteen million natural rubber trees. It was one of the great engineering feats of the war, begun by one of the great risk takers of the war, C.D. Howe.

The story of Polymer Corporation was remarkable in another respect. It was one of twenty-eight Crown Corporations set up during the war. The idea showed flashes of genius from Howe and his staff. The corporations, aimed at overcoming the inevitable bottlenecks and failures of government operations, revolutionized Canadian war production. Howe formed new companies with a specific role in wartime production. He would appoint a top executive or two to run each company, otherwise they were almost entirely independent. Was there a shortage of wood veneers for aircraft? A Crown Corporation could do the job. Machine tools? Howe's Citadel Merchandising (with its name from the Montreal phone book) could make sure they went where they were most needed. The Crown Corporations covered a broad spectrum of activities including manufacturing, purchasing and distributing, and supervising economic sectors.

Howe was American by birth, a through and through Yankee, born in Waltham, Massachusetts, on January 15, 1886. He went to Boston Tech, as the Massachusetts Institute of Technology was called at the time. He graduated as an engineer in 1908 but had no job. However, one of his professors heard of a teaching position at Dalhousie University in Halifax and recommended Howe. The young graduate accepted and spent the next five years on the Dalhousie engineering faculty, liking Halifax and enjoying his Canadian experience. In the spring of 1913 Howe was invited to work for the Board of Grain Commissioners in Fort William, Ontario, now part of Thunder Bay. Farmers had criticized grain companies for price gouging, so the board wanted its own terminal grain elevators. Howe would build them. Over the next two years he supervised construction of elevators at ports and cities across the country, elevators that were considered the best ever built in Canada.

During the First World War Howe resigned from government service to set up his own elevator-building company.[8] He became a British subject and expanded his business to include engineering, consulting, and general contracting work. Howe's company worked faster, cheaper, and better than the others. By 1934 he was a rich man and a prominent business leader in Port Arthur. He was then asked to run for Parliament as a Liberal even though he had no particular party leanings. He ran in the 1935 election, won, and was immediately included in Mackenzie King's cabinet as minister of marine and railways.

Howe might have stood out from his cabinet colleagues on one count. He wore Bond Street suits from London, but they always looked slept in. The topcoat he wore at Mackenzie King's funeral in 1950 was the same one he'd worn at his own wedding forty years earlier.

Throughout his life he was still partial to his childhood food favourites, including New England baked beans, but otherwise was indifferent to whatever landed on the dinner plate. He enjoyed bourbon, but he was not in the same league as Chubby Power.[9] When Howe travelled for business, which was often, the highlight of a train trip was playing cards, usually for small stakes, but on one long trip he went ahead by $2,500.

In Port Arthur his home commanded a dramatic view of Thunder Bay, but while his wife and five children might have enjoyed the panorama, he never much noticed. In Ottawa his office stayed pretty much as he found it, and not even a family photo was added. The only new object was a bright red phone on his desk that most people assumed was a "hotline" to the prime minister. It was actually just a gift from a friend. As a new arrival in Ottawa in 1935, Howe was described by veteran newsman Grant Dexter as "good natured, affable, with a ready sense of humor, but a mind that was razor-edged."[10] He became one of the more prolific cabinet leakers.

His early record was notable. In 1936 he introduced legislation to create the Canadian Broadcasting Corporation, and a year later he helped create Trans-Canada Airlines, which much later turned into Air Canada. He loved Trans-Canada, called it "my airline," and took it with him when he changed portfolios.

When he started his job as minister of munitions there was not a lot for Howe to do because Canada has never had a tradition of arms production. There were no Canadian equivalents to Krupp in Germany or Armstrong Whitworth in Britain. Canada's main contribution to the First World War in terms of supplies had been grain and mining. The nation did produce artillery shells, and rifles and total industrial production added up to about one billion dollars' worth of goods, a considerable sum at the time. But there were purchasing scandals and it became obvious some government favourites had become rich while supplying shoddy and defective goods.

In the interwar years any industrial momentum that had been built up in the First World War was completely lost. Even as late as 1936 a survey concluded that little industry would be needed in Canada if another war came. The Canadian army, navy, and air force were too small to warrant production of most equipment. Similarly, there was no hope that any Canadian company could get an American order because of competition, neutrality laws, and different equipment standards. For a Canadian company, everything depended on getting orders from Britain, but in the pre-war years there were only two orders placed. Marine Industries of Sorel, Quebec, received an order for one hundred artillery guns, while the Inglis Company of Toronto received an order for seven thousand Bren light machine guns. Regrettably, the Inglis order turned into a political scandal because the order was never put out to tender, nor were competing bids considered. Another order, this one for one hundred Bren gun carriers, was inexplicably cancelled just after the outbreak of war.

After the war began, and through the fall of 1939 and early months of 1940, Prime Minister King had a "limited liability" economic policy. Canada would help Britain with raw materials — especially grain — and whatever military supplies could be sent to the United Kingdom, but everything had to be done within existing finances. This framework, broadly similar to Britain's own at the time, lasted for the duration of the "Phony War," from September 1939 to May 1940. Even after the war began, there were few industrial orders from Britain because the British wanted their own companies to get the business and the jobs first and because Ottawa had set tough limits on profits.

There were a few exceptions, including the first corvette contracts and construction for the Commonwealth Air Training Plan, while work had also started on Canadian-produced Hurricane fighters. They at least gave a hint of big plans to come as Howe began his work.

Two pieces of breathtaking legislation transformed Howe from an ordinary cabinet minister into Canada's industrial czar. The Department of Munitions and Supply Act was put into effect by an Order-in-Council just before Howe was appointed. With it he would have the power to "mobilize, control, restrict or regulate to such extent as the Minister may, in his absolute discretion, deem necessary, any branch or trade or industry in Canada or any munitions of war or supplies."[11]

Corporate Canada would put its own money into wartime plants and expansion, but the government would also contribute loans or grants when needed to make sure it happened. In four years the total value of Canadian industrial plants doubled. The department coordinated all purchases made in Canada by British and other Allied governments for things like military trucks, tanks, cargo and military ships, aircraft, guns, and small arms, as well as uniforms, minesweeping equipment, parachutes, firefighting equipment, and hospital supplies. It purchased Canadian licences to build foreign-owned weapons and equipment and helped secure the British and American experts to let Canadian firms get up and running. The legislation was also the basis for setting up Crown Corporations like Polymer. It limited competition for scarce resources. The resources would be sent to wherever a national assessment deemed them to be most important.

The second piece of critical legislation was the National Resources Mobilization Act.[12] This later became the basis of conscription for the army (dealt with in Decision Nine). However, the new law enacted on June 21, 1940, was also the basis of much of the new wartime industrial planning. It allowed the government to restrict employment in dozens of fields such as retail sporting goods or confectionery shops and to require employers to apply to hire new workers. That way national employment priorities could be set.

Only weeks after Howe's appointment came the defeat of France, and with it the realization that the war was now a fight to the death. With that, with the new legislation, and with C.D. Howe rolling up his sleeves, things began to look entirely different. On July 1, 1940, *Maclean's* magazine commented on the effect on Ottawa: "The quietest war capital in Christendom has become a cauldron of excitement.... Where once reigned smugness [and] self-satisfaction, there is now a wholesome fear; with it fortunately, more of war stir and vigour."

A munitions and supply organization sprang up out of nowhere. By August, one newspaper noted that to organize purchasing, 650 workers had set up shop in a "grey wooden building, hurriedly constructed following the outbreak of war."[13] It added, "Every order from a toothbrush to a greatcoat; from a rifle to a fully equipped and armed bomber" is looked after. As much as one million dollars' worth of contracts were being approved every single day. In April 1940, there had been $11.6 million in new contracts placed with Canadian industry. But with the French collapse and with Howe bombarding both Mackenzie King and the British with demands for more orders, in May there were thirty-one million dollars' worth; in June $45 million; in July $82 million; in October 1940, $148 million.

Among Howe's first priorities was to scoop up some of the best business brains in the country. He didn't offer big money — their employers paid their salaries — but rather Howe argued for patriotic service at a time of crisis. This was the start of the extraordinary work of the "dollar-a-year" men, and in time there would be 107 of them. Mackenzie King, incidentally, looked at them with disdain because they were mostly Tories. Some were prima donnas who caused upheavals and were a burden for Howe, but most performed well, even brilliantly. They included Harry Carmichael, who since 1936 had been running General Motors of Canada and whose expertise in mass production was invaluable, and Billy Woodward, the West Coast department store owner.

The most celebrated and spectacular dollar-a-year executive was Edward Plunket Taylor, originally from Ottawa. Taylor was an extremely ambitious thirty-nine-year-old when he was grabbed for wartime service and made president of War Supplies Limited. He was dispatched to the United States, where he "thrived in the Byzantine atmosphere of wartime Washington," selling Canadian products in multi-million-dollar deals in the midst of U.S. wartime shortages.[14] After the war he turned into one of the greatest tycoons Canada has ever seen. He became the head of Argus Corporation, the sprawling investment and holding company that owned Dominion Stores, Hollinger Mines, Canadian Breweries, Crown Trust, Domtar, Standard Broadcasting, and many others. He was an avid horse breeder and owner of Northern Dancer, a Kentucky Derby winner.

The challenges for the dollar-a-year men were enormous. As described by Peter C. Newman, "Howe's protégés set out to learn where all the important pieces were, who counted and who did not, and how to deal with each other, with cabinet ministers, and with the political system."[15] Ottawa wanted everything now, right now. "There was no time to consider production programs in detail. No one could hope to know when production would actually come on stream — merely that a commitment to produce must be made, often orally, and ratified with government dollars."[16]

Howe said he had no idea of the cost of turning out vital weapons and supplies. "But before the war is over everything will be needed so let's go ahead anyway. If we lose the war nothing will matter."[17] Among the difficulties were that British industrialists had withheld blueprints, designs, and secret processes from Canadians to make sure British companies did not lose profitable orders. Another huge challenge was that Howe could not discover what British priorities were. Fighter planes or bombers? Warships or cargo ships? What kind of tank? What could the British do themselves and what couldn't they do? Howe resolved to visit Britain in person to settle matters.

He left New York City for Britain on December 6, 1940, for what he thought would be a restful trans-Atlantic trip aboard the liner *Western Prince*. Not so: on December 14, three hundred miles off Iceland, the ship was torpedoed and sunk. Howe was fortunate to be among those hustled into lifeboats only moments before a shattering blast sent the liner to the bottom.

The seas were rough and most people in the lifeboats were retching with seasickness, but by pure luck some hours later a tramp steamer appeared on the horizon. It was not supposed to stop to rescue people but did anyway, picking up more than two hundred survivors, including Howe and aides Taylor and Woodward, although another aide, Gordon Scott from Montreal, died while being rescued.

After reaching shore and recovering, Howe went to London to meet several top British officials, including Sir Andrew Duncan, Britain's minister of supplies. Duncan pointed out that, for one thing, the British needed bomber aircraft more than fighters.

Aircraft production became one of the biggest headaches of all for Howe. As of December 1940, production was at a modest 120 planes a month. The British Commonwealth Air Training Plan needed hundreds of aircraft, and the Royal Canadian Air Force needed hundreds more for its expanding operations. Britain, in its 1940 crisis could not supply much of anything, despite earlier plans. As Grant Dexter said at that time, "Our war program is in chaos.... Our aircraft industry which is based on British engines or frames not produced here, was brought permanently to a dead stop."[18] The only solution for the aircraft problem, and every other problem for that matter, was a crash building program.

Work on the Avro Anson, mentioned earlier as one of the most important of the BCATP aircraft, came to exemplify everything that could go wrong. The British-designed Anson, which dated back to 1935, was quirky to say the least. Retracting the landing gear required the pilot to make no fewer than 140 turns of a hand crank. Short flights were made with the landing gear down because raising it was just too much trouble. On retirement from front-line service in 1939 the Anson came into its own as an aircrew trainer.

Canadian production of the Anson was bogged down partly because of the primitive state of the industry but also because the aircraft had to be re-engineered using North American measurements and tool sizes. Eventually, the various versions of the aircraft were produced by companies including Canadian Car and Foundry in Amherst, Nova Scotia, Federal Aircraft in Montreal, and de Havilland in Toronto. But as if finding manufacturers and re-engineering the aircraft were not enough, the original Anson used British-built Cheetah engines, which were not available, and, as noted earlier, Canada never did produce an aircraft engine. Before the war Ford had produced a few copies of one engine in Windsor, Ontario, but the Canadian government was monumentally uninterested and Ford could not pursue the plan without government orders.

Canadian producers had to scrounge around the United States to find an engine, but by this time most producers were committed to filling new American orders. Finally, an obscure company in Pottstown, Pennsylvania, Jacobs Aircraft Engines, was found and was able to supply L6-MB engines. Even by 1941 only eighty-eight Ansons had been finished. Howe appointed Ralph Bell, the head of a Halifax fishing and shipping firm, to be director general of aircraft production and straighten out the Anson production delays. Bell's only previous aircraft expertise was as an enthusiastic amateur pilot. By 1942 the total of Ansons produced shot up to 1,432, while eventually nearly three thousand of them were built.

Another of the troubled programs was the Lancaster bomber, produced by Victory Aircraft in Toronto. Originally, the plant had been building the Lysander ground co-operation aircraft, but by the time the Lysander got into production it was obsolete. For some time the plant could not get any new production because the British couldn't decide what new aircraft to produce, but eventually the decision was made to build the Lancaster.

That was a tall order because the Lancaster was a big and complex aircraft. There were about five hundred thousand individual manufacturing operations required, excluding engines and some smaller items. Deliveries were delayed and delayed again. For one thing, while the plant was contracted to build the plane in September 1941, the first drawings only arrived the following January. A British Lancaster was flown across the Atlantic as a pattern aircraft, but it became clear that a Canadian version would have to have different engines, instruments, and radio equipment. The Canadian Lancasters ended up using Merlin engines manufactured to American standards by Packard in the U.S. rather than the original Rolls-Royce type. The differences were substantial, including such things as screw threads and bolt sizes. In the end, production was finally smoothed out and 450 Lancasters were produced, but the process demonstrated all the complications that could develop on big projects.

Despite the setbacks, in time the aviation industry became a huge success story. The industry grew to employ nearly 120,000 workers, many of them learning valuable skills they could use in the postwar years. Canadian plants delivered 16,418 aircraft to the Royal Canadian Air Force, the British Commonwealth Air Training Plan, the Royal Air Force, and even the United States Armed Forces. Canada produced a long list of aircraft in addition to the Ansons and Lancasters, including the de Havilland

Mosquito (more than one thousand produced), Catalina flying boat (almost seven hundred), and Harvard trainer (two thousand).[19]

Canada was not only an aviation powerhouse during the war but also a shipbuilding powerhouse, too. At the peak, Canadian shipyards were building three ten-thousand-ton merchant ships a week. The cargo ship SS *Fort Romaine* was built in fifty-eight days.[20] In all, Canada built 410 merchant ships. There was even more production in warships for the Royal Canadian Navy and the Royal Navy. The story of the corvette has already been outlined in Decision Two, and 206 of them were built during the war, but Canada also produced frigates and minesweepers, along with smaller craft such as tugs and landing craft. The Halifax shipyard started work on four Tribal destroyers, but as with the Lancaster the enterprise turned out to be more than could be managed. The Tribals were not finished by the end of the war.

Canada produced a variety of armoured vehicles, including scout cars and Universal Carriers (Bren gun carriers). The nation produced more than 1,400 Valentine tanks at Canadian Pacific Railway shops in Montreal that had been used earlier to build railway locomotives. The Valentine was becoming outdated by mid-war, but most of the Canadian production was shipped to the Soviet Union, where all armoured vehicles were welcome and all desperately needed. Another ambitious project was the one and only Canadian tank ever built — the Ram. It was a modified American Grant and nearly two thousand were produced. In the end building them at all was an extraordinary achievement, but the gun on it was too small, and the Ram was overtaken by the Sherman. The Rams were valuable as training tanks, however, and in the end they did have a place on the battlefields of northwest Europe as armoured personnel carriers.

Hundreds of other weapons of war, including machine guns, artillery pieces, shells, and optical instruments, were produced, but perhaps the one that became the most famous of all was an ugly truck. The legendary snub-nosed Canadian Military Pattern (CMP) truck looked like it had just run into a wall, but it came off the General Motors and Ford production lines in a seemingly unending stream. The design looked odd, but it was meant to save as much shipping space as possible. In all, Canada produced a staggering five hundred thousand CMP trucks.[21] For its part,

Chrysler produced another superb truck, the D60. While the Canadian army became the most "motorized" in northwest Europe during the war, it still only used about 30 percent of the total truck production. The rest went to the British and other Commonwealth armies. Toward the end of the war, the trucks rode on synthetic rubber tires produced by Polymer.

Apart from trucks, planes, tanks, and ships, other Canadian wartime production was equally vital to the war effort. Canada produced 95 percent of the nickel used by the Allies and about 40 percent of Allied aluminum. Without Canadian aluminum the Royal Air Force could not have fought the war.[22]

Among the most classified projects of the war was the mining and production of uranium. Howe secretly secured majority control of Eldorado Gold Mines, the only uranium producer among Allied nations. Eldorado had started off as a radium mine in 1932, extracting radium from pitchblende for use in treating cancer. Uranium from Great Bear Lake in the North West Territories was sent to Port Hope, Ontario, to be refined.

The Ugly Truck — *The rugged Canadian Military Pattern truck, manufactured by both General Motors and Ford, came in many shapes and sizes. The vehicle saw service in virtually every theatre of the war. Originally from a British design, the vehicles all had right hand drive.*

Canadian uranium played a key role in the research and development of the atomic bomb.

The massive wartime industrial and commercial expansion led to extraordinary changes in the lives of many ordinary Canadians. Jobs were everywhere and wages increased dramatically, rising from $956 a month in 1938 to $1,525 in 1943.[23] In contrast to the 1930s, several members of an extended family might be working, boosting the fortunes of everyone. Companies began to cater to workers as the war continued because they became hard to find. In the first week of January 1942, the Unemployment Insurance office in Halifax announced that not a single claim had been filed.[24]

One of the features of wartime industry was that work was spread across the country. This was a political necessity in any event, but the shortage of workers in some locations also made the move imperative. Companies such as MacDonald Brothers Aircraft of Winnipeg (later part of Bristol Aerospace) did well. MacDonald had started in 1930 as a small aircraft repair and maintenance company. At its peak in the war MacDonald Brothers employed as many as two thousand workers assembling Anson aircraft and repairing and overhauling other planes for the BCATP.[25]

An unlikely story was that of the tiny Pacific Veneer Plywood of Vancouver. Its owner was Poldi Bentley, who had fled Austria in 1938 one step ahead of the Nazis. In Vancouver Bentley started from nothing in the lumber business, but by the middle of the war Pacific Veneer began to make wooden wing parts for the Mosquito fighter bomber. The company went from a handful of employees to about one thousand. After the war Bentley's company eventually became the enormously successful Canadian Forest Products.[26]

Labour-management battles were a great challenge and put a severe dint in production in some industries. Unions were among the leaders in bringing about huge, if painful, social change. Before the war and during the war years, some companies took vicious action to prevent plants from being unionized. From 1939 on, unions looked at the war as a chance to regain losses from the Depression. In 1943 there were more than four hundred strikes or lockouts involving thousands of workers while in 1944 there were two hundred strikes.

At the peak of the war, shipbuilding was Canada's largest industry, and Halifax Shipyard, for one, employed a labour force of seventy-five thousand workers. The company challenged the union check-off system, which touched off a month-long walkout by three thousand workers.[27] Another damaging strike began in July 1941 at the Aluminium Company of Canada plant in Arvida, Quebec. Seven hundred workers spontaneously walked off the job, and the next day another 4,500 men decided to occupy the plant. Aluminum production had been declared an essential service, so the strike was illegal. More than two hundred soldiers were sent in to protect the factory. The problems included language difficulties between English-speaking managers and French-speaking workers, late pay, and a brutal heat wave. A royal commission found underneath it all was a struggle for better salaries and working conditions. Another company-union battle dragged on for years at the lead-zinc smelter in Trail, British Columbia, one of the largest in the world. Part of the conflict was that some unionists were long-time communists, including Harvey Murphy, who called himself "the reddest rose in the garden."[28]

Howe was no labour visionary, but his attitudes changed as the war continued, becoming more conciliatory toward labour and recognizing that many complaints were well justified. Also Mackenzie King, who had made a name as an industrial conciliator before the First World War, was generally sympathetic. In 1940 the government had recognized labour's right to organize and bargain collectively in industries subject to federal jurisdiction, though it did almost nothing on enforcement. Union membership increased by almost 100 percent in Canada in the war years.

There were historic changes for women in the workplace. By 1943–1944 there were as many as 439,000 women in the service sector and a further 373,000 in manufacturing, including many in the munitions industry. In August 1943 Canadian Pacific Railway advertised for women to do maintenance work on railway tracks in Windsor, Ontario, and for the first time in the history of the CPR's yards in Calgary, "grimy women in traditional blue overalls worked alongside men, clambering over snorting, dirty locomotives."[29]

Among the most prominent women employed was Elsie MacGill, the first woman aircraft engineer in Canada and possibly the first in the world.[30] MacGill was born in Vancouver in 1905 to prominent lawyer Henry James MacGill and his wife Helen MacGill, British Columbia's first female judge. At a time when many fields were closed to women, MacGill's appointment as chief aeronautical engineer at Canadian Car and Foundry in Fort William was astounding. MacGill and other top managers supervised more than 4,500 employees at the plant. Her achievements are even more remarkable because she overcame polio to continue her career. MacGill was referred to as "the Queen of the Hurricanes" for her work in adapting the Hurricane fighter to Canadian production.

Another remarkable woman was economist Phyllis Turner (Phyllis Ross after she remarried). She was the most senior and highest paid woman in wartime Ottawa ($4,500) working for the Wartime Prices and Trade Board. She lived in the Sandy Hill area of Ottawa, and when her teenage son, John, walked the family dog, he would often meet and chat with Mackenzie King. That teenager, of course, later became Prime Minister John Turner.

Most women had absolutely no industrial training. Dorothy Hendsbee was just sixteen when she left the isolated Nova Scotia fishing village of Half Island Cove to take a job as a welder in a Halifax shipyard. She first had to look up "welder" in a dictionary to find out what they did.[31] Although women made enormous progress in taking industrial jobs, their salaries lagged behind men's, and few became engineers or managers. Ella Gilfouy, among thousands of workers at the Research Enterprises Limited in Toronto, a Crown Corporation, said she could not recall a single woman manager.[32]

In the main Howe managed to steer the war effort clear of profiteering scandals. There were relatively few instances of financial gouging or exorbitant profits. Indeed, Canadian business paid its full share of the war's cost. Business contributed billions to Victory Loans, which helped finance the war. Corporate taxes increased from a rate of 18 to 40 percent, which generated $850 million in taxes in 1944.[33] Profits above a certain percent were taxed at 100 percent, although companies would receive a 20 percent rebate on excess profits after the war to boost recovery.

One of Howe's truly innovative ideas was the use of sub-contractors. Sub-contracting is widely used today, but at the time, except for the auto industry, the practice was little known. Dozens of companies with no experience in making military equipment whatsoever suddenly learned all about it. The Canadian Cycle and Motor Company of Weston, Ontario, was famous for its "CCM" brand bicycles and hockey skates, but it also began making gun parts, tripods for Bren guns, and cradles and pivots for anti-tank guns. Cockshutt Plow of Brantford, Ontario, made parts for aircraft and hand grenades.

Howe himself had to focus on the essentials, and his office was protective of his time. "There would be no lines of mad inventors or patronage-hungry politicians," according to biographers Bothwell and Kilbourn.[34] At the height of the war, Munitions and Supply was placing six hundred contracts a day.

Howe was not without faults, nor was he lacking for enemies. His temper was a handicap. Having both Howe and Mackenzie King sitting around the same cabinet table must have been something to behold: Howe with his temper and Type A personality; fussbudget King with all his twiddling pencil stubs. Nevertheless, it was always clear that King was the boss, and the prime minister backed up Howe when support was needed.

Howe's most acidic and relentless critics were Finance Minister James Ilsley and Defence Minister Layton Ralston. The truth is, the prime minister was not above encouraging feuding among his ministers because it strengthened his hand. Ilsley complained that Howe was running a one-man government, often leaving the finance department in the dark about key decisions[35] — which was true. Journalist Bruce Hutchison, who knew all the players in Ottawa, described Howe as "temperamentally a lone wolf, [who] ran his own show from the start. The cabinet seldom knew what he was doing and no one, probably not Howe himself, [knew] how he did it. His method, like King's, was to appoint good men and leave them alone; to drive himself sixteen hours a day; and, as he told a friend in the worst days of the war when everything seemed lost, to refuse to consider for a single moment the possibility of defeat."[36]

Early on in the war, there was backstabbing by lumber baron H.R. MacMillan, who was working at Howe's behest in Ottawa. In one attack

MacMillan wrote a report critical of Munitions and Supply, which had Howe as its thinly veiled target. That attack and others were leaked to the Tory-friendly *Financial Post* and other papers. Howe lashed back, referring to the *Financial Post* as "the number one saboteur in Canada."[37] MacMillan was subsequently sent to Montreal as director general of shipbuilding, where, in contrast to his Ottawa stint, he was a notable success.

For a man who was very tough, Howe displayed one unlikely weakness: he could almost never fire anyone. He would move a weak reed from one job to another, but otherwise he shrank from giving failed executives the boot.

Howe was not interested in theory of government or policy on a grand scale; rather his genius was to carry out plans. "He was an operating executive — one of the greatest this country has ever had," according to one of the great Ottawa mandarins, John Deutsch.[38] Part of Howe's success was his openness to new technology, which was undoubtedly helped by his background as an engineer. He was the first important Canadian politician to prefer the telephone to the written word. Fifteen-page memos were despised. Decisions, even ones with profound long-range consequences, were often made in one day after consultation with key advisers and experts. There was no time for anything else, anyway.

In summing up his achievements, one caveat should be noted. Neither Howe nor the Department of Munitions and Supply led the industrial war alone. Other government agencies and departments played crucial roles as well. The Bank of Canada and the Ministry of Finance kept the lid on inflation throughout the war, which allowed relatively stable pay levels for workers (the steel strike in Sydney, Nova Scotia, being an exception). Dr. Clifford Clark, the deputy minister of finance, in particular, was extraordinarily able.[39] The dollar-a-year men were vital. Howe was among those who recruited men and women of outstanding ability for the public service. He saw government as a powerful agent for social and economic change. The top public servants in wartime were, as a group, among the most active promoters of new ideas in Ottawa.[40]

Howe picked up some unlikely friends along the way. While Tory Gratton O'Leary was a fierce political opponent, he was also a

Dollar-a-Year Man — Ottawa native E.P. Taylor was among top business leaders co-opted for Canada's war effort. He went on to become one of the greatest tycoons in Canadian history.

devoted friend. Similarly, Co-operative Commonwealth Federation leader M.J. Coldwell — at political odds with Howe on many issues — was another admirer. Even H.R. MacMillan turned into a booster after the war. At one point he referred to Howe as "the greatest organizer Canada has ever seen."[41]

Howe's public service continued after the war until the catastrophe of his career — the "Great Pipeline Debate" of 1956. It was at that point the Liberal government used closure to ram a new pipeline project through Parliament, with the closure motion itself contributing decisively to the demise of the St. Laurent government. This was considered hugely arrogant and dismissive of Parliament. However, it should be noted that the comment — "What's a million?" — often attributed to him, was never uttered. It was dreamed up by John Diefenbaker, who, on this score at least, would have been right at home in today's "post-factual" political world. Diefenbaker used the comment in the 1956 and 1957 debates to imply that Howe did not much care about the public's money.

Canada's economic achievements during the Second World War were monumental. The people of Canada forged the nation's plants and factories into a war-winning weapon.[42] Eleven billion dollars' worth of munitions alone were produced. By 1943 war industries employed more people than did the three armed forces. The gross national product more than doubled during the war to a total of twelve billion dollars. Canada by the end of the war was the fourth greatest industrial nation among allies, an astonishing feat for a nation of eleven million people.

Mackenzie King and C.D. Howe set up something that was remarkable and unique — a single centralized agency to administer war production. That was quite different from the various conflicting empires in both the United States and Britain, empires that were tailor-made for conflict and competition. Howe's biographers summarized that "he shaped Canada's war program, renewed Canada's industrial plant, and reconstructed the Canadian economy with the aid of his chosen advisers and a blank cheque from the Canadian government."[43]

Howe's appointment as minister of munitions and supply was one of the best and most far-reaching decisions of the war. It is hard to imagine that any other person could have achieved what he did. No one before or since has been so successful in bringing together business and government. On his death on January 4, 1961, the *Toronto Star* described Howe as "the chief builder of modern industrial Canada" and "one of the greatest Canadians of all time" while Bruce Hutchison said he had made himself "one of the nation's immortals."[44] Among Canada's business elite in the postwar years, no badge of honour was more revered than the phrase, "I put in time under C.D."[45]

DECISION SIX

The Ogdensburg Agreement — Canada Turns to America

In the summer of 1940, with a mighty air battle raging over England, Britain faced its worst moment of the Second World War. If the Royal Air Force could not turn back the Luftwaffe in the Battle of Britain, the island nation faced the prospect of invasion and defeat. In London a then-obscure Canadian diplomat, Lester B. Pearson, said everyone understood that Britain "might lose the war, and we had to face that fact."[1]

Apart from what it would have meant to Great Britain, a British defeat would also have been a disaster for Canada. That was because at that moment Canada was virtually defenceless. That summer there were only two Canadian Army divisions — the 1st Infantry Division, which was already in England, and the 2nd Infantry Division, which was on its way there. The Royal Canadian Air Force was completely absorbed in the British Commonwealth Air Training Plan, with only a few squadrons available to patrol Canadian coasts. All other RCAF squadrons and personnel were in Britain. All the Royal Canadian Navy destroyers in the Atlantic were in the English Channel. When the warships were dispatched to Britain in May, Prime Minister King wrote grimly in his diary: "One wonders if [the] … destroyers will come back. We may find our own coasts left bare in giving our last possible aid to the Mother country. That, however, to my mind is right. We owe to her such freedom as we have. It is right we should strike with her the last blow for the preservation of freedom."[2]

Adding to the bleak outlook was the fear that if Britain fell, the Royal Navy might fall into Nazi hands. This was not fantasy; it was a prospect that greatly worried Winston Churchill. By mid-July secret preparations were being made in case the fleet had to fall back to bases in Canada.[3] In the midst of it all influential American newspaper columnist Walter Lippman described the effect on the United States, comments that applied equally to Canada: "How grave the situation is few of us have realized as yet ... we may find that the Allied fleets which now guard the Atlantic against the Axis will become part of the power of the Axis."[4]

With Canada undefended there were two options for the Canadian government: Prime Minister King could continue to support Britain and hope for the best or look for an ally who might be willing to help defend Canada if the worst happened. Even though it was still a neutral nation at that point, that ally could only be the United States.

On Saturday, August 17, 1940, in the midst of it all, and with the Battle of Britain still hanging in the balance, King was invited to meet with U.S. president Roosevelt. The prime minister made his way by car from Ottawa to Prescott, Ontario, and then via a special ferry across the St. Lawrence to Ogdensburg, New York. There Roosevelt greeted him in a private railcar. After a relaxing chat and dinner, the president had a proposal to make. He offered an agreement in which the United States would stand with Canada if it were attacked while proposing that both countries work together on continental defence over the long term.

It only takes a look back at a bit of history to realize what a revolutionary moment this was. Canada had long feared the threat from America. There had been the "Fifty-four forty or fight!" election campaign of 1844, in which James Polk called for the U.S. to grab a huge swath of territory north of the forty-ninth parallel. There were the Fenian raids between 1866 and 1871. Then, as late as 1893, Prime Minister Sir John Thompson said in a speech in Toronto that the United States was "intensely aggressive" and constituted a menace to Canada's existence.[5] In that same year an association was formed in New York that included John Jacob Astor,

Theodore Roosevelt, and Andrew Carnegie, which aimed to promote Canada's complete independence from Britain as a stepping stone to U.S. annexation.

In 1927 Canada and the U.S. exchanged diplomats for the first time, although not military attachés. Still, there was some leftover antipathy. By the 1930s no one seriously expected Canada or the U.S. to invade each other's territory, but Canada's Defence Scheme No. 1 remained on the books at the Department of National Defence, calling for a surprise invasion of the United States in the event of any serous American threat. The United States's own "War Plan Red" outlined the same thing in reverse. To the embarrassment of the American government, War Plan Red was revealed by the *New York Times* in 1935 and as a result was quietly shelved.

Despite all that, in the years before the Second World War, things were starting to look different. Economic ties had begun during the First World War and continued to build when Mackenzie King signed a trade agreement with the U.S. in 1935 that reduced some tariffs. It was the first such deal since 1854 and the first ever breech of the imperial trade preference. The trade deal offered a hint of the emerging diplomatic grand design of President Roosevelt.

For the next several years Roosevelt pursued what might in today's terms be called a "two-track" North American security policy. It was expressed in several ways but essentially it came down to this: the Americans wanted Canadian friendship, but they would never allow a foreign nation — perhaps Germany or Japan — to use Canadian territory to launch an attack on the United States. Roosevelt was especially disturbed by the lack of Canadian defences on the West Coast.

A number of Roosevelt speeches and American moves can be seen as expressions of the "two-track" policy. More than once the Americans requested permission for U.S. military aircraft to fly from Washington State in stages through British Columbia to Alaska, to see how quickly Alaska could be reinforced in an emergency. A pet project of Roosevelt's was an Alaskan highway through B.C. An American report in 1932 said the highway could be built for about $27 million and, with completely unwarranted optimism, said that Canada might contribute to building it.

The Canadian military wanted nothing to do with the idea, saying that in the event of a U.S. war with Japan, the highway would be an open invitation for the Americans to ignore Canadian neutrality if, in fact, Canada remained neutral.

Roosevelt was so keen on getting the highway started that in 1937 he boarded a U.S. destroyer for a trip to Victoria to sell the idea in B.C. He received a boisterous welcome there, but his ideas received a noticeably quieter reception on Parliament Hill. The King government knew all too well the weak state of defences on the West Coast and that the Americans had raised the possibility of moving some U.S. armed forces into B.C.

Roosevelt looked at trying to open up military bases in Newfoundland (of course, still a British colony at the time) and the Caribbean and, as well, wanted some kind of access to the port of Halifax. In 1936 during a Caribbean cruise he again examined the possibility of acquiring air and naval bases in Bermuda, the Caribbean, and Newfoundland if they were threatened by Germany. Mackenzie King had no objection in principle to giving American warships access to the Halifax naval yard or supplying fuel to the U.S. Navy, but he told the U.S. that access would depend on the circumstances and Canada was not interested in leasing or selling any base.

Franklin Roosevelt is warmly remembered in Canada, and justifiably so, for his groundbreaking "good neighbour" policy. Leaving behind the Fenians, War Plan Red and all the rest, Roosevelt declared in a number of speeches from 1936 onward that Canada and the United States were neighbours and had shared a "genuine friendship for over a century."[6] In August 1936 he said in a speech in upstate New York that "our closest neighbours are good neighbours." His "good neighbour" message was repeated during a state visit to Quebec on July 31, 1936, when he reminded listeners that his Canadian connections dated back to childhood days at his family estate in Campobello, New Brunswick.[7] Perhaps the most memorable Roosevelt comments came in August 1938, just before the Munich crisis, when he travelled to Kingston, Ontario, to receive an honorary degree from Queen's University and open a nearby international bridge. His text was written by the State Department, but in comments inserted in his own hand, he declared, "The Dominion of

Canada is a part of the sisterhood of the British Empire. I give to you assurance that the people of the United States will not stand idly by if domination of Canadian soil is threatened by any other empire.... We as good neighbours are true friends because we maintain our own rights with frankness, because we refuse to accept the twists of secret diplomacy, because we settle our disputes by consultation and because we discuss our common problems in the spirit of the common good."[8]

This was a significant comment, a significant turn in policy. Suddenly, Roosevelt was talking about involvement with Canada if there were foreign threats, quite a change for a nation steeped in isolationism.

Two days after Roosevelt's speech, in an address in Woodbridge, Ontario, Mackenzie King replied that while Roosevelt's pledges were welcome, North American defence meant Canada had obligations, too. "Enemy forces should not be able to pursue their way, either by land,

New Partnership — Prime Minister King and President Roosevelt developed a solid working relationship in a series of meetings, including this one in 1938. It was a later session at Ogdensburg, New York, on August 17, 1940, that proved historic.

sea or air to the United States across Canadian territory."⁹ In other comments at this time that stretched credulity to the breaking point, King indicated that Canada had at last got its defence program in good shape. The West Coast defences in 1938 were next to nil, amounting to a few archaic aircraft, some First World War–era coast artillery guns and a handful of modern warships.

It is worth remembering that Roosevelt was more positive about relations with Canada than any president in U.S. history. It helped that over the years the president and prime minister developed a considerable personal rapport.* Both men were Harvard graduates, and King had worked in the United States early in his career, so they had some things in common. King was friendly but not deferential. The U.S. president generally liked the prime minister, "perhaps because King was a good listener, who rarely asked for much," according to historian Tim Cook.¹⁰

King was a guest at the White House in March 1937 to discuss Atlantic and Pacific coast defences, one of a number of meetings held between the two. There were also discussions between Roosevelt, King, and King George VI in Washington during the 1939 Royal Tour. Roosevelt spoke about possibly establishing Atlantic naval bases, again expressing interest in Halifax. He said in the event of war, the U.S. "had a perfect right" to keep other European countries from sending warships into coastal waters of the Americas. For his part, King said as far as Canada was concerned, "We should not object to getting all the help we could." Roosevelt was so concerned about the situation on the Atlantic coast, he was determined to have a first-hand look, cruising through the area in a U.S. Navy warship in August 1939 and stopping one night at Halifax.

In sum, at this point there was a notion of continental defence, and there were discussions between the United States, Britain, and Canada about various defence questions, but there was no formal agreement on the subject. The military staffs in Canada and the U.S. did not exchange much military information, and there was no permanent machinery

---

* Roosevelt wanted to be informal and called King "Mackenzie." However, that was a bit odd because King was "Rex" to his close friends. King usually called Roosevelt "Mr. President," but sometimes used "Franklin."

for military co-operation or joint planning. When the war broke out, Mackenzie King was faced with conflicting messages from the U.S. When President Roosevelt declared that the United States would remain neutral in the war, he also said that North America would be defended against any attack.

The president faced serious domestic political problems in 1940. He had decided to run for an unprecedented third term as president in elections that November. His challenger was maverick businessman Wendell Willkie, who crusaded against Roosevelt's perceived failure to end the Depression and his supposed eagerness for war. Acutely aware of isolationist sentiment, Roosevelt promised that if he were elected there would be no involvement in foreign wars. That was behind his delay in dealing with Winston Churchill's urgent request for forty or fifty older destroyers. There were many political reasons for Roosevelt to be wary about getting entangled in the European war that summer or entangled in international agreements.

But there were other factors at work in favour of presidential action. It was abundantly clear that Americans did not want to join the war in Europe, but it was also clear that opinion about the U.S. defending itself was changing. On June 19 the *Chicago Tribune*, a staunchly isolationist newspaper, called for a formal Canada–U.S. defence agreement. Earlier in the spring, the U.S. Congress had passed an astronomical defence appropriation, the largest in American history. In June Congress passed legislation approving a massive military draft. Neither the draft nor the defence appropriation could have been done without significant public support.

Further, when Prime Minister King visited Roosevelt in Warm Springs, Georgia, on April 25, Roosevelt voiced concern about inadequate Canadian defences on both coasts, worrying that this posed "a real danger" to the United States. The president had already asked railway officials how they would move three hundred thousand troops to the Maritime provinces, if needed. Then on May 23 King sent a message to the president saying that all available Canadian destroyers had been sent to Britain — meaning that Canada's Atlantic shores were practically undefended. An American military assessment on July 3 painted "a very dismal picture" of the situation.[11]

Public opinion in Canada was changing, too. Not only Americans but Canadians, wrote historian David Beatty, "had grown fearful for the security of North America."[12] On August 3, the *Montreal Standard* commented, "A treaty for [North American] defence would give form to fundamental understandings that already exist. It would be something that could be read and grasped on both sides of the border. It would provide the basis for arrangements for defence against common danger."

Pressure for Canada to act in concert with the Americans also came from an influential group of twenty academics and business leaders at the Canadian Institute of International Affairs. An Institute report said the United States was determined to take whatever measures it needed in its own defence and Canada would have to act in light of that, voluntarily or involuntarily. The best way to prevent an "involuntary" solution, the report concluded, would be to admit Canada's inability to protect its air, sea, and ground frontiers and to request U.S. co-operation in mutual defence.[13]

All this time King (still his own external affairs minister) was being kept informed by Hugh Keenleyside, a senior official at External Affairs, who was going back and forth between Ottawa and Washington. Keenleyside recognized the need for Canada and the United States to work together. In a shrewd assessment he wrote that it was likely that the U.S. would expect Canadian assistance in continental defence and that an alliance between Canada and the U.S. would soon be inevitable.[14]

At this time there were also new joint military staff talks, far more candid and comprehensive than any previous exchange. But there was a problem; though the talks were valuable, the military had no power to really do anything concrete without political approval. By the end of July they had reached an impasse about what to do to improve the defence situation. Regular military channels were clearly inadequate to handle joint defence matters.

With all this in play — changing public opinion on both sides of the border, the urgent British plea for destroyers, the life and death struggle in the skies over Britain, and American worries about Canadian vulnerability — Roosevelt decided to act. It was just before two o'clock in the afternoon of August 16, 1940, when the president called Mackenzie

King at his country home near Ottawa. The prime minister picked up the phone himself. "I am going tomorrow night in my train to Ogdensburg," a jaunty Roosevelt said. "If you are free, I would like to have you come over and have dinner with me there."[15] He had, he added, taken the liberty of informing the U.S. press that the two would meet. "Are you free tomorrow night?" King was.

Historian C.P. Stacey has said that the president's decision to meet King at Ogdensburg was "one of Roosevelt's characteristically impulsive acts."[16] True, the meeting was arranged without the president getting advice from military or congressional leaders. However, the president's action was made in light of long-term U.S. interests and long-range policy objectives. In any event, he had asked his assistants on August 3 to arrange a troop inspection tour to either Canton or Ogdensburg, New York, on the seventeenth. There does not seem to have been much impulsive about it.

The morning newspapers broke word of a Roosevelt–King meeting. That was the cue for Defence Minister Ralston and the chief of the general staff to rush over to King's office with a list of urgently needed military equipment. As if King were going to the grocery store, the two said, "Why not pick up a few things for us." King then went to inform the newly arrived governor general, the Earl of Athlone, about the plan. King had no real idea of what Roosevelt was going to propose, but he told Athlone he thought the president would "probably be establishing some joint conferences on defence between heads of staffs, etc."[17] Then after getting a haircut, King picked up the U.S. minister to Ottawa, Jay Pierrepont Moffat and, with long-time chauffeur Robert Lay, set off for the drive to Prescott.

Roosevelt "looked exceedingly well," King noted as he arrived at the president's private railway car about seven o'clock in the evening.[18] The president was tired but in a happy mood, having just reviewed seven divisions of regular and National Guard troops. They were first of the legion of American soldiers who would later end up storming to victory in Europe and Asia. Once King was aboard, the presidential train moved to an obscure siding outside Ogdensburg to keep prying newspaper reporters away.

Secretary of War Henry Stimson joined the two men for drinks, chat, and dinner (at which, to King's amazement, Roosevelt demolished a gigantic steak). Roosevelt's mind was focused on the pending destroyers-for-bases deal, with the president saying he hoped the first destroyers might be turned over to Britain soon. However, he said the United States would have to get a string of bases in the Atlantic in return for them. There was an awkward discussion as Roosevelt raised the possibility of the U.S. purchasing or leasing a military base on Canadian territory. King made it clear that could not be done. "I … explained we would not wish to sell or lease any sites in Canada but would be ready to work out matters of facilities."[19]

Then Roosevelt came to the point. As Stimson later recorded in his diary, "[The President] suggested that there should be a Joint Board composed of representatives of the Army and Navy and Air Force in Canada, together with one layperson, and a similar group for the United States. The function of this Committee should be to discuss plans for defence of the Northern Half of the Western Hemisphere … he pointed out how vitally important it was that there should be conferences, discussions, and plans made … in case there should be an attack."[20]

King was pleased. Roosevelt's plan would mean that Canada would not fight any new battle on home territory alone, while the United States would not have to worry about Canada being turned into a base for an attack against America. The president wrote those ideas out in pencil on a piece of paper retrieved from a wastebasket. What he wrote became the historic Ogdensburg Agreement.

A key part of the agreement was that it was not a one-off arrangement. It set up the Permanent Joint Board on Defence, which despite the grey and bureaucratic name turned out to be a valuable connecting point for joint defence long afterward. The Ogdensburg Agreement proved to be one of the most important and far-reaching decisions of the Second World War for Canada and one that continues to be felt today.

Many things have been said about Mackenzie King, but in a situation like this he was in his element, clearly seeing the significance of what was being suggested. Roosevelt was offering no less than a military alliance. King said he was "perfectly delighted" with the idea while Stimson later said King was so taken with the offer that there were almost "tears in his eyes."[21]

The next morning the three men attended a military church parade and then retired to the railcar for a second time to fine-tune the

> Ogdensburg Agreement
> Press Release
> August 18, 1940
>
> The Prime Minister and the President have discussed the mutual problems of defence in relation to the safety of Canada and the United States. It has been agreed that a permanent joint board on defence shall be set up at once by the two countries. This permanent joint board on defence shall commence immediate studies relating to sea, land and air problems including personnel and material. It will consider in the broad sense the defence of the north half of the western hemisphere. The permanent joint board on defence will consist of four or five members from each country, most of them from the services. It will meet shortly.

agreement and sort out the final wording. King queried the word "permanent," which had been included. King said he did not object to it, but it was not clear what the president had in mind. Roosevelt replied that the board was meant not just for the short term, but also to deal with problems in the years ahead. King was fine with that.

With the title of the board and its membership determined, and its responsibilities briefly outlined, the Permanent Joint Board on Defence took shape. The whole agreement amounted to only six sentences (see above textbox). The word *defence* appeared five times in the 109 words of the statement, once in each sentence but the last, as if meant "to reject completely any suggestion of aggressive intent."[22]

With equal membership from each country, the deal gave the appearance, at least, of both nations having an equal voice in protecting North America. The arrangement did promise to allow full expression of the Canadian view and to give Canada some control over the defence measures that might be proposed for northern North America, despite the obvious disparity in military strength. However, it is worth noting that, as significant as the Ogdensburg Agreement became, one of the U.S. president's aims in arranging the meeting — to obtain one or more American naval bases in Canada, especially one in Halifax — failed to find its way into the press release because of Mackenzie King's resistance.

While there was thought of holding a press conference, in the end the two simply decided to issue a press release. It was handed out just before one o'clock in the afternoon, and King left Ogdensburg almost immediately. While the newspapers were aware there was going to be a meeting between the two men, until the moment the news release was handed out, few in Ottawa really had a clue about what was going on.

It is extraordinary that the two leaders simply issued a press release, an action unheard of in the world of diplomacy. As C.P. Stacey said, "No international arrangement of comparable importance has ever been concluded more informally."[23] The document was never signed and it was not a treaty. It was simply an agreement. The Americans called it a purely presidential decision, nothing more. Roosevelt was anxious at all costs to avoid calling it a treaty because that would have required U.S. Senate approval, something that would certainly have been divisive and taken months. Roosevelt did not want it to become an election issue.

The deal was entirely political. The professional heads of the fighting services had nothing to do with it, nor did they even know of the president's intention to set up a board. For his part, King had chosen not to get advice from anyone in his cabinet, which, again, might have exposed divisions on the Canadian side. This was bold on the part of both men.

That press release marked a turning point for Canada — the country's first international defence agreement. It moved Canada from a British political and military orbit toward a North American orbit. It was prompted not so much by a Canadian wish for continental defence or by an overwhelming love for the United States but, rather, by Britain's weakness.

Its effects and its wisdom have been fiercely debated since the Second World War. At the time there was stout opposition from Conservatives, but otherwise Canadians broadly welcomed Ogdensburg. Apart from guaranteeing Canadian security, it also allowed Canada to make an all-out effort to assist Britain because Canada would not have to hold back any war supplies, planes, ships, or troops for home defence.

No one was more surprised about the outcome than King, but the deal was masterful in its timing and in meeting the needs of both leaders. It was limited to mutual defence problems, which made it politically acceptable in the United States. For both Canada and the U.S. it expressed the realization that in the case of a hostile attack, Canada could not defend itself alone, while the United States could not be defended without defending Canada.

Reaction was exceptionally positive. U.S. Minister Moffat, who returned to Ottawa with King, called the deal "a daring improvisation." King's chief aide, Oscar Skelton, said, "It was certainly the best day's work done for many a year." External Affairs later examined fifty-four articles in Canada newspapers on the deal, and none offered outright opposition. In Britain there were forty-eight positive articles. In the U.S. there was widespread positive comment, with some isolationist newspapers expressing reservations but little outright opposition.[24] A poll in November in the U.S. put support for the agreement at almost 84 percent. (As late as April 1941, more than two-thirds of those polled in the U.S. still opposed sending army or navy units to Europe to help Britain.)

In Ottawa Conservative leader Richard Hanson attacked Ogdensburg as "window dressing" and a Roosevelt election campaign stunt.[25] More vitriolic was former prime minister Arthur Meighen, who accused King of abandoning Britain. He said, "[I] lost my breakfast when I read the account this morning and gazed on the disgusting picture of these potentates posing like monkeys in the middle of the blackest crisis of this Empire."[26]

King likely brushed off those comments but was shattered by one reaction. As soon as he returned to Ottawa, he telegraphed a detailed account of Ogdensburg to Winston Churchill in London. The British leader bristled. Churchill's response "contained traces of sealed disgust and disappointment at how the Canadians were shielding themselves under the American umbrella."[27] His telegram to King said, "There may be two opinions on some of the points mentioned. Supposing Mr. Hitler cannot invade us ... all these transactions will be judged in a mood different to that prevailing while the issue still hangs in the balance."

King read and reread the message with dismay.

Clearly, Churchill failed to recognize what Ogdensburg meant for both Canada and for Britain. A secure Canada could send everything it had overseas. What might Churchill have done in similar circumstances? To King's enormous relief, there was a second telegram later that was much more conciliatory, in which Churchill seemed to realize that the agreement was logical and for the best. Reconsidering Ogdensburg, but also having received King's congratulations on a stirring speech in Parliament, Churchill wrote, "I am very glad to have this opportunity of thanking you personally for all you have done for the common cause and especially in promoting a harmony of sentiment throughout the world."

The Ogdensburg meeting had another positive result. King's message to Churchill also related that it was clear the Americans were never going to turn over destroyers to the British without getting bases in return. Churchill had been hoping to avoid — or at least minimize — that. Bruce Hutchison said this valuable information from King to Churchill helped smooth the way for the eventual destroyers-for-bases agreement. As a result, said Hutchison, at this moment "King probably exercised greater influence on world events than any Canadian prime minister before him."[28]

The Joint Board sprang into existence only two weeks after Ogdensburg. Each side appointed members immediately, the Americans choosing New York's flamboyant Mayor Fiorello LaGuardia as its chairman while Oliver Biggar, a prominent Ottawa lawyer, was appointed to head the Canadian delegation. It was never an executive body, but it began surveying defences on both coasts and shortly came up with a joint Canadian–U.S. Defence Plan to deal with the immediate military situation.

Later in 1940 during discussions in the Joint Defence Board, Canada gave strategic control of its forces to the Americans in the event that Britain were overrun. But that was reversed. The issue, when raised a second time, caused a major blow up between the two governments in April and May 1941, after the Americans proposed a plan called

ABC-22. It called for Canadian defences in the Maritimes, the Gaspé, and Newfoundland (where Canadian troops were stationed) as well as those in B.C. to be folded directly into the American Northeastern and Western Defence Commands. Debate became heated. However, as he had done at Ogdensburg, Mackenzie King reject the proposals, asserting Canadian control over Canadian military operations in North America. There would be "coordination of the military effort" that was "to be effected by "mutual cooperation." If there was an emergency, the situation could be reviewed. It was all far removed from the original U.S. goal.

Ogdensburg was historic. Cook called it "One of the epoch-changing moments in Canadian-American relations."[29] Stacey said Canada (for better or worse) was moving closer to the U.S. He also termed it a "landmark" that signalled the United States was taking a further step toward war.[30] Granatstein said the agreement marked the first realization of the "changed shape of the world."

Despite those comments, in more recent years a number of prominent writers have said that Ogdensburg was simply a sellout. In one day in that railway car, the argument goes, Canada moved from being a British to an American colony. It was the first of many steps taken both during and after the war toward the American economic and political domination of Canada. As one writer said, Canada was Panama with snow or, by another description, Mexico with sweaters. One of the most prominent champions of the sellout allegation was George Grant, author of the bestselling *Lament for a Nation*.[31] Grant's book argued that Canada has lost its identity and soul, losses which can be traced right back to Mackenzie King's "continentalist" regime. *Lament* mourns the end of Canada as a sovereign state. Although Grant says its days are numbered, the book came out in 1965 and the days since have reached a fairly high number despite his prediction.

The background is that in the late 1950s and 1960s Grant was an ardent supporter of Prime Minister John Diefenbaker and a foe of the Liberals. He was stung by the defeat of the Diefenbaker government in 1963 after its refusal to accept nuclear warheads. Diefenbaker's loss was, for him, "the defeat of Canadian nationalism." According to Grant, Diefenbaker was thrown out because of the central Canadian establishment and its Liberal Party allies. "The election of 1963 was the first time in our history that a strongly nationalist campaign did not succeed," Grant writes, "and [the first time] that a government was brought down for standing up to the Americans." Grant's book is awash with nostalgia for a British Canada, while, rather surprisingly, many New Left commentators have cherry-picked their way through it, seizing on his abundant anti-Americanism, but ignoring his support for Diefenbaker. A second opponent was one of the most colourful historians of his day, and a man of volcanic eruptions, Donald Creighton. He was once called "the bard of British Imperial power."[32] Like Grant, Creighton loved most things British, including his attachment to the Red Ensign flag. During the flag debate of 1963 and 1964 he called the new maple leaf flag design "a tomato squashed on a handkerchief."

Nevertheless, Creighton was a serious and extremely influential writer. His book *Canada's First Century* said Canada was established as an independent northern economy based on a transcontinental east–west axis but one that was undermined by the American "instinct for continental domination."[33] Creighton loathed Mackenzie King, who "broke up the Britannic union without even attempting to devise policies for a separate and independent Canada." King was no "bulky St. George confronting a slavering imperial dragon," said Creighton, but a prime minister who "behaved like a puppet" in 1940.[34]

One of Creighton's arguments was that King consulted neither his cabinet nor his defence minister, let alone Parliament, before approving the Ogdensburg agreement. "Yet it effectively bound Canada to a continental system dominated by the United States," said Creighton, "and largely determined Canadian and defence policy for the next thirty years."[35] Creighton skipped over the favourable public reaction to the agreement and omitted the fact that King asked for and received approval for his actions from both his cabinet and Parliament after he returned to Ottawa.

Many other authors have made similar arguments to Creighton's, including W.L. Morton, who, in *Kingdom of Canada*, regretted British Canada's succumbing to Americanization. Charles Lynch, a long time Ottawa journalist, denounced Mackenzie King in 1974 as a "compromiser, an appeaser, a sort of fat Neville Chamberlain."[36] King transferred us, said Lynch, "from the bosom of the British mother onto the bony lap of the American uncle."

It is easy to make the argument that Mackenzie King and subsequent governments have sold Canada down the river. Today, the American colossus is overpowering in its political, corporate, and cultural domination of Canada and much of the world. Still, a couple of points deserve mention. First, the United States, for all its faults, has generally supported Canada both during and after the Second World War. As Greg Donaghy commented, Canada and the United States always managed to find "ways to accommodate each other's diverging political interests without seriously impairing bilateral cooperation."[37]

If Canada were located alongside Russia or China, could the same thing be said? Would the country even exist? Many other people bordering great powers — the Latvians and Poles, for example — have not been so fortunate. To cite one minor example of the United States's real power in world politics, recall its actions in the Suez Crisis in 1956, in which the very threat of U.S. financial reprisal was enough to trigger British and French retreat from Egypt. The British currency could have been driven into the ground if the United States had wished.

The second point is this: What exactly were the alternatives? What were the options Mackenzie King had in 1940? Among the most prominent and outspoken defenders of Ogdensburg, and scourge of the Ogdensburg critics, has been historian J.L. Granatstein. He has written extensively about the agreement, including penning a short book called *How Britain's Weakness Forced Canada into the Arms of the United States*. The title says it all. The "sell out" at Ogdensburg, and indeed the Liberal "sell out" in general, is one of the "hoary central myths" of Canadian history.[38] "It was not Mackenzie King and the Liberal Party that sold us out and forced Canada into the arms of the United States, but Great Britain's economic and military decline."[39] Not only at Ogdensburg but also in the years following the war, said Granatstein, both Liberals and Conservatives turned to the south only when their efforts to form a viable economic links with Great Britain failed. "It was less a Canadian desire to share Washington's bed, in other words, than London's impotence that compelled our seeking shelter within Uncle Sam's all-encompassing embrace."[40]

Not that everything was sparkling at Ogdensburg, not that the deal turned Canada into a power equal to the United States. Ogdensburg did not change reality. "That Canada has come increasingly under the American political, economic and military sway I must accept," said Granatstein. But, he goes on, the idea that Mackenzie King or his successors collaborated in or willed this surrender to the United States is ridiculous. The Creighton-Grant-Lynch argument assumes Canada had the ability to make many other choices. "This, however, was precisely what the Canadian governments of this century did not often have."[41]

Ogdensburg showed that King had properly assessed Canada's national interest and at the same time showed his willingness to offer all possible assistance to Britain. Hutchison has gone rather far out on a limb to say, "As the Prime Minister of Canada he would have been mad and treasonable to refuse it [Ogdensburg] under conditions of that summer."[42] It is important to emphasize as well that the outcome at Ogdensburg was not simply one-sided. "The PJBD [Permanent Joint Board on Defence] played a signal role as an 'equalizer' of sorts between Canada and its powerful neighbour, reducing the pressure that the latter would otherwise have been able to apply to Canada."[43] The Ogdensburg Agreement was a pragmatic approach to a Canadian crisis.

Canada and the United States were among the very few nations that emerged from the Second World War stronger economically, politically, and militarily than before the war. Who else was there to stand with a nation that was, in population terms, one hundred miles wide and three thousand miles long? Could Canada thrive or even survive as a stand-alone Sweden or Switzerland? In his most telling comment, Granatstein concludes that in that "terrible summer of defeat and despair ... no matter how often I try to appraise the situation, I cannot see any other option for Mackenzie King." He said, "King did what he had to do to secure Canada's security."[44]

King, despite his chummy arrangement with Roosevelt, had absolutely no illusions about America. He was always wary of American power. Since Ogdensburg, Canada has taken a number of steps to try to at least limit American dominance. As Desmond Morton noted, "Canadian governments have realized that having other partners would help to counterbalance American power. An organization like the North Atlantic Treaty Organization meant that Canada would have a number of allies to curb America's occasionally wilful actions. A few years of bilateral defence arrangements with the United States made Ottawa yearn for additional partners. 'Twelve in the bed meant no rape' became an Ottawa slogan."[45]

The Ogdensburg Agreement cast a long shadow. In April, 1941, there was the financial equivalent of the Ogdensburg Agreement between Canada and the United States. Called the "Hyde Park Agreement" it was meant to offset huge Canadian purchases of American military equipment. With the signing, the American government began a massive buying campaign and Canadian companies very quickly got between $200 million and $300 million in military contracts. In subsequent years it has led to the establishment of several military treaties and operations including the construction of the Distant Early Warning radar line, the creation of the North American Air (later Aerospace) Defence Command in 1958, the bi-national operation of the underwater acoustic surveillance system, and many others. It was the beginning of a long and, for the most part, successful military relationship between Canada and the United States — close defence allies for seventy-five years.

However, there remains one irony. The Ogdensburg Agreement was agreed to in 1940 because Canada was entirely defenceless. In the Cold War and after, one counterweight to American dominance would be for Canada to take a strong role in collective defence; yet recent Canadian governments have declined to do that. Canadians would rather be unarmed and complain about American dominance than spend money on defence and moderate it.

Ogdensburg should be remembered as an effective solution to a short-term crisis but, quite unexpectedly, remembered also for its long-term effects. It has remained, through crises and upheavals, through sunny days and storms, through the Cold War and after, through successive Canadian governments and even a recent erratic American president, a symbol of what Canada and the United States can achieve standing together.[46] Not many neighbours can say as much.

DECISION SEVEN

Dieppe

The Dieppe raid on August 19, 1942, marked the worst day in Canadian military history. On that day five thousand Canadian soldiers stormed ashore from landing craft and assault boats at Dieppe. Within hours 60 percent of them were dead, wounded, or prisoners of war. Some of the battalions in the attack were almost entirely wiped out. Of the 554 Essex Scottish who embarked, only fifty-two returned — a casualty rate of 90 percent. In the Royal Hamilton Light Infantry, Captain Denis Whitaker was the only officer to land on the beach, fight into the town itself, and return to Britain unscathed. More Canadian soldiers were captured at Dieppe than in the entire campaign in northwest Europe in 1944 and 1945. With the horrifying death toll, with the hundreds of men wounded and taken as prisoners of war, Dieppe remains to this day an open wound.

The raid has often been called a dress rehearsal for D-Day, an answer to the question, "could Allied troops mount a successful cross-channel attack?" But, for one thing, that was not stated in the original plans. The idea outlined then was to launch a raid to destroy coastal defences, port structures, and military buildings, gather intelligence, scoop up some barges that were in the harbour, and get out. One recent, and rather unconvincing, book even proposes that the entire operation was a front for stealing an Enigma machine, the secret German coding device.[1]

Among other things, Dieppe was also meant to demonstrate a firm British commitment to open a second front and, not incidentally, to set some grabby newspaper headlines at a bad moment in the war.

Dieppe has been described and explained in many ways, but perhaps the single most telling comment about it came from Major Brian McCool of Toronto, the beach master on the main beach, who was captured that day. Among the most pressing questions put to him by the Germans was why such an obviously suicidal attack had been launched at all. He was asked, "Look, McCool, it was too big for a raid and too small for an invasion. What was it?" McCool replied, "If you can tell *me* the answer, I would be very grateful."[2] General Konrad Haase, the German commander at Dieppe, considered it "incomprehensible" that less than a single division was expected to overrun a defending force that was dug in, well protected by anti-tank obstacles and barbed wire and supported by heavy artillery. An entire panzer division was only a few kilometres away.

The Dieppe attack was one of a number of raids planned by Combined Operations in 1942. It was a relatively new British organization that included, as the name implies, elements from all three armed forces. It had enjoyed some previous success that year, including a raid at Bruneval, east of Le Havre, in which 120 commandos grabbed secret radar gear and brought it back to England. Another successful, although costly, raid took place on March 28 when the Royal Navy and British commandos targeted the heavily defended French dry dock at St. Nazaire. It was the only dry dock big enough to handle German battleships like the *Tirpitz* on the Atlantic coast. The obsolete destroyer HMS *Campbeltown* was rammed at high speed into the dry dock gates. The ship had been packed with hidden explosives, which, as planned, detonated later that day, putting the dock out of service and killing a large number of German officers who had gone aboard out of curiosity. The dry dock was still out of operation five years after the war.

Dieppe was something else altogether, far more complicated than all earlier operations. Instead of a couple hundred commandos, the Dieppe raid was to involve two infantry brigades plus tanks. It would require a huge Royal Air Force air operation and hundreds of Royal Navy ships and smaller landing craft. A briefing book outlining the plan ran to 122 pages.

Most commando operations aimed to put a small force between the cracks of the defences, and as a result defenders would suffer more losses than attackers. Large-scale raids were generally viewed skeptically as running head-on into defences and suffering more damage than they caused. Those at the top of the military ladder in London knew that Dieppe was an extremely hazardous operation, and as Tim Cook put it, some senior staff regarded the idea as "mad and bad."[3]

Politics always lurked in the background of Dieppe. The Allies were losing the war and there had been a numbing parade of catastrophes — Pearl Harbor, Hong Kong, Singapore. The Battle of the Atlantic was going badly, and there was a crisis unfolding on the Eastern Front. Stalin had delivered a speech that dropped heavy hints about signing a peace deal with Germany and dropping out of the war. The Soviet leader was convinced the Allies wanted the Germans and Soviets to slug it out to their mutual destruction, then see the Americans and British sweep in afterward and conquer both.

Dieppe Disaster — The Dieppe raid marked one of the worst episodes in Canadian military history. Sixty percent of the soldiers who went ashore were killed, injured, or became prisoners of war.

In late June 1942 the Germans launched their summer offensive. The Soviets expected that Moscow would be the main target even though the first attack was farther south. Although not necessarily the end of the war militarily, the fall of the Soviet capital would be a political disaster of the first order. Stalin's relentless demand was for a Second Front, a Second Front — now. Even in Britain some newspapers were screaming for the same thing. There had to be *something*. Something to relieve the pressure, to get the Germans to move as many divisions as possible away from the Eastern battlefields. Churchill looked around for any kind of response to aid the Soviets, but a Second Front in France in 1942, as the Russians wanted, was simply out of the question.

For their part, the Americans were putting on their own pressure for a Second Front. With their "defeat Germany first" plan, they wanted no delays in mounting some sort of invasion. They were looking at a cross-Channel attack in 1942 called Sledgehammer. It was a kind of do-or-die plan to be used only if the Soviets were down to their last gasp. Eight or ten Allied divisions would seize areas around either Brest or Cherbourg during the early autumn and then hold on for dear life until there could be a buildup and breakout the following spring. Churchill and the British chiefs of staff knew full well that Sledgehammer was a fantasy, given the weakness in British and U.S. forces available and the lack of air superiority and landing craft. A bigger plan for 1943 was Operation Roundup, a full-scale invasion of France, but even Roundup would be nearly impossible. The British were right about Roundup, but still the Americans were unconvinced.

It was not as if the British were doing nothing. The Royal Navy and the Royal Canadian Navy were still fighting hard in the Battle of the Atlantic and the 8th Army was fighting and not giving up in North Africa. But the only real alternative in Europe anyone could come up with for 1942 was a division-sized "reconnaissance in force." That was thin soup for both the Soviets and Americans, but it was virtually the only thing possible. Top planners at Combined Operations knew that cancelling Dieppe would cause big political trouble and it was getting too late in the summer to organize any other operation. Dieppe almost had to be launched — no matter what. Dieppe was not planned solely as a sop to the Soviets, but with the operation already in the planning stages, it was seized on by Winston Churchill and others as part of a political response to them.

A large-scale raid also fitted Churchill's character and personality. He always wanted action everywhere and at all times. His restless mind was forever dreaming up unlikely plans to invade somewhere or attack something. He had gotten rid of the chief of the imperial general staff, Field Marshal John Dill, calling him "Dilly Dally" because he was not bold enough. Commanders in North Africa were constantly being bombarded with calls to attack — ready or not, hurry up. The successor to Dill, Sir Alan Brooke, spent hour after acrimonious hour trying to curb Churchill's more far-fetched schemes. Brooke recorded one meeting in which Churchill was carried away with wanting "lodgements all around the coast from Calais to Bordeaux." Brooke told General Wavell, the commander in Egypt, "The process of trying to control the Prime Minister ... is fraught with difficulties."[4] Still, Churchill's ideas were not all bad, and anyway at least he was a bulldog. Perhaps it was better to attack and keep the Germans off balance rather than just stare across the Channel.

Churchill had appointed "Dickie" Mountbatten, a cousin to the king, as chief of Combined Operations in October 1941.* Before that he was a rather junior naval captain who had been bumped up to acting commodore. He was only forty-one and a celebrity — "the glamour boy" of the British press. Churchill wanted a driver and Mountbatten was surely that. He was also a smooth political operator and mendacious but, nevertheless, an unquestionably brave man. His claim to fame was having had three destroyers sunk under him. He had initially balked at being involved in Combined Operations, wanting instead to take command of a British aircraft carrier. In an apparently lighthearted comment, but one with unintended foreshadowing, Churchill said Combined Operations offered a much greater challenge than the carrier, in which Mountbatten

---

* Mountbatten was known as Dickie, even though Richard was not among his given names. He was Louis Francis Albert Victor Nicholas Mountbatten, born Prince Louis of Battenberg. The family dropped its German titles during the First World War. His wife was Edwina Ashley, principal heir to the rich merchant banker Sir Ernest Cassel.

would only have a bigger and more expensive ship shot out from under him. With Churchill's sponsorship, Mountbatten was double promoted in short order (triple if you count that he was a substantive captain) to the rank of vice-admiral. Such a thing had not been seen in the Royal Navy since Nelson's day.

Mountbatten joined the heads of the army, navy, and air force on the chiefs of staff committee. They seethed at having to sit with a new colleague they considered an over-promoted publicity hound and blowhard. They hated the whole Combined Operations set-up while Mountbatten tried in every way he could to prevent them from meddling in his plans.

There were other pressures that summer. The Canadian Army had thousands of soldiers in England. Some of them had been there since December 1939, and all of them were fed up with twiddling their thumbs. Their demands for action were getting to the point of explosion. Strome Galloway, from Humboldt, Saskatchewan, said all the training and more training left him and his soldiers "fed up, browned off [and] disillusioned."[5] A member of the Essex Scottish, Arthur Rossell from Hamilton said, "We were really just boys … we were young and we were hyped up for action."[6] When the time for the Dieppe raid came, many Canadian soldiers pulled all kinds of strings to take part in it. No one wanted to be left behind.

Back in Canada Mackenzie King was in the midst of yet another conscription battle and faced taunts in Parliament as a do-nothing prime minister. Senior Canadian Army commanders too just wanted "something." There were unflattering comparisons between the idle soldiers and the sailors in the midst of their life-and-death battle against the U-boats.

So, with the Russians near apoplexy, the Americans demanding an invasion, Churchill in a jam, Mountbatten in a turf war, the Canadian Army itching for action, and much more besides, many hopes and dreams were cast upon the next big thing that came along. It turned out to be Operation Rutter — the attack on Dieppe. The British had been looking at possible targets for some time, and Dieppe seemed to fill the bill. There was nothing of strategic value in Dieppe except a radar station, but it was close enough for ships and landing craft to reach it in one short summer night, and it was within fighter aircraft range. It was small

DECISION SEVEN 157

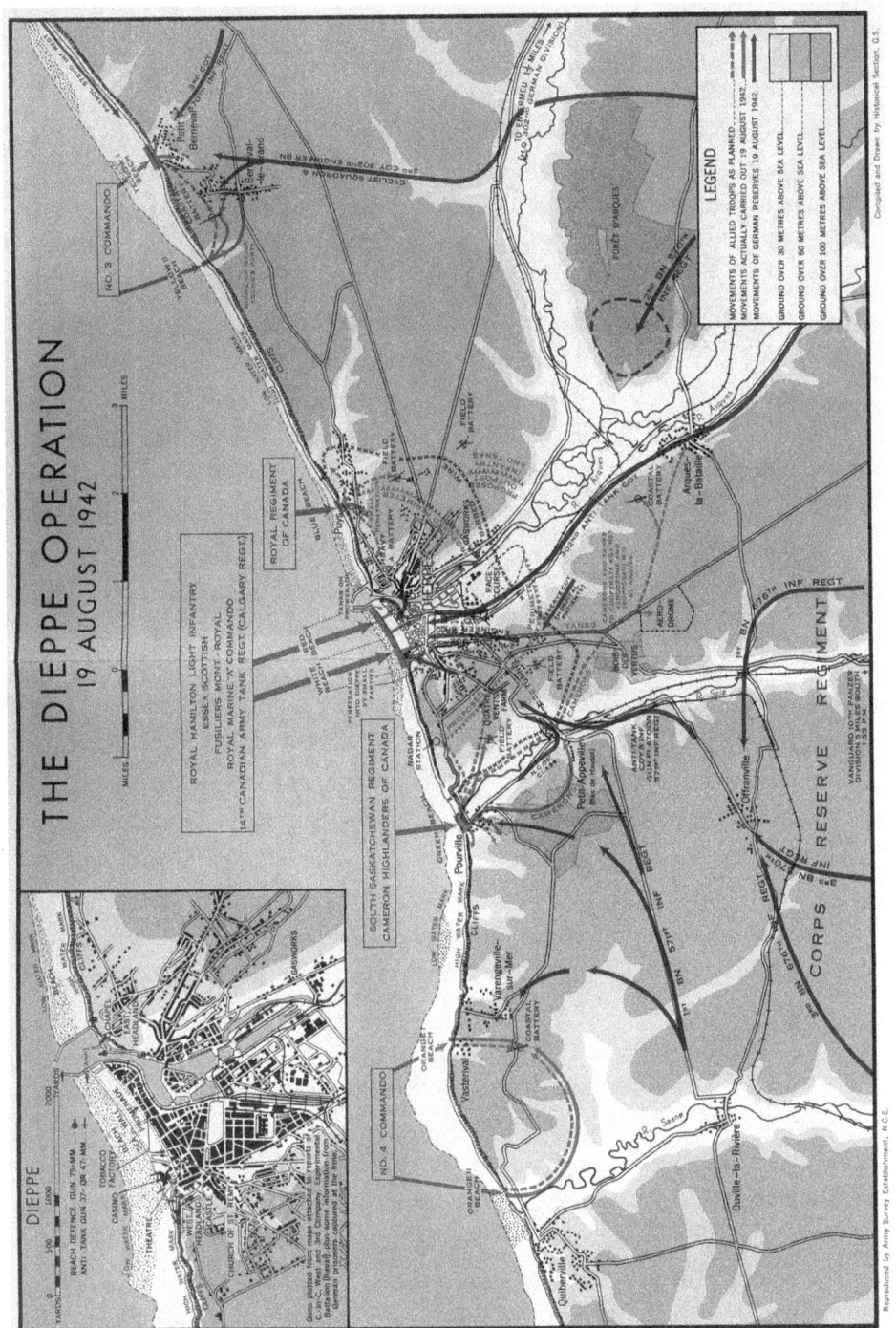

enough that it could be hit in one attack. But that was always the big problem with Dieppe — if the British thought it was an obvious target, the Germans did, too.

While Dieppe had advantages, it was quite dreadful in other respects — described at one point as "an attacker's nightmare."[7] It was shaped like a Roman amphitheatre so that weapons set above Dieppe would have a clear field of fire down onto the beach itself. The Germans had turned Dieppe into a fortress manned by the well-equipped and capable 302nd Infantry Division. The place bristled with well-hidden machine guns, artillery, anti-aircraft guns, and mortars.

At the start there were actually two plans on the table for Dieppe, but the one favoured by Mountbatten was essentially a pincer movement. It would start with British airborne and glider attacks to the east and west of the town and then attack Dieppe from the rear. Massive air and sea bombardment would destroy German fortifications. One problem was that the plan intended to use new British Churchill tanks, and no one was sure bridges around Dieppe were strong enough for them.

Combined Operations could not mount an operation that size on its own. The plan called for two infantry brigades, so it was hardly a surprise that the army wanted a say in how they would be used. Enter Bernard Montgomery, at the time a little-known lieutenant-general. Montgomery was always dodgy about Dieppe and considered the plan to be amateurish and impractical. Indeed, after the war Montgomery's official biographer, Nigel Hamilton, said the Dieppe operation bore the traces of "hasty planning, of obtuse enthusiasm on the part of those units desperate to see 'action' and of amateur, even tragic, overambitiousness."[8]

Montgomery said a pincer attack would simply take too long. The port would have to be attacked quickly and directly; in other words — there would have to be a frontal attack. Mountbatten, ever afterward, accused Monty of making "a shambles" of the original plan. Meantime, Bomber Command chief Arthur Harris called the intended bombing a sideshow and refused to take part. There were also fears that bombing would result in large-scale French civilian casualties, and additional worries that rubble in the town would make it impossible for the tanks to move. So much for the bombing campaign.

Presently, there was another fateful decision: there would be no heavy naval bombardment. To his credit, Mountbatten pushed hard for a battleship to be part of the operation. He acknowledged that putting a battleship in the English Channel in daylight was risky. Still, he argued that a ship such as HMS *Malaya*, of 1915 vintage, was too slow to be used in fleet operations anyway, but its eight big guns would be invaluable. Mountbatten was not alone in that view. Lieutenant-General Frederick Morgan — later on, the chief D-Day planner — remarked about the "explosion that shattered the cloistered calm of the Chiefs of Staff Committee Rooms" when he suggested one or two capital ships be used in the raid.[9] The response of the First Sea Lord, Dudley Pound (perhaps recalling the fates of *Repulse* and *Prince of Wales*, sunk by aircraft off Singapore) was unequivocal. "A battleship in the Channel! Dickie, you must be mad." There would be no battleship or even cruisers but only six small Hunt-class destroyers with their 4.7-inch guns to offer fire support.

A central question was which troops were going to do the attack. Earlier operations had all been run with commandos. For some time Lieutenant-General Harry Crerar, at this point the acting commander of the Canadian Corps, had been lobbying the old boys' network to have a Canadian division take on some kind of operation.* His boss, Lieutenant-General Andy McNaughton, the corps commander, was away on extended leave. (McNaughton was later general officer commanding-in-chief, First Canadian Army.) McNaughton had a key role later in the Dieppe operation. At this point the main actor was Crerar, and he was finally successful in having Canadian troops chosen for Dieppe.

Once that was decided, Monty looked over the available Canadians and picked the 2nd Canadian Infantry Division because he thought it was the best-trained formation in the Canadian Corps and because he was impressed with its commander, Major-General Hamilton Roberts.

---

* Lieutenant-General H.D.G. Crerar, a gunner from Hamilton, Ontario, was one of the central Canadian military figures of the Second World War. In addition to his crucial role in the Dieppe operation, he also had an important part in the career of Lieutenant-General Guy Simonds (Decision Eight) and a pivotal role in the conscription crisis of 1944 (Decision Nine). He held various appointments, including that of chief of the general staff and commanding officer-in-chief of the First Canadian Army.

Actually, there was not much of a choice. Monty thought the First Division commander, Major-General George Pearkes, was a failure and the Third Division was new. Roberts, the eventual scapegoat in the disaster, was a gunner and had a good reputation, but he was in a tough spot.

This would be his first big command, and if he became too difficult he would likely be replaced. An intense training program was laid on for the entire force.

A plan was finalized in early May and approved by the top Allied army, navy, and air force commanders on May 13. An amphibious force would do a frontal assault on Dieppe without bomber support but with large-scale fighter and light bomber attacks and the naval support from destroyers. There would be secondary attacks by parachutists to neutralize guns on the cliffs high above Dieppe. Unquestionably, with the bombardment pared back surprise and the tank support became fundamental to the success of the raid.

Once the troops and naval forces had completed their training, everything was set. Only a bit earlier, Lieutenant-General Crerar wrote that Canadian commanders "expressed full confidence in being able to carry out their tasks — given a break in luck." The soldiers embarked on their ships and landing craft on July 2 and July 3 and were "sealed." The paratroops made final preparations. Everything was set, but there was a final, crucial issue — the weather.

Everyone waited and waited, but what followed was a relentless series of storms, leaving conditions well below minimums for the airborne troops. Finally, on July 8 time ran out. The window of required tide and moon conditions closed, and to the frustration of everyone the attack was called off. The troops were disembarked, and at that point, undoubtedly, the plan was blabbed about all over the pubs of southern England. To all intents and purposes Operation Rutter was done. Certainly, Montgomery thought it was. He recommended that the operation be cancelled for all time because the security issue made it impossible to do otherwise. But at this point, on August 1, he was whisked off to a rendezvous with history in the African desert and had nothing more to do with things.

The cancellation of the raid came at a particularly bad time for Churchill and the Royal Navy. Just at that moment, far to the north, the PQ-17 Arctic convoy disaster was unfolding. The convoy, carrying urgently needed supplies to the Russians, was being hunted down by German naval forces and was ordered to scatter on July 4. Twenty-four of thirty-five merchant ships were lost. Further convoy runs were cancelled. The Russians were outraged.

What came next must be accounted one of the strangest moments of the war: the operation lurched out of the crypt. The Dieppe attack was dusted off, renamed Operation Jubilee and remounted. Mountbatten reasoned that if the Germans heard anything about it, they would hear that the operation had been called off, so that remounting it would — after all — be a surprise. There were questions afterward about whether or not the Germans did hear about it, but it seems unlikely.[10]

The Dieppe operation came back from the dead but with three changes. In Jubilee, commandos would replace the airborne units (minimizing the weather problems). Second, the U.S. Army Air Force, not part of the original plan, would bomb a single German airfield near Dieppe as a diversion. Third, the time ashore would be reduced from two tides to one, without scaling back the raid's objectives on the ground. In its final form, the plan was made up of attacks at five points, spread over an area sixteen kilometres long. Starting from the outside and working inward, there would be a pair of assaults by separate British Army commando teams, one east and one west of Dieppe, to destroy big coastal guns on cliff tops. Then there would be two attacks closer in, at Puys, just east of Dieppe, and at Pourville, just to the west. Then the biggest part of the force, including the tanks, would storm ashore at the port of Dieppe itself.

Hundreds of soldiers were quickly recalled from leave or rounded up from surrounding towns. British Commando Alan Saunders said he went to his base that afternoon believing his group was getting ready for another exercise. "We went to the dockside where ammunition boxes and explosives were laid out. We saw it was live ammunition.... We knew then we were going into an operation, but where we didn't know."[11] Finally, the much altered, much delayed, but certainly much hoped for attack was set. In all, 253 ships, landing craft, and boats then crept out of British ports, some in the soft evening light, others, just after dark. The operation was underway.

The team ordered to attack the cliffs to the far west of Dieppe was made up of the 252 members of the British Army's No. 4 Commando, led by one of the war's most colourful characters, Lord Lovat, the 25th chief of Clan Fraser of Lovat. Armed for the occasion with his favourite hunting rifle, Lieutenant-Colonel Lovat was an able combat leader and the No. 4 Commando attack turned out to be the most successful part of the entire operation. The team swept ashore, split into two groups, climbed the steep cliffs, and went on to destroy six 5.9-inch coastal guns. Lovat's commandos suffered casualties, but Lovat himself and most of his men made it home safely.

On the extreme opposite flank, it was far different for No. 3 Commando. Four of the landing craft, with a total of about one hundred men aboard, developed engine trouble and had to turn back. Meanwhile, as the twenty-three other vessels approached the French coast in the middle of the night, they ran into a small German convoy, and a sustained and deadly firefight erupted. Radio traffic and gunfire from the German ships alerted some, but not all, of the coastal defences.

Several analysts and writers have claimed that this was just "bad luck," an unexpected event that wrecked the entire operation. But the Germans frequently ran small resupply convoys from one port to another at night, so this should not have been completely unexpected.[12] Two warnings about the possible route the German convoy would take were sent by the commander-in-chief at Portsmouth to the Jubilee forces in the Channel, but the messages were apparently not received.

The vessels carrying No. 3 Commando were badly scattered in the firefight, and several landing craft, shot full of holes, were forced to join those already limping back to England. While a large group of commandos landed, only one small party was able to get close to the massive 170-mm guns. Some of the German guns were prevented from firing because of sniper fire, but most kept up their shelling throughout the main attack. This part of the operation was a failure.

Between the point where No. 3 Commando attacked and Dieppe itself was the narrow beach at Puys, the target for Toronto's Royal Regiment of Canada. The Royals were to land, climb the cliffs, and take out the defences overlooking Dieppe. This was absolutely critical to the success of the entire plan. If it turned out well, it would significantly reduce German fire onto the Dieppe beach, but if it failed, the soldiers landing there would face a firestorm. In the end, Puys was, simply, a "death trap."[13] It was an obvious place for a landing, and there was only one single gully for soldiers to climb to the cliff top, a gully that was mined and covered in barbed wire. As the commander of the regiment, Lieutenant-Colonel Douglas Catto, had pointed out before the raid, this is where heavy bombardment from a cruiser or battleship might have been most effective. However, in response to his observation, he was simply asked whether he intended to take the regiment ashore or wished to be replaced.

The Royals approached the beach more than thirty minutes behind schedule because some landing craft initially headed in the wrong direction. The troops arrived with German flares arcing overhead. The result was that the Royals lost not only the advantage of surprise, but of darkness too. There was some fire support from the destroyer HMS *Garth* and an armed motor launch, but it was entirely inadequate. Touching down amid a wall of machine-gun and mortar fire, about half the Royals were casualties within ten minutes. According to Canadian Press reporter Ross Munro, who went ashore with the regiment, "It was just carnage ... the whole slope was just littered with khaki bodies."[14] Those who made it to a barbed wired seawall could get no farther. There was nobody to look after the wounded, and if there had been, it would have been impossible to get near them. Three platoons of reinforcements from the Black Watch (Royal Highland Regiment) of Canada arrived but were similarly pinned down. Such was the curtain of fire that by 8:30 in the morning the Royals and the Black Watch were forced to surrender. Only sixty-five members of the Royals were able to return to England; only thirty-three of the Black Watch. The Puys operation, despite heroism and sacrifice, was a failure.

The other flanking operation was at Pourville, just to the west of Dieppe, where the South Saskatchewan Regiment (SSRs) and Queen's Own Cameron Highlanders of Canada had some degree of surprise as they landed. German defences did not appear to be able to return fire right at the start. Nevertheless, one survivor, Corporal Donald Wolfe of the Camerons, said, "to me it was suicidal ... as soon as we got off the landing craft, boy it was murder."[15] The aim of the two regiments was to charge up the headlands above Pourville overlooking Dieppe. Unfortunately, some troops were landed on the wrong side of a small river, which caused serious delays. They had to cross the river, but heavy fighting developed and the SSRs were stopped cold. It was in this part of the operation that the regiment's commander, Lieutenant-Colonel Cecil Merritt, repeatedly ran back and forth across an open bridge to get reinforcements despite continuous fire. This act of bravery earned him the Victoria Cross. Remarkably, the SSRs were able to get about two thousand yards inland before the order to withdraw arrived, but they were not able to reach the headlands, nor the guns on them. The exceptional bravery of crewmen aboard naval landing craft allowed for re-embarking 341 men, but that was all that could be done.

The result of all this was that there was no hope of surprise when, thirty minutes after the first attacks, the main force charged head-on into the inferno of Dieppe itself. Five squadrons of Hurricane aircraft launched attacks while the fire support from destroyers offshore began. The attacking force was made up of the Royal Hamilton Light Infantry, the Essex Scottish, No. 40 Commando of the Royal Marines, and the Calgary Tanks. In reserve still offshore was another infantry battalion, Les Fusiliers Mont-Royal. The untouched German 150-mm heavy coastal batteries on top of the Dieppe escarpment joined the battle.

The Royal Hamilton Light Infantry, known to all as the "Rileys" from their initials, landed on the mile long beach, near a casino. The defences were much stronger than expected and progress was very slow. Casualties continued to mount, but a few members of the regiment were able to clear the strongly held building and the nearby pillboxes and enter the town. There was toe-to-toe street fighting. As dozens of men lay wounded and dying, among those who braved danger to try to help them was Honorary Captain John Foote, the regimental chaplain. On landing, Foote went to the Regimental Aid Post that had been set up. During the next several hours he ministered to the wounded — injecting morphine, giving first aid, carrying soldiers to the Aid Post — and undoubtedly saved many lives. As the tide went out, Foote had more than one opportunity to scramble aboard a landing craft but chose to become a prisoner of war rather than leave the wounded. He was also awarded the Victoria Cross.

One of the many problems of the raid turned out to be high casualties among signalmen. Neither they nor their radios survived long enough to send information back to General Roberts in the destroyer HMS *Calpe*. One of the few messages he did receive was confusing and garbled and led Roberts to believe — wrongly — that the Essex Scottish had arrived in force in the town. This led to one of the most disastrous decisions of the entire operation, to launch Les Fusiliers Mont-Royal toward the beach. The Montrealers rode through unrelenting enemy fire all the way in, with high casualties even before they set foot on dry land. Originally 584 members of the regiment had set off from England but only 125 of them eventually made it back.[16]

The planners had high hopes for the tanks. In an operation without battleships or big bombers, here at least was some firepower. The attack would be history making. The Calgary Regiment (Tanks) would be the first Canadian armoured regiment to go into action while the operation marked the first time in history that tanks would be used in an amphibious landing. It is not often mentioned that fifty-seven Churchill tanks left England that fateful night but twenty-eight of them, intended for a second-wave attack, were held back. The landing of the first wave was late and the landing craft on the shore were being pulverized. The decision was made — wisely — not to send in the remaining tanks. They would have made no difference to the outcome whatsoever.

The thirty-nine-ton Churchills were the goliaths of their time, but the planners really did not have a clue about how to use them.[17] The plan intended that the tanks would cross the Dieppe seawall, go into the town proper, through narrow streets, shoot up the place, go out the other side to link up with the Camerons coming in from Pourville, and then withdraw back through the town, back over the seawall, and re-embark. All in a few hours. This was patently impossible. Moreover, the idea of using tanks in narrow streets in a defended town was absurd. The Germans had put huge concrete tank obstacles at the street entrances such that they were never able to go through the streets anyway.

Two of the tanks sank in deep water even before they reached the beach, and others were hit immediately after landing. The first wave of tanks was put ashore ten to fifteen minutes late, leaving the infantry without support during the first critical minutes of the attack. Fifteen minutes may not sound like much, but in those first few minutes, the battle on the main beach was probably lost. As has often been commented, the beach was covered by layers of smooth stones called *chert*, which clogged the tank treads. The chert was several metres deep, so there was no chance that a spinning tread could gain traction. All the treads did was keep spinning until the tank was grounded or the stones that were caught up in the treads broke the track pins. A few tanks had mats to help them get traction.

The plan was for engineers to put wooden ramps down so the tanks could mount the seawall along the beach, but most engineers became casualties, and neither they nor their ramps ever appeared. Only fifteen tanks were able to get past the seawall. Although the tanks were able to engage the defenders in the town, their main guns could only fire anti-tank shells, rather than high-explosive shells, which would have been more help to the infantry. Most of the tanks spent the entire time as immobile pillboxes, although they kept up firing until their ammunition ran out.

The last troops to land were Royal Marine commandos. Their job was to seize landing craft in the port and try to sail them back to England. In an interview years later, commando Alan Saunders said the German defenders were "just popping them [the Canadians] off left, right and centre. There was nothing we could do. We were only ashore for five or ten minutes at the most before the order came … to withdraw."[18] None of the commandos managed to move even a few yards from the shoreline.

While the disaster unfolded on the ground, in the skies above Dieppe an epic battle raged all morning. The Allied air forces, which included Blenheim and Boston bombers as well as hundreds of fighter aircraft, were able to provide protection for the ships off Dieppe and, to some extent, do strafing runs on shore. But the Royal Air Force lost 106 aircraft and the Royal Canadian Air Force lost five, the highest one-day total of the war. Of the nine hundred Luftwaffe aircraft that took part in the action, forty-eight were destroyed. At sea, more than thirty landing craft and one of the supporting destroyers were sunk. The ground troops had high praise for the naval crews, which suffered 550 killed, wounded, or captured.

Just before 11:00 a.m., only nine hours after the first troops hit the beach, General Roberts ordered a withdrawal. Bad as things were at this point, the evacuation proved to be even worse. Men who had miraculously survived the mortars, the machine guns, and all the firepower an infuriated defender could mount tried to scramble back to the landing craft only to be killed by the score. At 1:58 p.m. the firing stopped.

As the last of the landing craft coughed its way into the smoke offshore, Marine Saunders scanned the waterfront and said, "You couldn't see the beach as there were bodies, body parts ... and all the detritus and chaos and carnage of war there." At the water's edge, the tide rose, leaving the sea stained red. Many of the dead and wounded floated away in the waves. At least one body was recovered as far west as the Cherbourg peninsula, 180 kilometres away.

Canadians alive but still on shore were rounded up by the score. Lieutenant-Colonel Robert Labatt of the Rileys said what came next was "the most unpleasant decision of my life."[19] A German prisoner was released with a white flag. "He waved to his pals and thirty or forty of them leapt onto the sea wall and covered us with sub-machine guns or rifles. Everybody stood up, and that was that." They were prisoners of war.

The soldiers and commandos had done everything that they could do. It was amazing that any of them got off the beach and back to England. Lieutenant Les England of the SSRs was seriously wounded and put aboard a landing craft, but it was sunk. He was then picked up by a destroyer, but it was bombed. He crawled out of the hole in the side of the ship and was picked up by a third vessel that finally delivered him to England. Lance Sergeant G.A. Hickson, an engineer, returned to England uninjured but with two bullet holes right through one sleeve and one through his pant leg.

And so ended what C.P. Stacey called "the brave and bitter day."[20]

It was far worse than anyone had imagined. It was only when the ships and landing craft began to return to England — or failed to return — that the true depth of the disaster began to sink in. The military attempted to dampen down the worst of it. Public relations staff had a plan titled "In Case the Raid is Unsuccessful." In it Defence Minister Ralston was urged to "lay extremely heavy stress on stories of personal heroism ... in order to focus public attention on *bravery* rather than *objectives not attained*."[21] Initial newspaper accounts hailed the operation as a victory. "Canadians Spearhead Battle at Dieppe … Help Smash Nazi Opposition," beamed the *Toronto Star*. It was short-lived. The next day, Ross Munro reported, "Canadian shock troops had a rough time of it at several points and losses will probably not be small."[22] When the endless lists of killed and wounded began to be published in Canada, it shocked the nation.

In a memorable description, the eminent British historian John Keegan said that Dieppe "in retrospect looks so recklessly hare-brained an exercise that it is difficult to construct the official state of mind which gave it birth and drove it forward."[23] A blizzard of after-action reports flew all over Canadian and British headquarters for months in the fall and winter of 1942. None of them contained much that was surprising. Lord Lovat said, "Only a foolhardy commander launches a frontal attack with untried troops, unsupported, wired and mined approaches, in daylight against veterans … it was a bad plan and had no chance of success."[24] Lieutenant-Colonel Charles Carrington, an army officer attached to the Royal Air Force headquarters for the operation, thought there was "nothing to be learned from Dieppe, except how not to do it."[25] More recently one Canadian officer who examined that plan concluded it was "impossible to execute."[26]

For a start, Operation Jubilee had no single commander but instead three of them, which was surely a prescription for disaster. Also, historian Robin Neillands said the plan came with a fundamental error. "If the Canadians landed on the main beach while the enemy were still in possession of the headlands, their destruction was inevitable…. There was no provision whatsoever for action in the event of failure — if the attack stalled, if the enemy reacted strongly and held the invaders on the beach, if there was any major hold up of any kind, no arrangements were in place either to call off the attack or divert parts of the landing forces to some other beach."[27]

The Germans questioned many of the prisoners, including, as mentioned earlier, Major McCool, but after that they did their own investigation. They captured a complete set of the plans (copy No. 37) and examined them closely. "The planning down to the last detail limits the independence of action of the subordinate officer," the Germans felt, "and leaves him no opportunity to make independent decisions in an altered situation."[28] If there were any lessons at Dieppe, the Germans were learning them, too.

One of the more startling comments about Dieppe came in an article a few years ago by Lieutenant John Edmondson of the South Saskatchewan Regiment. He wrote that while the plan leaned heavily on surprise, junior officers were sure that surprise would be impossible. At a briefing Edmondson attended before the raid, he asked senior officers how there could be surprise when every time the moon and tides were favourable for a German attack on England, British forces were put on increased alert? He got no answer, and a naval officer told him to be quiet and not repeat the question.[29] Indeed, on the eve of the Dieppe attack the German defenders *were* on a higher state of alert — a category called "Threatened Danger" — because of the tides and the moonless nights of early August.

Timing was also critical. All 252 vessels had to release their landing craft at exactly the right moment. The coastal batteries at Berneval and Varengeville had to be silenced on time. The tanks had to land on time.

In the event, the cancellation of the bombers may not have changed things much. Bombers proved to be very inaccurate and made little difference on the Normandy beaches on D-Day in 1944. However, not having a big naval bombardment definitely did make a difference. Brigadier-General Lucian Truscott, a later U.S. army commander, watched the battle from a destroyer and said the naval and air attacks were not nearly as heavy as required.[30]

There was a lot of wishful thinking about Dieppe. The initial plan said Dieppe was not heavily defended. The intelligence chief was the flamboyant Wing Commander the Marquis de Casa Maury. "Bobby" de Casa Maury was a controversial figure whom one senior Royal Navy officer described as "utterly useless."[31] One intelligence source was a collection of pre-war postcards. Intelligence depended heavily on aerial photos, but the Germans were masters of camouflage, and the photos failed to pick up most gun emplacements. Neither did they show many barbed wire defences.

The withdrawal is always the trickiest part of any raiding operation. It would be obvious that as soon as the attackers stopped advancing and began to withdraw, the defenders would be close on their heels. Those withdrawing would have to take time to carry wounded or prisoners, and inevitably there would be confusion. Re-embarking the tanks would be a cumbersome affair. Little provision was made for any of it.

But bad as all the above is, one point seems most damning of all. At the time, almost all the Canadian and British top brass who looked at the plan believed that the Dieppe operation would be successful. Mountbatten's biographer said Dieppe "was accepted by all concerned to be an ideal target."[32]

Prime Minister Churchill, the chiefs of staff — General Brooke, Admiral Pound, and Air Chief Marshal Portal — and other top officers have to accept their share of the blame for the carnage. They knew long before Dieppe that large-scale raids were fraught with danger. Final authority lay with the chiefs and the war cabinet. After the initial plan was cancelled, the chiefs were aware the operation might be remounted but raised no objection.

Beyond that, no matter which way you look at it, it was Admiral Mountbatten's show. He was the man in charge, and what he was in charge of was an appalling, calamitous disaster. Another commander might have been fired or pushed aside, but Mountbatten was not a man to be trifled with, and he had Churchill's backing. Montgomery's biographer, Nigel Hamilton, accused Mountbatten of being a "master of intrigue, jealousy and ineptitude" and of having "insatiable, even psychopathic ambition."[33] But Mountbatten had his response ready. He was not a man to go down on this or any count. He argued that for every one man who died at Dieppe, twelve more must have been spared in Normandy in 1944. It became his mantra for years to come.

The claim that lives lost at Dieppe were crucial to success on D-Day has been repeated many times by Mountbatten and others. But most of the lessons were entirely obvious as Lord Lovat said. Canadian-born newspaper tycoon Lord Beaverbrook had been one of the admiral's biggest boosters, but after Dieppe he became a relentless accuser. At a dinner party Beaverbrook confronted Mountbatten: "You have murdered thousands of my countrymen … their blood is on your hands."[34] It became an ugly vendetta. General Eisenhower's aide, Henry Butcher, quoted

Mountbatten as saying that the "unlucky" contact with the German convoy in the Channel "couldn't happen once in a hundred times, but it did this time."[35] But, of course, the evidence is far different.

One telling example of how Mountbatten was able to deflect blame came with the publication of Winston Churchill's six-volume epic *The Second World War*.[36] After the war, Churchill was still troubled by Dieppe. He wrote a version of what happened for his book but asked one of his collaborators to get Mountbatten's comments. Mountbatten was alarmed by the draft, which pointed to casualties of more than 60 percent among the Canadians. Instead, Mountbatten penned an entirely new version of the raid that downplayed his own responsibility.[37] In the end Churchill's interest turned elsewhere and Mountbatten's version — almost untouched — appeared in Churchill's war history.

But even with that, questions about Mountbatten have continued. A book by Brian Villa titled *Unauthorized Action* raised the issue of who gave final approval to launch Operation Jubilee. Villa's answer is — no one did. Mountbatten did it on his own.[38] Years later, Mountbatten claimed Churchill gave a verbal go-ahead, something that Churchill could not remember. In the 1960s, the British Broadcasting Corporation produced an autobiographical documentary about Mountbatten that totalled twelve hours in length. The Dieppe raid got three and a half minutes.

Major General Roberts agreed to the many changes in the plan — no bombing, no battleships. He should have insisted on better naval support, but as noted earlier his real power was limited. The raid would have gone ahead whether he was in command or not. Roberts made the dreadful decision to send in Les Fusiliers Mont-Royal, but communications were terrible. Once the ships left England, not even a Patton could have pulled this one out of the fire. Lovat was outraged that Roberts was later made the scapegoat.[39] Strictly speaking, Dieppe did not end Roberts's career. He did poorly in a major exercise in 1943, was shuffled off to minor jobs, and then left the army.

As for the two Canadian generals, McNaughton and Crerar, they had direct responsibility for selecting the mission and for signing off on the final plan. They had a much more critical role in the operation than has sometimes been stated. Crerar pushed hard for Canadians to

Decision on Dieppe — Lieutenant-General A.G.L. McNaughton played a key role in approving the Dieppe plan.

Hard Lobbying — Lieutenant-General H.D.G. Crerar held backroom meetings with Admiral Mountbatten and others to urge that Canadian troops be included in the Dieppe raid.

be involved in the first place. At the start, the British did everything possible to keep McNaughton away from the decision and have Roberts report to Montgomery alone. However, by the time Jubilee was launched, things were completely different. There was vicious infighting between McNaughton and Crerar, on the one hand, and the British Army, on the other, over who would have control of the Canadian troops. By the time Jubilee was launched, the British commanders had been pushed aside. Both McNaughton and Crerar argued successfully that only Canadian commanders could decide whether and how their troops would be used in battle.[40]

One crucial moment came even as the troops started boarding their ships for Rutter. It was clear that General Roberts still had misgivings about the set-up. He went to Montgomery, but the problem was punted to Crerar. On July 2 Crerar met with Roberts and told him that no operation ever goes 100 percent according to plan. Crerar's advice was that swift decision making would keep things on track, as if that would have made any difference on the Dieppe beaches. The message was that he — Crerar — was behind the plan and the operation. Crerar reported back to McNaughton that he told Roberts, "I should have no hesitation in tackling it."[41]

An equally important decision came in the switch from Rutter to Jubilee. Crerar looked at the changes and on August 11 reported to McNaughton, "I … am satisfied that the revisions made in respect to the previous exercise plans add, rather than detract, to the soundness of the plan as a whole. I am, therefore, of the opinion that, given an even break in luck and good navigation, the demonstration [i.e., operation] should prove successful."[42]

Far from being manoeuvred into the raid by British authorities, the Canadian Army was driving hard for it. In reality, the raid would probably not have taken place if McNaughton and Crerar had not backed it so aggressively.[43] As Brian Villa commented, "It is sadly true that if anyone could have stopped the Dieppe raid it was the Canadian commander, General McNaughton."[44] The Dieppe operation, in the way it was planned by both British and Canadian officers, was a disaster. The British undoubtedly deserve a part of the blame for what happened. However, Canadian commanders accepted the plan and pushed it forward, so for their part of

Dieppe Today — *What is a quiet-looking beach today was the scene of carnage on August 19, 1942. The casino that was the focus of some attackers was located approximately where the rectangular structure now is.*

the decision making, going to Dieppe must be judged among the worst Canadian decisions of the war.

Afterward McNaughton accepted that verdict, telling Vincent Massey, the Canadian high commissioner in London, that he had "examined the plans carefully and assumed full responsibility for the Canadians taking part."[45] It was different with Crerar. He adopted the "Mountbatten Defence," never varying from his view that Dieppe was a "tragic, but necessary, lesson."[46] As with Mountbatten, Crerar has very largely escaped blame for Dieppe, and as J.L. Granatstein has said, he "led a charmed life."[47]

One final point should be made. Beyond the failed plan and the culpable commanders, Dieppe showed a wider, deeper malaise. If there was a lesson in Dieppe it was surely this: it showed that after three long years of war British and Canadian commanders could not plan a full-scale invasion of the continent; they could not even put together a successful one-day operation. There was not going to be any cross-Channel invasion anytime soon.

Perhaps the last word should go to a soldier who survived Dieppe. Private Jack Poolton of the Royal Regiment of Canada said, "I lost my friends and I think it was a waste, a waste of a lot of good soldiers … they didn't have to die, at least like that."[48]

DECISION EIGHT

Simonds Appointed to Command II Canadian Corps

Lieutenant-General Guy Simonds is Canada's most compelling, most written about, and most discussed army commander of the Second World War. That is hardly surprising because his abilities as a battlefield commander were unmatched by any of his Canadian contemporaries. From his early days the word that followed Simonds around like a shadow was *brilliant*. He was a brilliant student at Royal Military College, a brilliant young officer before the war, and in 1939 with the outbreak of the war, a brilliant star headed right to the top. The most famous among those who praised him was his great patron Field Marshal Montgomery, who said, "Canada produced only one general fit to hold high command in war and that was Guy Simonds."

But there was another side to him. For all his gifts, he was not a popular figure in the army. He was much respected but viewed as a cold and remote mannequin. Major-General Chris Vokes, Simonds's friend and RMC classmate, famously said he was "the finest Canadian general we ever had, but as a leader of men he wasn't worth a pinch of coonshit."[1]

Although born in Britain in 1903 Simonds was raised mostly in British Columbia. His father was a lieutenant-colonel in the British army who, after the First World War, headed for B.C. in straitened financial circumstances. Early in life Guy Simonds faced formidable barriers. His mother was an unbalanced and outrageous spendthrift who used money meant for her children on herself. At one point the young Simonds was forced to leave school for a year to earn enough money to continue his education.

That financial hardship continued during his years at Royal Military College in Kingston, but he was helped by loans from a sympathetic RMC commandant. He took part in athletic events and even theatre and was admiringly nicknamed "the Count" by RMC peers. He won numerous distinctions in his final year, including the Sword of Honour, the college's highest prize for conduct and discipline, while at the same time he was the cadets' own choice as best all round student. He was commissioned into the tiny regular army in 1925.

Simonds was first posted to the Royal Canadian Horse Artillery in Kingston, where his battery commander was Harry Crerar, later the chief of the general staff and then commander of the First Canadian Army. Their paths would cross often. Simonds's assessments in the 1930s gave him top marks for imagination, tactical knowledge, technical ability, judgment, and leadership but, significantly, only average marks for sociability.[2] He returned to RMC as a staff member before the war and was remembered by Cadet Ned Amy, a later tank officer, as "very brilliant."[3]

At the British Staff College in Camberley, England, in 1936 Simonds was "one of the outstanding men."[4] He returned to Canada in 1938 and was the author of three articles in *Canadian Defence Quarterly* that focused on the shape of a future war.[5] When the war broke out, Major Simonds was sent to Britain and appointed a staff officer with the 1st Canadian Infantry Division. Quick jumps followed. In July 1940, he was a lieutenant-colonel and appointed to command the 1st Field Regiment, Royal Canadian Horse Artillery and after that, commander of the first Canadian Junior War Staff Course. In August 1941 he was promoted to brigadier and assigned to Canadian Corps Headquarters, becoming principal staff officer to Lieutenant-General McNaughton. At some risk, Simonds criticized McNaughton, telling him he spent too much time on the administration of the First Canadian Army and not enough on training troops. McNaughton's shortcomings became obvious in Exercise

Spartan, a huge training scheme in 1943 that, according to General Alan Brooke, the chief of the imperial general staff, ended in "an awful muddle."[6] It helped bring about an abrupt conclusion to McNaughton's career as army commander.

Simonds was fortunate to have spent a short time as an observer with the famed Eighth Army in North Africa. Both Montgomery and Lieutenant-General Brian Horrocks were impressed by him. Simonds could see that the days of the 1940 blitzkrieg were over, doomed by German defence-in-depth and deadly anti-tank weapons.

In April 1943, Simonds was promoted to major-general and appointed to command the 2nd Canadian Infantry Division, with Montgomery having possibly had a hand in the appointment.[7] At this point there was a fateful turn. The 1st Canadian Infantry Division commander, Major-General Harry Salmon, was killed in a plane crash. On April 29, 1943, Simonds was appointed to replace him. The appointment was notable because the 1st Division was training for Operation Husky, the invasion of Sicily, only two and a half months away. The appointment was also noteworthy because Simonds, just turning forty years old, was nine years younger than Salmon. Command of the Canadian Army was making a generational leap.

It is important to look at the timing of Simonds's appointment in broader terms. Until October 1942 — that is, six months before he was appointed to the 1st Canadian Division — the British and Canadian armies were still gripped by a crisis of confidence. There appeared to be real questions about whether the British and Commonwealth armies could ever take on and defeat the German army. The electrifying victory at Alamein and the following defeat of the Germans in North Africa changed everything. The invasion of Sicily, therefore, could begin with a record of victory behind it. In Operation Husky, the 1st Canadian Division and the 1st Canadian Army Tank Brigade, both under Simonds's command, would also be part of the legendary Eighth Army.

For the Canadian Army there was a second psychological boost. After two and a half years of training to defend Britain against possible German invasion, and after the Dieppe disaster, here in April 1943 were new marching orders. The Canadian Army, at long last, could start planning to attack, to take the war to the enemy.

There were challenges for the Canadians going to Sicily, including that the division was completely untested. It would be a challenge to turn theoretical combat doctrine into reality and to learn the hard way what it takes to win a battle. Simonds was similarly untested. He would be on a short leash and under intense scrutiny as the first Canadian officer to lead troops in a sustained campaign.* Perhaps worst of all was that the Sicily operation would begin with that most formidable of challenges: the amphibious assault.

Fortunately, in addition to the psychological boost mentioned earlier, better equipment was also at hand. Most conspicuously, the army could set aside its Canadian Ram tanks in favour of the Sherman, although the Canadian armoured regiments heading for Sicily — the Ontario Regiment, the Calgary Tanks, and the Three Rivers Regiment — had to be quickly retrained on the new vehicles. The failings of the Sherman have been well documented (it readily caught fire and was nine feet tall, to mention only two). Still, it was sturdy, rugged, and reliable. The Canadians were also handed the six-pounder anti-tank gun and the new PIAT anti-tank weapon (Projector, Infantry, Anti-Tank). The PIAT, the British equivalent of the bazooka, had a short range and a vicious kick but was at least effective. Similarly, the army had a new three-inch mortar.

For Canadians the worst setback in Operation Husky came on the way to Sicily when U-boats sank three cargo ships with the loss of fifty-eight Canadians, five hundred vehicles, and forty guns. Then, a summer gale made for confusion when the British, Canadians, and Americans did finally sweep ashore on July 10. Still, the operation went much better than some had feared, and initial casualties were light. Within hours Canadians at home were electrified to hear the prime minister break the news about the operation. "Armed forces of Britain, the United States and Canada are now in the forefront of an attack which has as its ultimate objective the unconditional surrender of Italy and Germany. All Canada will be justifiably proud to know that units of the Canadian Army are a part of the Allied force engaged in this attack."[8]

---

*   Hong Kong and Dieppe were too brief to be considered campaigns.

As the Canadian division pushed inland, Simonds quickly gained a reputation for prowling the front lines. On July 16, near Piazza Armerina, he came under mortar fire and had more than one close call. There was intensive newspaper coverage, including an article in the *Winnipeg Free Press* that described him as carrying "the bronzed stamp of the Canadian outdoors" on him.[9]

There were mistakes, notably in attacks in late July near Agira that featured uncoordinated artillery support and high casualties. The Germans made a determined stand and had to be beaten back several times before a fresh brigade succeeded in dislodging them. It was only on July 28, after five days of fighting, that Agira was taken.[10] In one day of battle the Hastings and Prince Edward Regiment had five officers and seventy-five other ranks killed, wounded, or missing — the heaviest losses suffered by any Canadian unit during the Sicily campaign. The Royal Canadian Regiment lost its commanding officer, three other officers, and sixteen men. As a result there were a lot of accusations, some them aimed it at 1st Brigade commander Howard Graham. But Graham said the plan was overly ambitious, while even Simonds's biographer conceded that the detailed artillery plan "seemed excessive."[11] There was also a blow-up between Graham and Simonds, possibly complicated by the fact that Graham was a militiaman. Simonds wanted to fire Graham for not being aggressive enough, but both Montgomery and British Lieutenant-General Oliver Leese, who was Simonds's boss, said that was too hasty. The new division commander was forced into a humiliating climb down.

The Sicily campaign is generally considered a strategic failure. True, the Germans were soundly trounced; the Allies secured air bases necessary to support the liberation of mainland Italy; and the operation contributed to the downfall of Mussolini. However, Allied air and sea power utterly failed to prevent the defenders' escape to the mainland, where the same German troops would have to be defeated a second time. Nevertheless, in their part of the operation the Canadians and Simonds did well. It has been said that the key to victory was Guy Simonds and lots of artillery. Simonds had tended to over-control subordinates, and his dealings with Graham had shown a nasty streak, but in the big picture he had learned a great deal. Lieutenant-General

Leese was complimentary, describing Simonds as "a young Regular Canadian soldier and very intelligent."[12]

In November 1943 Harry Crerar, Simonds's one-time battery commander and boss at RMC, re-entered the picture in Italy as a lieutenant-general and commander of the newly created I Canadian Corps. The Corps was more of a political statement than anything, not really a battlefield requirement but more an opportunity for Canadians to gain experience in operating in a larger formation. With Crerar as corps commander, Simonds was appointed to the newly arrived 5th Canadian Armoured Division.

There was soon friction between Crerar and Simonds over a trivial incident. At one point Simonds returned to his personal trailer to find a young officer working inside it without his knowledge. Simonds loudly dressed down the offender in front of others and sent him packing. It turned out Crerar had dispatched the officer to measure Simonds's trailer because Crerar wanted one built the same. Crerar was outraged at the treatment of the young officer, criticizing Simonds for "personal discourtesy." There was a further complication when Simonds fired a senior officer without Crerar's approval.

Neither man could claim any kind of glory in the episode. It touched off a vicious attack by Crerar. In a report sent back to Ottawa, Crerar claimed that Simonds had become mentally unbalanced and that his nerves were "overstretched."[13] This bit of poison was meant to be kept on file for future use, if needed. Crerar then attempted to have psychiatrists secretly observe Simonds under stress. Here was the ugly side of Crerar, a man with ruthless ambition and an evil eye on possible rivals. Crerar complained to Montgomery about his junior commander, only to have Monty take Simonds's side. Montgomery commented that Simonds was "a first class officer … [and] you have no one else with his experience."[14]

Now the stage was set for the epic of Normandy and the following campaign in northwest Europe. It would be historic for many reasons, including that it would be the first time Canada had placed an entire army on the battlefield. The D-Day landing would include the 3rd Canadian Infantry Division and the 2nd Armoured Brigade, while the First Canadian Army would gradually build up and become operational in late July. The Army, made up principally of two corps, one British and one Canadian, would be part of General Montgomery's 21st Army Group.

But in late 1943 and the first weeks of 1944, with D-Day only five months away, the First Canadian Army's leadership was in turmoil. McNaughton was on the way out. There was additional uncertainty about who would lead II Canadian Corps — the main punch in the army formation. At this point the corps commander was Lieutenant-General Ernest Sansom, an early McNaughton appointee and a nonentity.

McNaughton had been First Canadian Army commander since the formation was put together in early 1942, but as mentioned earlier, he had botched Exercise Spartan. He had also been in a furious dispute with Defence Minister Ralston and the Canadian army chief, General Stuart, over the dispatch of Canadians to Sicily the previous July. McNaughton heatedly opposed taking part in Husky because it meant the breakup of the army in England. Ralston and Stuart wanted it to give Canadians much-needed battlefield experience. Things reached such a fury that, in an unprecedented move, McNaughton wrote to Prime Minister King saying he had lost confidence in the defence minister.

McNaughton could not remain long as commander of the First Canadian Army, but there was a behind the scenes battle over his replacement.[15] The British pushed to have a British commander because they thought no Canadian general was up to the job. On December 23, 1943, Montgomery wrote to Brooke saying that Crerar was "quite unfit to command the army in the field at present."[16] Having a British commander, however, was politically impossible, which left Crerar as the only candidate. Ralston made the final decision on December 22 while he and Stuart went to London to break the news to McNaughton.[17]

When it came to II Corps, Montgomery lobbied hard for Simonds, saying he had the makings of a future army commander. Crucially, Crerar also recommended Simonds in early January 1944, acknowledging that while the young general was "highly strung" he was the best candidate. One might say this represented Crerar rising above personal disputes and taking the high road. That may be true, but as with Crerar's own situation, Simonds was the only candidate. Crerar could not possibly appoint someone the British did not want when it was clear they wanted Simonds.

Brilliant Commander — *Lieutenant-General Guy Simonds, shown here in Italy in 1943, was only forty-one when he was appointed to command II Canadian Corps in 1944.*

Simonds's appointment required ministerial approval, although it is likely it received only brief consideration. The appointment was discussed at the meeting between McNaughton and Ralston, but since the defence minister was really there to axe McNaughton, that consumed most of the oxygen in the room. Simonds was formally appointed to command II Corps on January 30, 1944. Given his later achievements, this appointment turned out to be one of the best and most far-reaching Canadian decisions of the war.

On his return to England Simonds hit II Corps "like a khaki tornado."[18] He quickly concluded the corps was not combat ready, but he had little time to make all the changes he wanted. Out went a string of senior officers, including tank expert Major-General Frank Worthington, commander of the 4th Armoured Division. Worthy was fifty-four years old and not a great trainer. Later division commanders were in their thirties or early forties, and in August 1944 Robert Moncel was promoted to brigadier at the age of twenty-seven.

From January through to June the corps undertook intensive training for the breakout phase of Operation Overlord. Simonds stressed what he had learned in Italy. All attack plans had to aim at jumping forward at least four thousand yards to overrun German mortars. Time and again, mortars had proven to be among the deadliest enemy weapons on the battlefield. One key to success was to defeat counterattacks that invariably followed any German loss of ground. Another "must" in the attack was to keep the corps artillery within range of the infantry. However, this Simonds hallmark later became the source of considerable dispute as being too rigid and inflexible. It was extremely unfortunate that, in the time remaining, neither Simonds nor the 4th Armoured was able to conduct full-scale exercises.

The historic D-Day landing was a hard-won success, with the 3rd Canadian Division and the 2nd Canadian Armoured Brigade among the first to go ashore. The life and death challenge for the Allies was to build up forces faster than the Germans did. The Germans had about sixty divisions in France, including six top-rated panzer divisions. II Canadian Corps opened its first tactical headquarters not far from the Normandy beaches on June 29, 1944, and it became operational on July 7. The troops in the Corps eventually included the 2nd Canadian Infantry Division (Major-General Charles Foulkes), the 3rd Canadian Infantry Division (Major-General Rod Keller), the 4th Canadian Armoured Division (Major-General George Kitching), the 2nd Canadian Armoured Brigade, and the Army Group, Royal Artillery (AGRA). For most of the campaign the corps also included the Polish 1st Armoured Division, while a number of British divisions were attached at different times.

The troops were well trained, well equipped, and motivated, but as with the Sicily landings, the whole apparatus was untried. The 3rd Division had had three weeks' experience in Normandy by the time II Corps got going and at least some officers had fought in Sicily. One of the best tank officers of the war, later Brigadier-General Sydney Radley-Walters, said the Canadians in Normandy were "no flaming hell until about the third or fourth week" but in reality it was much longer before II Corps operated well.[19]

In all, Simonds fought four battles in Normandy. The first was Operation Atlantic, part of a larger British operation that took place from July 18 to July 29. The British made limited gains while losing over three hundred tanks, and Montgomery was subject to savage criticism. On the western flank of the battle, II Corps had some limited success in capturing the remaining German-held sections of the city of Caen and advancing south from there.

Next, in Operation Spring Simonds had two British divisions attached to his Corps, but despite that the battle ended with major losses and few gains. The operation included the bloodiest single day of combat since Dieppe and the virtual destruction of the Black Watch Regiment. Simonds has been criticized for not using all the armour available in the battle while he, himself, was critical of the tanks for not giving better support to the infantry. Two division commanders were disappointments. The heavy-drinking Rod Keller in the 3rd Division was criticized by the British, but Simonds, unaccountably, failed to replace him. Simonds was unhappy with Charles Foulkes in the 2nd Division, saying on at least three occasions he was going to get rid of him. However, Foulkes was likely protected by Crerar. More than anything, the two operations revealed II Corps' inexperience, and as a result Simonds resolved to do things differently next time. Crerar set up his First Canadian Army headquarters on July 23. Montgomery had likely delayed that as long as possible because he preferred to rely on Lieutenant-General Dempsey to handle several corps rather than deal with Crerar.[20] When it began operations, the First Canadian Army and ancillary troops in Europe added up to about 175,000 soldiers.

The next operation defined Simonds as a corps commander. Operation Totalize was meant to be a leap forward as far south as Falaise and was described by Tim Cook as "a deep armoured thrust through the guts of the Germans."[21] While Crerar had overall command, it was Simonds's plan, worked out by him almost without staff assistance. The highly unorthodox operation, set for August 7–8, showed Simonds's brilliance, some of his failings, but also the limitations of the sword in his hand. In the end it was a victory but not a complete one, and as a result it became hugely controversial.

One of the most electrifying moments of Totalize came not on the battlefield but in the briefing room beforehand. Outlining his plan to senior officers, the corps commander said, "Gentlemen, we will do this attack at night with armour."[22] There was stunned silence. Never mind what the Germans might do, the prospect of a night operation with hundreds of tanks milling around on a battlefield, shooting at each other, ramming into each other, running over infantry soldiers, and falling into ravines was almost too ghastly to contemplate. But as chaotic and risky as it might have seemed, there was brilliance in what Simonds proposed. So far in daylight attacks the Canadians had had to advance against an enemy on the high ground, an enemy who showed unsurpassed ability to hide mortars and anti-tank guns, an enemy whose tanks could outrange their Allied equivalents, and an enemy who could, therefore, destroy an Allied armoured regiment before it could fire a single shot. A night attack would be a complete surprise and would neutralize all the German advantages. For Totalize, Simonds's corps had, in addition to its two infantry divisions, the 4th Armoured Division (just arrived from England), the Polish Armoured, a British division, and two British armoured brigades along with

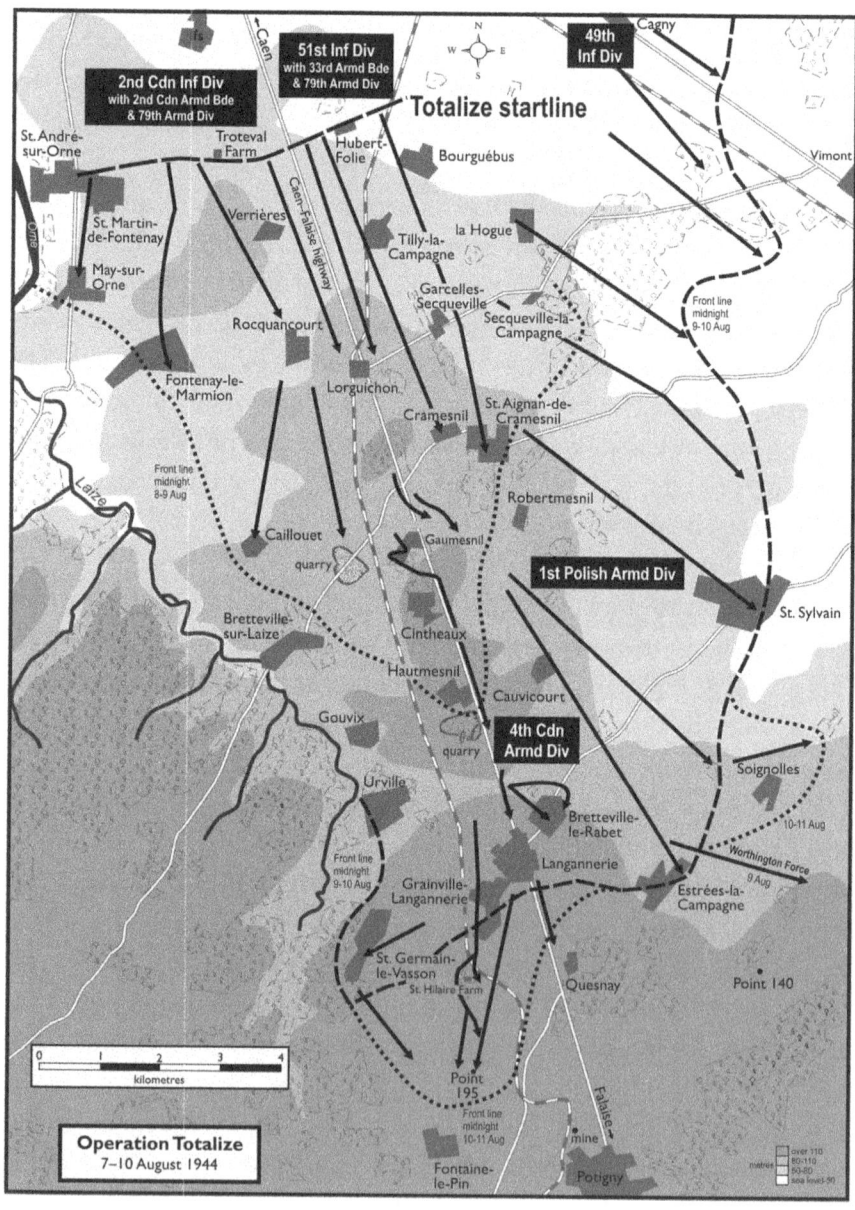

anti-mine flail tanks from the 79th British Armoured Division.* All in all, it was a powerhouse on the battlefield.

The operation also called for the use of sixty tracked armoured personnel carriers, a remarkable Simonds innovation. The Germans and Americans had used half-tracks to carry soldiers, but this was the first real appearance of APCs in battle. The vehicles had been used earlier as anti-tank guns, but for this operation the guns were taken out and ten soldiers put inside instead. It gave the infantry protection and allowed them to keep up with the tanks in an attack.

There would be two phases to the operation. In Phase One, Simonds essentially lined his divisions up in six columns almost as if on parade. The entire force would be nose to tail, on an extremely narrow front, with the armour and the infantry in their carriers in front and infantry on foot behind. The only things missing were a band and a reviewing stand. The attack would begin behind a rolling artillery barrage. Two key problems remained: how to deal with the German defence in depth, especially its flanking forces; and, in an era long before night vision equipment, how to prevent this gigantic parade from getting lost.

The first problem was answered by using heavy bombers. Enemy troop concentrations, tank harbours, and artillery on either side of the planned line of advance down the Caen-Falaise highway would be plastered by more than one thousand RCAF and RAF heavy bombers, the 1944 version of shock and awe. The second problem was dealt with by Bofors guns firing fire tracer rounds well over the heads of the attacking force to indicate the line of advance, while searchlights would create artificial moonlight by bouncing light off clouds.

When the entire force was lined up, according to one Fort Garry Horse officer, "as far as the eye could see [there] were armoured vehicles stretching for two miles."[23] Totalize began in the last hour of August 7. There were problems almost immediately with the air operation. The

---

* The 79th Armoured employed specialized vehicles usually referred to as "the funnies," which included flame-throwers and anti-mine "flails," among others. The flails were Sherman tanks with a series of chains in front that operated from a powered, rotating horizontal bar. The chains would beat the ground in front of the tank and set off mines.

first aircraft dropped their bombs on target, but in the ensuing smoke and dust later bombers ended up dropping right on top of Canadian troops. Wisely, the last third of the planes were ordered not to drop their bombs.

Then near midnight the parade rolled. With smoke and dust already kicked up by the bombers, the artillery began firing the first of eight tons of shells, and the flail tanks started to pound the ground, making direction-finding impossible for the ground troops. There were collisions, vehicles got lost, and platoons of infantry drifted away and vanished into a maw. Some officers dismounted from their vehicles to act as ground guides. Some tanks turned on their tail lights. Still, somewhere in the confusion, the 4th Armoured Division and the Polish Division — the mailed fist of the operation — rolled south.

Despite it all — the dust, the dark, and the bombs dropping short — rather miraculously, at first light on August 8, many units had advanced as far as eight kilometres. This was breathtaking; the longest jump forward by the 21st Army Group in the campaign to that point. It was a truly remarkable feat, but there was no time to stop and admire it. The attack had not completely broken through the last German defences — a demonstration of how challenging it was to deal with their multi-layered defences. A complete breakthrough meant seizing this very moment to keep moving, but that simply did not happen.

The artillery was not available for Phase Two because by this time it was out of range. It had to be packed up and moved after its initial firing to be in position for a further bound forward. That barrage would instead come from a second bombing operation, this time by seven hundred bombers from the U.S. Eighth Air Force. The bombing was not scheduled for several hours, but at this point it was too late to call it off. This was one of the great failures of the campaign — that ground forces were not in direct touch with the bombers but had to relay requests back to Bomber Command. When every minute counted, II Canadian Corps sat and waited with engines ticking over because any advance would be past the bomb line. That delay was just long enough for the commander of the 12th SS Division, Kurt Meyer, to sniff the battlefield air, sense the moment, and whip together an improvised defence line.[24]

Finally, the second bombing went ahead. Again, bombs dropped short, taking a deadly toll, with Major-General Keller among the wounded. Some bombs landed a kilometre or more behind the Canadian front lines. Polish troops in particular suffered severe casualties, while among Canadian battalions, the North Shore (New Brunswick) Regiment suffered one hundred dead and wounded.

Even with the delay, and after the bombing, there was still a second opportunity for the tanks to step on the gas, but this is where inexperience came into play. At least one armour-infantry battle group stopped in the early evening to allow its forces to reorganize, which, of course, allowed the Germans to do the same thing. More disastrous was a move that night by another battle group, "Worthington Force," led by Lieutenant-Colonel Don Worthington.

Worthington's British Columbia Regiment tanks had only landed in France a few days before. Unfortunately, the BCRs, working with Algonquin Regiment infantry, became completely disoriented in a night move forward. The force ended up five kilometres away from its objective, and in the confusion that followed, was destroyed. Ironically, Worthington had broken right through the German defences, but in what must be one of the most unaccountable failures in the entire campaign, hours went by with the brigade headquarters not taking direct action to find out where Worthington actually was.

There had to be one more push. Operation Tractable, set for August 14 and under Montgomery's command, would be conducted by Canadian and Polish troops supported by one brigade of British tanks. The aim was to capture Falaise and the smaller towns of Trun and Chambois. Before the Canadian operation began, Simonds delivered a rocket of immense calibre to top commanders, demanding they be more aggressive.

Like Totalize, Simonds's plan for Tractable was innovative. It called for a daylight attack using two squares of 150 tanks each, both directed to move straight forward. The flanks would be covered by smoke and bombed by eight hundred heavy RAF and RCAF aircraft. However, when the operation was launched, there was another disaster. For the third time, bombs dropped short, killing nearly four hundred men. At the same time, the Germans captured a completely marked battle map.

The operation also included one of the legendary dramas of the war. Thirty-two-year-old Major David Currie of the South Alberta Regiment was in command of a small force of tanks, anti-tank guns, and infantry companies from the Argyll and Sutherland Highlanders of Canada and the Lincoln and Welland Regiment. They were among those trying to seal the gap between Anglo-Canadian–Polish forces in the north and the Americans in the south to prevent Germans near Falaise from escaping. After Currie led an attack on the village of St. Lambert-sur-Dives his group repulsed repeated enemy counterattacks. Currie and his ever-diminishing band destroyed seven enemy tanks, twelve guns, and forty vehicles. As many as 2,100 Germans were captured in addition to those killed or wounded. Currie was awarded the Victoria Cross.

While the 2nd Canadian Division arrived at Falaise on August 17, the pivotal role was played by the Polish Armoured Division, which was able to partly close the Falaise Gap by August 19. It trapped about 150,000 German soldiers, including more than two hundred fanatical Waffen SS Grenadiers, who would neither surrender nor run. By August 19, only two of the SS soldiers remained.

The key position taken by the Poles was Mont Ormel near Chambois, which had a commanding view of one of the few German escape routes. During two days of nearly continuous fighting, Polish forces were surrounded but managed to hold off assaults by seven German divisions. The gap was narrowed to only a few hundred yards, but the II SS Panzer Corps prevented the final slamming of the door. One German commander recalled that two army commands, four corps commands, nine infantry divisions, and five Panzer divisions were pressed into a square ten kilometres wide and fourteen kilometres long.[25] Every Typhoon fighter-bomber that could fly and dozens of other aircraft kept the retreating forces under constant air attack. On August 21 elements of the First Canadian Army relieved the Polish survivors and sealed the Falaise Gap for good by linking up with the United States Third Army. The Poles had been reduced to the point that about fourteen hundred of their two thousand men had become casualties — wounded, killed, taken prisoner, or missing.

After the battle there were ten thousand dead left in the gap. Miles of debris and thousands of bombed-out vehicles and horses, still used by the thousands, traced the agony of the German army trying to escape to the east. Two German armies were written off, while the much-hated 12th SS Division ceased to exist. The road to Paris finally lay open.

The Canadians had fought with great courage and had finally prevailed. Still, the delay in closing the Falaise Gap, which allowed thousands of enemy soldiers to escape to the east, was a failure of historic proportions. If the Germans had been completely trapped it could have led to a much wider collapse. Simonds sacked the 4th Armoured Division commander, George Kitching — Simonds's closest friend. By the end of the campaign Simonds had also fired six of nine brigadiers and fourteen of twenty-four battalion commanders. This was a brutal but clear message that second best was not good enough.

Most conspicuously, there was a fatal lack of co-ordination between the Americans on the one hand and the Canadians, Brits, and Poles in the 21st Army Group on the other. At one point the 4th Canadian Armoured Division could not directly communicate with American forces only a few kilometres away. Another issue was that Montgomery did not use all the forces available to him and did not put his most experienced divisions at the sharp end. The British 11th Armoured, the 59th Division, and the 53rd were all available. Chester Wilmot and Tim Cook are among the writers who criticized the field marshal on this score, with Cook saying not using the more experienced troops was "a grand failure of vision."[26]

It fell to the neophyte Canadians to close the gap.

The Americans were not blameless even though they were loud in criticizing Montgomery's "plodding." General Omar Bradley was scathing, saying "a golden opportunity had been lost," but Bradley himself was most reluctant to cross into ground that had been earmarked as 21st Army Group territory or get the boundary changed.[27] His failure to do so, said Cook, was "not a little bit stupid."[28]

The Canadians have been portrayed as too slow.[29] On that account, J.L Granatstein has said, "Yes, the Canadians were too slow, too unco-ordinated, some too poorly trained and too weakly led in a complex, fluid battle, and simply too green to beat a desperate, skilled enemy."[30] In mitigation, it is well to point out that, to that time, no army had found a way to effectively deal with the German defence in depth. Wilmot commented, "There is no doubt that if the armoured divisions had been more experienced and aggressive, the Canadian offensive would have been completely successful."[31] There is an assessment of Simonds's role in the Normandy campaign later in the chapter.

The cost of the Normandy campaign had been terrible, with as many as 18,444 soldiers killed, wounded, missing, or taken prisoner.[32] Back in Canada that cost was being revealed one by one in moments of private despair. On July 26 Bruce and Nora Wagner of the tiny hamlet of Teeterville, Ontario, near Brantford, received a telegram from Ottawa. It said their son, Ivan, known to friends as "Chub" and a stretcher-bearer in the Royal Regiment of Canada, had been killed near the village of Louvigny in Normandy. On August 19 the Wagners received a second telegram telling them that another son, Harry, a member of the same regiment, had been killed. Months later the Wagners received news that a third son, Howard, had died while fighting in Holland. It was shattering, all but unbearable for the Wagners, as it was for so many families in the war. Three sons gone in less than six months.[33]

After the German retreat across the Seine, the First Canadian Army, on the far left of the vast Allied array, was given the thankless job of clearing the Channel ports. It then moved along the coast of Belgium and the Netherlands. The 2nd Canadian Division swept into Dieppe without a fight and received a tumultuous welcome. There, on September 3, the Canadians mounted a victory procession through the streets and symbolically reclaimed their dead, lost more than two years before. It was an emotional day. Along the coast, the First Army also captured a number of German rocket-launching sites, putting an end to at least some of the attacks on southern England. The V-1 — the cruise missiles of their day — had caused havoc in Britain.

The battle in which Canadians made the greatest contribution to Allied victory in northwest Europe — the Battle of the Scheldt — is not much remembered today. It was conducted on a windblown bogscape that is difficult to imagine as a battlefield in the usual sense, sprawling as it did over about one hundred kilometres. Much of it ended up under water. Jeffery Williams, a member of the Calgary Highlanders, commented, "The

Family Shattered — Ivan "Chub" Wagner (left) and his brother Harry (right) from Ontario were both killed within weeks of each other in Normandy. A third brother, Howard, was killed months later in Holland.

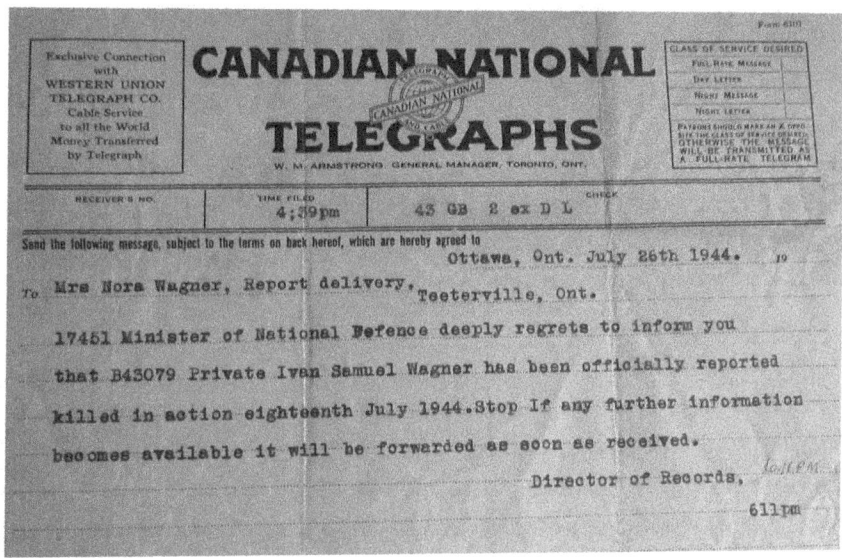

Every Parent's Fear — Next of kin were notified by telegram that a relative had become a war casualty. Bruce and Nora Wagner of Teeterville, Ontario, received three such messages.

abiding memory is of grey skies, rain, fog, bone-chilling dampness, boots, battledress and blankets soaking wet, cold food, matches that wouldn't light, the soldier's weariness that is as much fear as lack of sleep, and everywhere, mud and water."[34]

The Scheldt River wends its way through three countries, but most importantly the vast port of Antwerp lies on its banks. At that point in the war most of the Allied supply lines bumped and lurched all the way back to the Normandy beaches. Nearly one-third of all fuel brought in to northwest Europe was consumed by six thousand trucks as they drove fuel supplies to the front lines. Controlling Antwerp, which could handle a thousand merchant ships at a time, was, therefore, a great prize.

The problem was that Antwerp was far inland and any ship arriving or leaving had to pass along a fifty-kilometre estuary. By the fall of 1944 German defenders of the estuary totalled nine divisions — about one hundred thousand men. They had laid thousands of mines to prevent any attack by sea and the area bristled with heavy guns. It was near impossible to attack by land because much of it was below sea level, which left any attacker channelled onto narrow paths while some areas were protected by fifteen-foot dikes.

Apart from the mainland, the Scheldt Estuary was dominated by three features: there was South Beveland Island, shaped like an ice cream cone on its side with the big end facing west and an isthmus in the east connecting it to the coast; the smaller North Beveland Island was just above it; and, finally, the square-shaped Walcheren Island was just to the west and connected to South Beveland by a narrow causeway.

Tackling the Scheldt was even more daunting because Field Marshal Montgomery had committed one of the great blunders of the campaign by not taking Walcheren and the estuary earlier. The British XXX Corps, with the help of the Belgian resistance, had actually captured most of Antwerp and the docks intact on September 4, but instead of driving farther north, cutting off the Bevelands and Walcheren, it turned south. That was part of Operation Market Garden, the "Bridge Too Far," which Montgomery hoped would launch the Allies into Germany itself. In the event, it was only at the end of September after Operation Market Garden had failed that the order was given to clear the Scheldt Estuary.

DECISION EIGHT 195

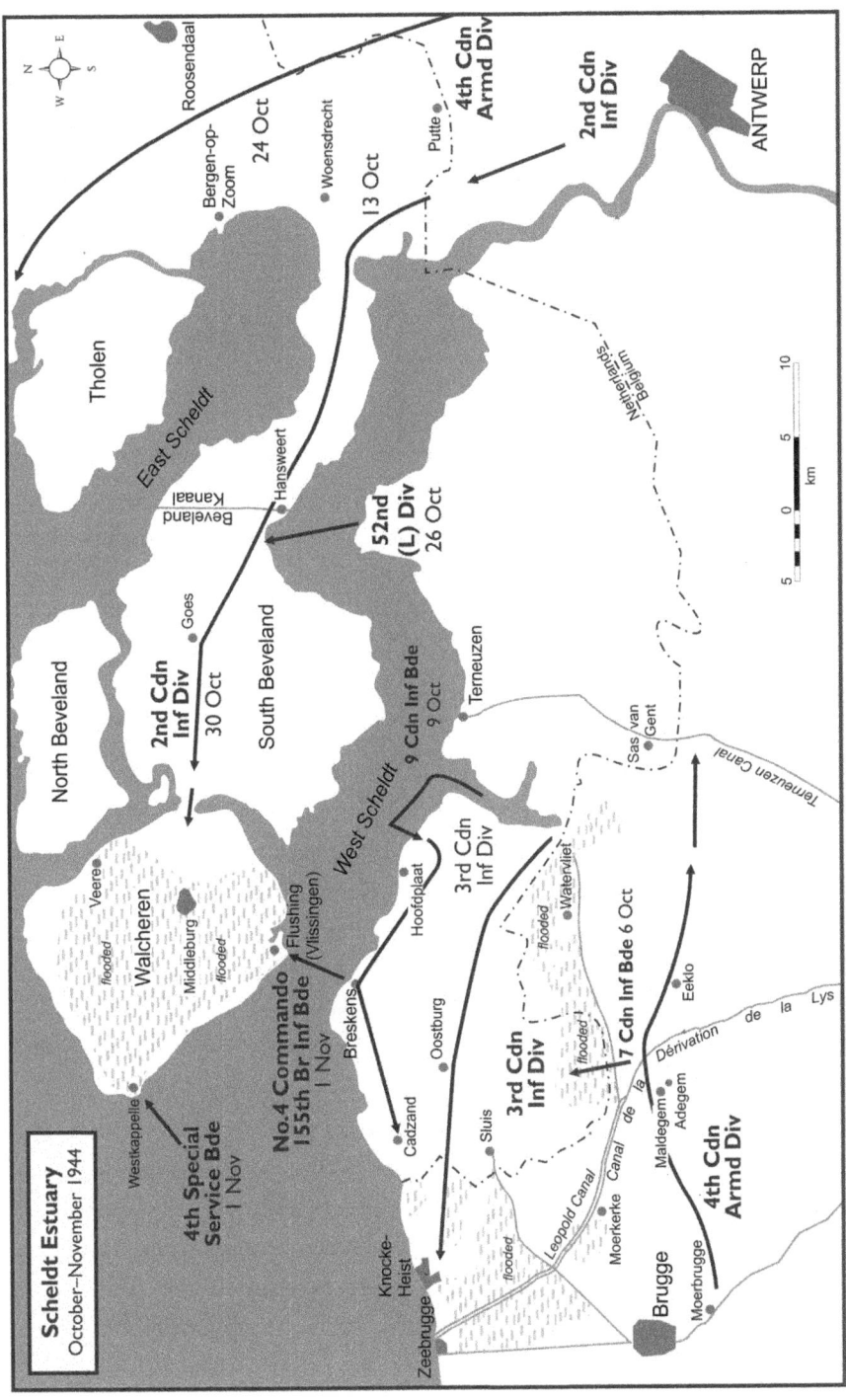

This grim challenge fell to the First Canadian Army. An immediate complication was that on September 27, 1944, as the battle was set to begin, General Crerar became seriously ill with dysentery and was evacuated to England with Simonds taking over as acting Army commander. Crerar had dealt mostly with the broad picture, but Simonds was determined to plan, direct, and control the entire battle himself. His mere arrival at the First Canadian Army headquarters to take command had an immediately bracing effect on the staff.[35]

The fighting on the Scheldt was as fierce as any during the war. The Canadians had to fight numerous separate engagements, and at the beginning it had to do so with only three tired divisions — the 2nd and 3rd Infantry Divisions and the 4th Armoured Division. Bill Davis of the Black Watch described one later incident, an indication of how exhausted the troops were. "We were moving up to a little town called Goes, on the Beveland Peninsula. And everybody took to the ditch all of a sudden and I ... went back to see what was going on. One of my guys had fallen on the road and the boys all thought a sniper had hit him. He just fell asleep walking and fell down. It was raining and snowing and everything. But that's how beat up the guys were."[36]

Not only were the divisions tired, but also combat losses were mounting and reinforcements were hard to come by. Many of the infantry reinforcements who did arrive were retrained members of the artillery, Service Corps, or Signal Corps.[37] Numerous companies operated with only half or two-thirds of their nominal strength, which meant that each company had to cover a long frontage with few men. At one point the Régiment de Maisonneuve in the 2nd Division was more than two hundred men short.[38] One platoon attack began with twenty-one men and finished with five, including the wounded platoon commander.

In broad terms, the Battle of the Scheldt could be divided into three distinct operations: first, a series of attacks to clear the Germans out of the south shore of the mainland, the so-called Breskens Pocket; then, second, the advance to clear the area north of Antwerp up to Bergen op Zoom to cut off the German forces on Walcheren and the Bevelands; and finally, the First Canadian Army (by this time with considerable British Army and Royal Navy help) had to take the three islands themselves.

Simonds would have to carry out several big amphibious operations with waterborne troop carriers in most operations.[39] One decision Simonds made turned out to be vitally important. He decided to bomb the dikes and flood much of Walcheren Island in order to cut off the Germans and force them into smaller and more isolated groups. It also made their reinforcement and supply more difficult.[40] The Royal Air Force and the army's chief engineer both thought bombing was unlikely to succeed.[41] But in a show of "real leadership," according to one officer, Simonds was determined to go ahead and finally convinced both.[42] It was a dreadful decision to make, but his proper concern was to clear the estuary and do so with minimal casualties.

The first of five RAF bombing attacks started October 3. One gigantic earth wall cracked open and three other dikes gave way, gradually flooding the area and leaving more than 80 percent of it under water. The bombing, as Simonds had planned, isolated German forces and put at least one-third of their artillery batteries out of operation.

In the Battle of the Scheldt, operations overlapped each other. However, an early part of it was Operation Switchback to clear out the Breskens Pocket. The only way the wet and miserably cold troops could advance was by using the remaining dikes and built-up footpaths, which, of course, were mined and covered by machine guns. The Germans had partly flooded some areas, so it was difficult for tanks to operate, while any slit trench soon filled with water. As one soldier said, "Digging in was like digging a well."

Initially, the 4th Canadian Armoured Division advanced to find itself facing two heavily defended parallel canals, the Leopold and Dérivation de la Lys. Some of the defended areas were under water or barely above ground. More infantry was needed for any further advance, so the 3rd Division had to be hurried in from more than a hundred kilometres away to make an assault starting on October 6. A part of the plan was to have one brigade launch an amphibious attack around to the east and behind the German defences using Buffalo and Terrapin troop-carrying vehicles.

While the canals were only about thirty metres (one hundred feet) wide, they still made formidable obstacles. Third Division commander Major-General Dan Spry organized 325 guns in support of the troop crossing, and while that was underway, other members of the division moved north toward the town of Breskens. In addition to the artillery, Spry also brought up twenty-seven Wasp flame-throwers mounted on Bren carriers. The Germans despised flame-throwers. The Bren carriers were driven partway up sloped hills so they would work like mortars. They would shoot flames right over the canal and land on the reverse slope of the opposite side, exactly where all the German mortars and machine guns were. When the attacks began, the flame-throwers caused panic among the defenders, at which point assault companies used boats to cross the canals.

Two companies of the Canadian Scottish Regiment from Victoria crossed successfully, but the Regina Rifles Regiment and elements of the Royal Montreal Regiment attached to them had a grim time once the Germans recovered. Both the Canscots and Reginas were able to make small lodgements, but over the next several days there were so many counterattacks that the Canadians lost track of the number. The affair turned into a stalemate. "For five days the Reginas were pinned to the Canal bank, separated in places by only ten yards from the enemy. It

Versatile Amphibian — The four-ton Terrapin amphibian was widely used in the Battle of the Scheldt. It was powered by two Ford V-8 engines.

became almost a grenade war, with each rifleman throwing as many as twenty-five No. 36 grenades every night."[43]

In the meantime, the two battalions were aided enormously by what historian Douglas Delaney called "superb" artillery support, which became a hallmark of the entire Scheldt battle.[44]

It was only on October 13 that engineers from the 4th Armoured Division were able to bridge the canals. In its attacks toward Breskens, on October 18 a company of the Queen's Own Rifles had to fix bayonets and charge some of the last holdouts in its area. Including the company attached from the Royal Montreal Regiment, the Regina Rifles had 280 casualties, fifty-one of them fatal. For the Germans, most of the 1038th Grenadier Regiment and 1st Parachute Training Regiment were wiped out or captured. It was not until October 24 that the south shore of the estuary was cleared and the Breskens Pocket battle ended.

After the failure of Operation Market Garden, Montgomery made the British 52nd (Lowland) Division available. It included Scots who were initially not happy to work with the Canadians but eventually warmed to the idea.

There were some strange moments in the second part of the Battle of the Scheldt near Antwerp. While the British had captured part of the city and the docks, not all German forces had been cleared out. At one point the 2nd Canadian Division remained stuck in and around the city for seventeen days fighting a bizarre "streetcar war." Both the Germans and Canadians used different parts of the Antwerp tramway system to move troops around. Those out of the line, meantime, could take advantage of Antwerp's nightlife.

The attacks planned farther north by the 2nd Division were set back by another wave of German reinforcements, which began arriving on October 7, among them two thousand fanatical young paratroopers. The very day they arrived and apparently without even doing a reconnaissance, the paratroopers launched a heavy attack on the Calgary Highlanders near the town of Hoogerheide. It was a disaster that left as many as four hundred Germans dead. German Colonel Augustus von der Heydte later said, "The Canadians fought brilliantly. To the rank of brigadier the officers stood side by side with their men on the front lines."[45]

On October 13 an attack in the same area decimated the Black Watch Regiment for a second time within four months. It lost 145 men and all its senior officers in a merciless engagement.

The 2nd Division then moved up to the Beveland Canal, which crossed the peninsula of South Beveland and proved to be a major obstacle. The German defences were only defeated by an amphibious landing by the 52nd Division. At that point the Canadians attacked the canal head-on in assault boats while engineers managed to establish a crossing on the main west–east road. Once positions on the Beveland Canal were cleared, German resistance on South Beveland collapsed and remnants of the German forces withdrew to Walcheren Island.

Simonds was "hands on" at every stage of the operations, visiting brigade and division headquarters almost daily in his Staghound armoured car. He frequently made spur-of-the-moment changes in the amphibious operations to adapt quickly to changing circumstances. Delaney says he was "not above 'tearing a strip' off a brigadier or two who were not performing or driving their formations hard enough."[46]

The 4th Armoured Division, after its fighting in the Breskens Pocket ended, moved north of Antwerp toward Bergen op Zoom, which was taken on October 27. That cut off any possible German retreat and set the stage for the third and last phase of the Battle of the Scheldt.

The spectacular climax of the battle was set to unfold much as Simonds had planned it weeks before. An enormous array of forces took their places for the complex assault on Walcheren Island. They included both Canadian and British troops and British Commandos from the 4th Special Services Brigade. There was also a contingent of French commandos and Belgian partisans. In the air the attack involved scores of Bomber Command aircraft and fighter-bombers. At sea was a huge armada of Royal Navy amphibious craft and RN warships. Among the latter was that stately survivor of the Battle of Jutland in 1916, HMS *Warspite*. For *Warspite* this was its last operational mission of the war and its last ever. The battleship, along with two big-gunned bombardment ships, pounded the German coast artillery before and during the attack.

The Walcheren flooding had forced the twelve thousand German defenders to concentrate on a circular outline of the island. Still, defences were formidable, with coastal artillery batteries facing outward and a second defensive perimeter facing landward (or at least toward such land as there was). German troops included the 70th Infantry Division, a so-called "stomach" division, made up of men recovering from stomach wounds or stomach ailments. The division performed surprisingly well.

The one and only land approach was a causeway a thousand metres long and just wide enough for a two-lane road, a rail line, and a bicycle path. Author Mark Zuehlke called it a "perfectly engineered killing ground" because German forces protecting it, backed up by as many as sixty guns, could see everything that moved and could fire straight down it.[47]

Starting on October 31 there were three separate ground attacks, the first by the Black Watch. The hope was to "bounce" the defenders by surprise so one Black Watch company launched itself headlong into the causeway with little artillery support. However, the attack was repelled, with deadly results. It was the same for following attacks by the Calgary Highlanders and the Régiment de Maisonneuve.

The regiments had balked at undertaking the attacks to begin with, suspecting how suicidal they might be. However, the timing was critical because the attacks prevented the Germans from moving troops to two other points that were attacked at about the same time by the amphibious forces. There was one attack on the south of the island and another on the western side. The 4th Special Services Brigade commandos were to land at Westkapelle and the British 52nd Division landed at the fortified town of Flushing, in the south.

The decision to launch the final assault bore echoes of Eisenhower's formidable challenge on D-Day, and for the same reason: the weather. In the event Simonds and the Royal Navy commander, Admiral Bertram Ramsay, determined to go ahead. It was a daunting challenge, in part because only small sections of the dikes had been breached, requiring the assault craft to funnel into a very narrow line before hitting land. However, with great determination and considerable losses, the forces succeeded in gaining a lodgement. That became the turning point. The fighting that followed was bitter but the outcome was not in doubt. On November 8 the fighting ended, bringing the Battle of the Scheldt to a close. It cost 6,367 Canadians killed and wounded and almost as many British casualties.

The estuary was then swept for mines, and on November 28 the first Allied ship, the Canadian freighter *Fort Cataraqui*, entered Antwerp. Eisenhower wrote to Montgomery, "The capture of the Antwerp approaches will have the utmost significance for us … will you please convey to the Commanding General of the Canadians my thanks and congratulations."[48] Montgomery, who was ever loath to admit any fault, wrote later, "I must admit a bad mistake on my part — I underestimated the difficulties of opening up the approaches to Antwerp so that we could get free use of the port."[49] The Allied high command organized celebrations to mark the opening of the port, but unaccountably, no one thought to invite anyone from the First Canadian Army.

In the end the First Canadian Army achieved the near impossible in the Battle of the Scheldt.[50] There were setbacks and losses, but there was no shortage of raw courage in the most dreadful conditions. The victory truly belonged to the soldiers and sailors who had endured the worst of it all. However, as for Simonds's role, one letter he received after the battle throws a light on his leadership. It said, "I would like to say myself how much I enjoyed working with you. You are always ready to discuss ideas: you have provided a whole series of new techniques and methods and have succeeded in surprising the enemy on many occasions."[51]

What was remarkable was not so much the fulsome praise but the fact that it came from Major-General Sir Percy Hobart, commander of the 79th Armoured Division (mentioned earlier). Hobart was brilliant but was one of the crankiest personalities in the British Army. Praise from him was praise indeed.

After the Battle of the Scheldt Harry Crerar returned to his post and then went on to command the First Canadian Army during the bloody Rhineland campaign in 1945. He led an army of 350,000 men, the largest force ever to serve under a Canadian general. John English has called it "the best little army in the world."[52]

Finally, how should Simonds's contribution to the Canadian and Allied victory be measured? As he had shown in Sicily, in Normandy, and again on the Scheldt, Guy Simonds was undoubtedly one of the great wartime corps commanders. Lieutenant-General Brian Horrocks called him a "first-class commander with a most original brain."[53] A chapter about him in *The Generals* by J.L. Granatstein is titled "Master of the Battlefield."[54] In Sicily his conflicts with Brigadier Graham and with Crerar showed sharp elbows and uncertainty, but in the end he became a capable division commander. In career terms he was fortunate because when the invasion of France was coming, successful, battle-seasoned commanders were in short supply.

With Operation Totalize, Simonds was the only commander to achieve a decisive corps-level penetration of a German defence line in Normandy.[55] The operation made his reputation even though his own and his corps' inexperience meant it was not strategically decisive. John English commented that an even more significant problem was that there was too little staff or tactical depth both above and below Simonds to properly support him.[56] Communications were terrible. Brigade and divisional commanders lost complete control of their forces. In any event, Simonds's plan turned out to be too rigid. He also suffered because of an unworkable communications set up between Bomber Command and the British and Canadian armies.

In his early going in France, Simonds ran a totally top-down operation, but at the time it was likely the only way such an inexperienced corps could have operated. Still, all in all, he had been impressive. He was aggressive and incredibly imaginative and his use of APCs was brilliant.[57] Simonds and other British and Canadian commanders have been criticized for their use of the set-piece battle in the Montgomery manner. Using thousands of artillery shells as a prelude to every attack may have been unimaginative, but it saved lives. As Cook said, "They did this, quite simply, because they could."[58]

As for his leadership in the Battle of the Scheldt, various writers have called it "unquestionably superb" and "the acme of Canadian generalship and professionalism," while his analysis and plans were called "brilliant examples of joint and combined warfare."[59] It was also a "battle that suited his background and talents" because of the important role played by the artillery.[60] In the last months of the war, Simonds became the Allies' foremost expert in amphibious warfare.

Despite his gifts, Simonds was a difficult man to work for; an officer who commanded but did not lead. He could not appeal to the human and emotional side of warriors. Major-General Bert Hoffmeister thought Simonds "paid no attention to the psychology of the situation, unlike the best British officers, and he showed no understanding of his subordinates' problems."[61] Like a modern-day version of Shakespeare's Coriolanus, he has been dubbed a "tragic hero" — a gifted man with a fatal flaw.[62]

A revealing view comes from Canadian Brigadier James Roberts who at one point in the Normandy campaign had seen Lieutenant-General Brian Horrocks at work. Roberts was hugely impressed, calling the British general one of the finest officers he had ever seen and yet a man completely without pretense. Horrocks talked to everyone, including private soldiers. He called his officers by their first names: Joe, Peter, or Reggie. Roberts said with Canadian officers such as Crerar or Simonds that warmth was entirely missing.[63] That is not to say that Simonds did not show a genuine concern about wasting young lives. He did, but he was missing one touch of greatness — the human touch. Roberts also had a further comment, noting Simonds "brooked no sentiment and demanded results. I felt toward him as I felt to Montgomery, an admirable battle commander but not a man one could love."[64]

The II Corps commander knew all too well that many of these criticisms were true. Guy Simonds must have been difficult to be around even for Guy Simonds. "Supremely confident, driven to succeed, and fiercely competitive ... he hated being anything but the best," said historian Roman Jarymowycz.[65] At one point Simonds said, "I know I have a hot and quick temper.... It is a fault I know, but it has always been with me and I am afraid it always will be.... I am impatient of stupidity, dullness and indifference."[66] He said it was his duty to be sure the leaders were the best that could be found, not simply those who were just good enough.[67]

What separated Simonds from most senior commanders was his ability to innovate, learn, and keep on learning. Totalize was the result of his seeing that German long-range weapons were defeating Canadian tank attacks. In another case, after seeing that advance fire plans were too rigid and did not work, he changed to having artillery on call when and where the infantry needed it. He became a much better commander as time went along, just as the First Canadian Army became a much better force on the battlefield. He was unique in terms of original thinking, intelligence, and the sweep of his imagination, while his performance as acting army commander marked the pinnacle of his wartime career.[68]

Simonds's legacy is shaded by the fact that he had no Alamein. In the First World War the Canadian Corps had its Vimy and, even greater, its Hundred Days, but there was no real equivalent in the Second World War. Still, J.L. Granatstein has said, "Guy Simonds was the best soldier Canada produced in the Second World War."[69] In all Canadian history, probably only Arthur Currie was a more outstanding military leader.

DECISION NINE

The Greatest Political Crisis of the War

With deft leadership Prime Minister Mackenzie King avoided crisis in Canada in 1939 that had, at its base, a French Canadian fear of conscription. Despite that, two conscription crises did shatter the nation later in the war, in 1942 and again in 1944. Those crises had a bit of everything: explosive news headlines, intrigue and suspense, crafty politicians, scheming generals, cabinet splits, and threats of resignation. The 1944 crisis, in particular, became the greatest political upheaval of the war, almost demolishing the government and bringing with it dangerous divisions in the country. To top it all there was even a surprise ending.

As soon as the war began the government announced its intention to send an expeditionary force of one infantry division overseas and to form a second division in Canada. The pre-war regular army was tiny, so the army would need tens of thousands of men to enlist right away, and it would need hundreds of thousands before long. But, as noted in Decision One, part of the unwritten bargain in going to war as a unified nation was the government's policy of "no neutrality, no conscription." So the new soldiers needed would all have to be volunteers.

For the first months of the war that was not a problem. In the waning days of the Great Depression six hundred thousand men were still unemployed, and being in the army was, at least, a paying job. A combination of patriotism and hunger brought long lineups to recruiting stations.

The situation started to change in mid-1940 with the defeat of France and the beginning of the Battle of Britain. Suddenly, the war was a fight to the death. That triggered public demand for a much greater war effort, a bigger army, and a new call from some in English Canada for conscription. In the House of Commons, opposition members pressed hard for it, while organizations such as the Canadian Legion joined the campaign. The Leader of the Opposition, Richard Hanson, called for Parliament to introduce something similar to Britain's Emergency Powers Act, which gave the government sweeping powers, including the ability to conscript soldiers. Many English-speaking Liberals backed the idea. When the issue came to the war cabinet, Prime Minister King found to his surprise there was considerable support for the new powers, including conscription, if — but only if — it was limited to service in Canada. King thought there would be serious division over the issue, but as things turned out there was general support.

On June 18, 1940, the government introduced the National Resources Mobilization Act (the same act that gave C.D. Howe such sweeping powers). Among its provisions was that men between the ages of nineteen and forty-five were required to register for conscription. The act — usually known by its initials NRMA — required them to serve in the army but that service must be "solely and exclusively for the defence of Canada." The government tried to downplay what it all meant, with one minister saying every individual would be given the "opportunity" to train in the use of arms "to come to the defence of Canada." It is hard to imagine being conscripted into the army as an "opportunity."

Quebec did not seem unduly alarmed by the plan, the loud exception being Montreal Mayor Camillien Houde, who said it was the first step on the road to overseas conscription. Apparently wanting to nip any outcry in the bud, the government arrested and interned him. The bill became law on June 21, with the plan providing for thirty days' training for those selected.

The first conscripts reported for duty on October 9, 1940. The army thought the whole thing was a waste of time because thirty days was too short to do any serious training and simply disrupted civilian war work. The plan went through its first change on January 28, 1941, when the training period was increased to four months. Then, another change came when the volunteers and the conscripts were ordered to train together. On April 23, 1941, the army hit on a new solution — retain NRMA conscripts for the duration of the war, which would free up the volunteers for overseas service.

Soon the army started to put very heavy pressure on conscripts, by this time universally known by the disparaging name "Zombies," to "volunteer" for overseas service. There were subtle and not-so-subtle digs. Unlike volunteers, the conscripts were not allowed to wear regimental hat badges and there were no "Canada" shoulder flashes on their uniforms. Often, those who volunteered got periods of leave, but conscripts did not. One unidentified Zombie was later quoted as saying, "I was put in platoons, twenty-five men active service and myself the only Zombie, and they were told ... I was fair game."[1] There were fights. In the Canadian Scottish Regiment those headed overseas "talked openly of cowardice" among the men who refused to volunteer.[2] One resident of Sydney, Nova Scotia, Donna Spalding, recalled an NRMA soldier breaking down in tears because he was despised everywhere he went in the town.[3]

By 1941 virtually all the six hundred thousand men who had been unemployed at the beginning of the war had either enlisted in the armed forces or taken civilian jobs. For the first time there was a shortage of army volunteers. In May 1941 the army and the government had to start a huge national recruiting campaign. Thirty-four thousand men did enlist that month, which met the target, but even so the army needed a relentless supply of new soldiers to accommodate planned expansion. Individual regiments were feeling the pinch. The Black Watch Regiment in Montreal, at its own expense, bought advertising to encourage recruiting. At the same time, more and more conscripts came to detest the intense pressure to volunteer.

At this point it is worth backtracking a bit to deal with one of the key elements underlying the 1944 conscription crisis — the army and its agenda. With the defeat of France in 1940, there surfaced the first glimmer of the military's campaign for a "Big Army."[4] Memos and reports from top generals to the government during the war made it clear the generals wanted a "full national commitment" overseas. Lieutenant-General Harry Crerar (who, as noted in the previous chapter, became the commander of the First Canadian Army later in the war) wrote, "It is essential from a military point of view that Canada provide the maximum force overseas that it is possible to organize and maintain."[5] Put in those terms, there is nothing wrong with that. In fact, one could argue that in a life and death struggle it was the army's duty to do everything possible to win the war.

Apart from the patriotic motives, however, it became clear that the generals wanted a Big Army in their own self-interest. Memorably, R. MacGregor Dawson, an early biographer of Mackenzie King, commented that the general staff "never at any time in any place advocated a small army if there was any conceivable chance of obtaining a large one."[6] Major-General (later Lieutenant-General) Tommy Burns said "national prestige" was among the most important reasons for the creation of the First Canadian Army.[7]

For the generals a Big Army was important not only during the war but afterward, even though that would very likely require conscription. General Crerar tried to pressure the cabinet for an early decision, arguing that unless there was conscription, "it will be impossible to plan and develop the future defence of Canada."[8] Late in the war the army again outlined its postwar plans, which included conscripted troops. As Richard Walker said, "The Army's commitment to conscription never deviated for a moment."[9]

It would be wrong to say that the 1944 conscription crisis was a clash between two visions of the army — the brass hats who wanted a Big Army overseas and the suits who wanted an all-volunteer army. There were, as we will see, other factors and complications. But certainly the plan for a Big Army played a role in the drama that unfolded. It made conscription much more likely.

There is something that should be included here, as well, because it is sometimes forgotten what Mackenzie King's basic view of conscription was. King never opposed conscription as a matter of principle. He said if it were absolutely essential he would implement it. Rather, he tried to avoid it because it had the potential to wreck the country. The army, on the other hand, tended to see the issue as strictly a military problem. We

Conscription Battle — *This 1944 cartoon by John Collins, popular editorial cartoonist at the* Montreal Gazette, *reflected the view of many English Canadians. The solution to the conscription controversy was in plain sight.*

have a big job to do, the generals might have said, and we cannot do it with one hand tied behind our back. Mostly, the army was completely blind to the political dimension of conscription, while English- and French-Canadian politicians saw conscription along linguistic lines. We will come back to the issue of the Big Army a bit later.

One turn in the conscription battle came in 1940 with the death of Defence Minister Norman Rogers in an air crash. Although Rogers supported conscription, he was wary of army expansion. He was an able politician as well as King's biggest ally in cabinet, and things might have turned out very differently had he remained a minister. His replacement, Layton Ralston, though a sincere, dedicated, and entirely honourable minister, got completely wrapped up in minutiae. Also, Ralston had been a battalion commander in the First World War, which was likely a factor in his support for conscription and his unwillingness to rein in the generals and their repeated demands for expansion. Later on, Mackenzie King accused Ralston of not standing up to them. King said, "I have asked not once but many times why he does not tell the generals what we, the cabinet, think instead of continually telling us what the generals think."[10]

The army then went on to undertake two dramatic expansions, the first in 1941. General Crerar, at this point chief of the general staff, proposed that the army set up a corps made up of three divisions plus an armoured brigade. Of course, there had been the legendary Canadian Corps in the First World War, so this proposal seemed hardly out of line. The prime minister, normally wary of expansion, was on board. King said the pride of the nation demanded it, but also "we owed it to McNaughton and his men."[11]

This was agreed to on January 28, 1941. But no sooner was that over than there was a new demand. Crerar, in a note to McNaughton in London, said, "Shortly after the Canadian Corps is formed, and a going concern, your elevation to Army Command would, I believe, give similar satisfaction to Canada."[12] Even at that point the military was looking ahead not simply to having one corps but an army made up of at least two corps, which would include an enormous number of additional administrative troops. In a letter dated October 1, 1941, Victor Sifton, the son of newspaper magnate Sir Clifford Sifton, warned Ralston, "It appears to me that we are permitting ourselves to drift into a position with respect to manpower for the armed forces which may bring about a very serious political crisis in the next six to eight months if recruiting fails to keep up." He also commented to one journalist that "Crerar is steadily increasing the establishment without Ralston getting on to it." He was "always boosting the establishment."[13]

Then in December 1941 the army unveiled its plans for 1942–43. The war cabinet met with the new chief of the general staff, Lieutenant-General Ken Stuart (Crerar had gone to Britain to command the 2nd Infantry Division) to hear his latest proposals. By this time Canada had an overseas army of three infantry divisions, two armoured brigades, and various support units. The military wanted to increase that to a total of five divisions, which would be organized into two corps. That would mean the army in Europe doubling in size in less than two years.

Two corps, if formed into one fighting organization for battle, is termed an "army." For example, the "army" in North Africa was the famous British Eighth Army. In this case the generals were proposing to create the First Canadian Army. So here we are back to the military's hopes and dreams, the Big Army. It should be recalled that there were also considerable army forces remaining in Canada for home defence, so even a Big Army overseas was not the end of manpower needs.

Given Canada's population and the many other demands on its manpower, including a huge air force and the massive requirements of agriculture and industry, how big an army could Canada realistically have? Prime Minister King noted right away that this formation would require not only new troops but in time a very considerable number of reinforcements. It was clear that the army's plans were colliding with other demands. At the cabinet meeting, General Stuart was asked, "Could the Army Staff give assurances that their proposed program could be carried out by the voluntary method?" And was this the "last demand"?

Stuart replied that "the program had been worked out so as to fit the government's policy of voluntary enlistments for overseas. That is what the staff had aimed at [and] had worked for." Were there enough reinforcements to meet the needs of the army once it became involved in battle? "Yes," replied Stuart, enough to cover "foreseeable circumstances."[14]

Some cabinet members were dubious. C.D. Howe thought that there was too much emphasis on the military and not enough on production. However, in the end, on June 6, 1942, King and the war cabinet accepted this "last demand." Stuart was delighted, saying that this was "absolutely all" the army wanted. He described the new formation as "the kind of army a soldier dreams of commanding, hard hitting, beautifully balanced, incredibly powerful. It was, for example an army that could beat Rommel in Libya."[15]

This was, without question, the turning point. Even Grant Dexter — a journalist and not a military expert — put his finger on the key issue sloughed off by both the army and the cabinet. He said the problem "will be one of reinforcements — not new units."[16] But here is a crucial point: King asked Stuart for assurances about the size of the army, but when he got Stuart's response he simply took the general at his word. Although King was under pressure from Ralston and Angus Macdonald (the navy minister) to accept the expansion, King failed to do his due diligence. In that, both King and Ralston failed.

Richard Walker called the decision to expand the army "a political time bomb,"[17] while J.L. Granatstein commented, "In retrospect, it is clear that the conscription crisis of 1944 became almost a certainty with this decision."[18] Like a ghost in a mystery novel, General Stuart's phrase "foreseeable circumstances" would reappear, haunting Mackenzie King and rattling its way through the conscription crisis.

A number of events suddenly collided to bring on the first conscription crisis. Its beginnings date to November 1941, when Conservative Party members met to organize a leadership convention to find a new party leader.* The influential conservative paper, the *Globe and Mail*, began heavily promoting former prime minister and ardent conscriptionist Arthur Meighen. In the middle of the Conservative conference there was a sudden change of heart and those attending decided to skip the convention idea and simply draft Meighen.

At this time the former prime minister was sixty-seven years old, a member of the Senate, and more or less on the political sidelines. He was reluctant to rejoin the battle but eventually decided to accept the call to duty and was named new party leader. Meighen was an undoubted heavyweight, the greatest debater of his generation, and the only Tory

---

*   Both earlier leader Robert Manion and his interim replacement Richard Hanson had been failures.

who could "put the fear of God into the Liberals."[19] The problem was that he came with the worst kind of political baggage. He was tarred forever as a leading member of the Union government of 1917–18 that had implemented conscription. He could expect absolutely no support from Quebec, and as a result his chances of forming a Union government were nil. The left-wing *Canadian Forum* magazine called the idea of drafting him "insane."[20] On November 13 Meighen issued a statement calling for full conscription and a Union government, writing, "This nation is in the throes of crisis." The Liberal policy on conscription was, he said, "a base and cowardly insult" to Canadians.

Amid all this came the Japanese attack on Pearl Harbor on December 7, 1941, which transformed the already desperate fighting in Europe, North Africa, and the North Atlantic into a worldwide war. The attack was a shock to Canadians. Victory was not even remotely in sight in the war against Hitler, and now there was a new and frightening war in the Pacific. It brought the United States into the battle, to be sure, but with the U.S. Navy's shattering losses in Hawaii, the situation would be bleak for many months.

The Japanese also attacked Hong Kong and wiped out a British-led force that included a Canadian brigade. Hundreds of Canadian troops ended up in dreadful conditions as Japanese prisoners of war. The British Columbia coast was now under threat. Japanese aircraft carriers might attack the naval base at Esquimalt or could help land troops on one of the West Coast islands. Japanese submarines could menace coastal shipping. It became clear that Canada would need troops on the Pacific coast as well as those already overseas. The Japanese threat brought with it new demands. Dr. Herbert Bruce, a Toronto Conservative member of Parliament said, "I call upon the government to take immediate steps to meet the present urgent situation and … bring our armed forces up to the strength that represents the fighting might of Canada."[21] In Toronto, two hundred prominent citizens met on January 10 to demand "Total War Now." The group placed huge advertisements in Ontario newspapers to stoke public debate.

For the Conservatives, the first step to getting a tougher conscription law and a union government was to get their leader into the House of

Commons. Meighen chose to run in a by-election on February 9, 1942, in the constituency of York South, bordering Toronto. It had a long history of Conservative support. At the time it was customary for other parties not to oppose a party leader in a by-election, so the Liberals announced they would not field a candidate. However, the Tories were outraged when the CCF decided it would enter the contest. A spirited campaign followed, with the Liberals quietly providing one thousand dollars to assist the CCF. In a radio address on January 9 Meighen made his main platform clear, declaring, "We are not organized politically as we should be … we are not organized militarily as we should be." Meighen claimed Canadians were solidly behind conscription.

Meighen may not have seen a poll by the Canadian Institute of Public Opinion just before Pearl Harbor that showed that was not the case. Sixty-one percent of those asked said they were satisfied with Canada's war effort, while only 35 percent were not.[22] Two-thirds of respondents were satisfied with Mackenzie King's leadership.

Prime Minister King had been thinking about holding a non-binding plebiscite. He had earlier committed the government *not* to send conscripts overseas, so the plebiscite was meant to release him from that commitment. King worried that at some point in the future — if the army faced imminent defeat on the battlefield, for instance — he might have to send conscripts to Europe. With Meighen in the field, it appeared the time might be approaching for a vote. A plebiscite is simply an expression of national opinion, so it would not have committed King to anything, but it would give him an opportunity to see if Meighen's campaign was gaining traction. There was a "heads-I-win, tails-you-lose" element to it. If plebiscite results came in to support King (that is, allowing him to send conscripts overseas in an emergency) it would de-fang Meighen. King could say he was right all along. If the vote went the other way, it would be a political disaster, but at least it would give the prime minister a convenient excuse to shift ground.

The problem with the whole idea was that there were sharp divisions in cabinet and in the Liberal Party. Defence Minister Ralston and Navy Minister Macdonald both wanted a plebiscite to clear the way for full conscription — immediately. Quebeckers in cabinet and in Parliament were overwhelmingly against overseas conscription. It all had explosive potential. King's challenge was to try to keep the government from flying apart. He could give ground on conscription but not to the point that the Quebec Liberals would desert him. He could hold the line on conscription but not to the point where Ralston and others would quit.

King hemmed and hawed until the last possible moment, but he finally announced the plebiscite on January 22, 1942. The question chosen was a marvel of wordsmithing, a cloud of evasion that never once actually mentioned the word *conscription*. The government had already promised it would not send conscripts overseas, so the actual question was: "Are you in favour of releasing the Government from any obligations arising out of any past commitments restricting the methods of raising men for military service?"

Conservatives and many Liberals led the charge for the "Yes" side, while there was a vehement "No" campaign in Quebec. Campaign leaders there said, "No one asks to be relieved of a pledge unless he is already planning to violate it."[23]

After much handwringing, Meighen was forced to support the "Yes" side, meaning he had effectively been manoeuvred into supporting King. In terms of timing, the York South by-election results would come in first, and then after that, the plebiscite vote. Both were life and death for Meighen but also vital for King.

When the York South voting day rolled around, Meighen was soundly defeated — an unheard of rebuke that virtually ended his career. The decisive factor may have been the CCF campaign, in which social welfare issues trumped conscription.[24] As for the plebiscite, Canadians gave King an overwhelming vote of confidence. They said "Yes" to the idea that he could send conscripted troops overseas if necessary. The vote was "Yes" 65.63 percent and "No" 34.37 percent. However, plain for all to see was that the French-Canadian vote was the reverse. In Quebec 72 percent were against and only 27.9 percent in favour, and most of those in favour lived in Anglo-Quebec areas. If anyone needed a reminder about how severe the divisions in Canada were, this was it.

In light of the plebiscite result, King had to introduce a bill in Parliament — Bill 80 — to give legal authority to overseas conscription if it became necessary. The issue brought furious controversy with it and debate dragged on for weeks. In cabinet both Ralston and Macdonald expected the plebiscite result would lead to immediate overseas conscription. They were outraged when King felt otherwise. The prime minister argued that the plebiscite only gave approval to send troops overseas *as a last resort*, and that this time had not arrived. Works Minister Cardin, a Quebec minister, quit. King was fortunate that Louis St. Laurent stuck by him. St. Laurent had just become the new justice minister and King's Quebec lieutenant, succeeding Ernest Lapointe, who had died the previous November.

On June 10, 1942, King finally joined the debate. This was the speech that included the famous hedging-of-bets, logic-bending comment that has been glued to him ever since: "Not necessarily conscription, but conscription if necessary." The phrase was not originally his but was in the *Toronto Star* newspaper. It certainly did describe his policy, but it made King look like a quintessentially shifty operator, a man of weasel words.

When debate finally ended, King told the cabinet that if he lost the vote on Bill 80 he would either resign or ask for a dissolution of Parliament. However, the government won the vote by a substantial majority, 158–54. While many Quebec Liberals publicly opposed Bill 80, or at least abstained, in reality the fight convinced them that King was indispensable. The only alternative was, if not Meighen, someone like him. Astonishingly, a poll in August 1942 found that fully 50 percent of French Canadians thought that Mackenzie King was the greatest living Canadian.[25]

The night before the vote Defence Minister Ralston, emotionally stretched, had finally resolved to resign because of King's foot-dragging. Ralston did submit a letter of resignation, but after a lot of arm-twisting from allies, he decided to stay on. However, the entire plebiscite affair poisoned the relationship between Ralston and King from then on. The two, said historian Tim Cook, were entrenched "on opposite sides of an ideological No Man's Land."[26] As for the letter, Ralston never did withdraw it, which turned out to be important later on.

The 1942 conscription battle was over. It ended with a victory for King, who had completely outfoxed the opposition and kept the cabinet together. Meighen was gone. King has often been criticized as a man whose chief aim was to put off trouble for another day, but in this case that was what he wanted and achieved. The longer overseas conscription could be delayed, the better.

For many months the conscription issue remained a kind of smoking volcano on the skyline, quiet for the time being but threatening pyrotechnics at any moment. That moment came in the early fall of 1944 and brought on the second conscription crisis. On September 19 a front-page article in the *Globe and Mail* carried the shocking allegation that Canada's army in Europe was being bled to death because of a shortage of infantry reinforcements. The author was Major Conn Smythe, an artillery officer who was well known across the country as owner of the Toronto Maple Leafs hockey team. At the age of forty-five Smythe had volunteered for active duty overseas only to be wounded in France.

Before returning to Canada, Smythe had talked to other wounded soldiers and had become incensed over the government's all-volunteer policy. Many of the reinforcements, said Smythe, quickly became casualties because they had been rushed onto the battlefield. He did not say it, but the implication was that, while this was happening, well-trained NRMA soldiers were sitting in Canada playing cribbage. Also it should be mentioned that by 1944 the Japanese were retreating everywhere such that any threat to British Columbia had all but disappeared. The army did not need all those troops in B.C.

Smythe wrote,

> The need for trained reinforcements in the Canadian Army is urgent. During my time in France and in the hospitals of France and England, I was able to discuss the reinforcement situation with officers of units representing every section of Canada. I talked to officers from Eastern Canada, French Canada, Ontario and all the Western Provinces. They agreed that the reinforcements received now are green, inexperienced and poorly trained. Besides this general statement, specific charges are that many have never thrown a grenade. Practically all have little or no knowledge of the Bren gun and

finally, most of them have never seen a Piat anti-tank gun, let alone fired one. These officers are unanimous in stating that large numbers of unnecessary casualties result from this greenness, both to the rookies and to the other soldiers, who have the added task of trying to look after the newcomers as well as themselves.

He went on, "The relatives of the lads in the fighting zones should ensure no further casualties are caused to their own flesh and blood by the failure to send overseas reinforcements now available in large numbers in Canada."

Was Smythe right?

On August 3, only six weeks before the article was published, Lieutenant-General Stuart had appeared before the Cabinet War Committee in Ottawa to report on the reinforcement situation. He said, "Although the Army had been fighting for some twelve months in Italy and two months in France, the reinforcement situation was very satisfactory."[27] Apart from that, many in the army and in Ottawa had thought the war with Germany might end in 1944. The generals felt Canadian divisions could continue on, shorthanded, for a few more weeks or a couple of months. But wars do not run on timetables, and the German army turned out to be far more resilient than anyone thought possible. The hope that the war would end quickly proved false.

The situation Smythe described had come about because the army had been involved in heavy fighting in the late summer of 1944. In Italy, Canadians were trying to crack the Gothic Line. There was a desperate shortage of infantry soldiers. As one of a number of emergency moves, the Princess Louise Dragoon Guards, an armoured reconnaissance regiment, was converted to infantry. As outlined in the previous chapter, in northwest Europe the First Canadian Army had cleared out Dieppe, Le Havre, and Boulogne and was heading northeast along the coast, facing granite-like German defences. Near the end of August both the Royal Regiment of Canada and the Royal Hamilton Light Infantry of the 2nd Division were far under strength and made up mostly of "reinforcement personnel with little training."[28] The Argyll and Southerland Highlanders of Canada and two other battalions in their brigade were at a little better than half strength.[29] Such had been the rush to get men forward that one man on the front lines with the Essex Scottish had been a civilian on the streets of Winnipeg only two months earlier.[30] Reinforcements sent to the Royal 22e Régiment were described at one point as "all bums."[31]

It turned out there was a big problem with what Stuart had been saying. The Canadian Army had been using a British calculation to estimate casualties, which proved to be disastrously wrong. The estimates were based on what happened in Italy, where Luftwaffe bombers caused casualties among infantry on the front lines and service corps, ordinance troops, and others in the rear areas. But the Luftwaffe was not a factor in northwest Europe, so there were, proportionately, many more infantry casualties. The net result was that there were too many Service Corps reinforcements but a dramatic shortage of infantry. The British Army had to disband two entire divisions and one brigade to provide reinforcements for its infantry battalions.

Defence Minister Ralston had already sensed trouble. He had been receiving messages that the army had to transfer troops from other branches to the infantry on an emergency basis. It began to dawn on him that despite what General Stuart said — and honestly believed — Smythe might be right.

Actually, there were replacements in England and behind the lines in France, but the army could not get them forward fast enough. The real infantry shortage was estimated at only 5 percent, but it was severely compounded by a critical logistics problem. Much later, Major-General George Kitching described the reinforcement organization in Britain as "a shambles," while Brigadier Bill Megill said of the reinforcement units in Britain, "All the duds were there."[32]

Similarly, General Tommy Burns in *Manpower in the Canadian Army 1939–1945*, concluded the army had not used its available men wisely.[33] The First Canadian Army was short because it had heaped on administrative and support troops. There were dozens of administration and supply bases, reinforcement depots, and corps troops. Part of the reason was that the army was running operations both in northwest Europe and Italy, but otherwise it was simply bad management. The fighting arms of the First Canadian Army amounted to 34.2 percent of total troops, but in the U.S Army that number was 43.5 percent.[34]

Meanwhile, huge numbers of volunteer soldiers (not just conscripts) remained in Canada. Dawson estimated that there were at least 120,000 of them, but few could be sprung for overseas service. The army brass said half the men did not meet physical requirements for overseas service, while almost all the rest were instructors, trainees, or administrators. Dawson was not impressed, suggesting some driver like C.D. Howe could have dynamited the log jam.[35]

But even then it was not just the bad casualty estimates, the slow trickle of reinforcements, the "tooth-to-tail" ratio, or even the number of volunteers swanning around in Canada. Underneath it all was — as dealt with earlier — the military's demand for the Big Army. Two years before this crisis, when the question was put to General Stuart about whether the enormous force could be maintained as an all-volunteer army, his answer had been "yes" in any "foreseeable circumstances." With the enormous casualties in Europe plus all the other problems, the army, to Stuart's chagrin, had run into "unforeseeable circumstances."

Grant Dexter commented earlier in the war that the size of the army could not be sustained.[36] However, it was not only the politicians who had questioned the wisdom of the Big Army. Some senior officers, including Major-General Bruce Matthews, one of Canada's best divisional commanders, said it was far too big for Canada to support.[37] It would have been better to have had a smaller formation and keep the divisions up to strength. A full army with all its specialist units, said Matthews, was forever begging assistance from the British. Earlier in the war the British Army contributed as many as nine thousand support and administrative troops to each Canadian division to complete its strength. John English said, "The First Canadian Army could not, and never was able to, operate entirely as a Canadian Field Force."[38] As Granatstein said, quite simply, "The army was too large."[39]

Over the entire length of the war, the army's total intake of men (volunteers and conscripted soldiers) was 730,625. If you added in 249,000 in the RCAF and 106,000 in the Royal Canadian Navy, the total came to over one million.[40] For a nation of eleven million, that was a stupendous effort, an incredible achievement. But even with the latest new enlistments in 1944 the situation was desperate. The army had eased the criteria for recruits so that eighteen-year-olds were eligible for the first time. However, the call-up notices were getting less and less efficient at coming up with new conscripts. At one point 185,000 call-up notices were sent out yet yielded only thirty-four thousand recruits. The rest were medically unfit, doing critical war work, or were heading for enlistment in the RCAF or RCN. As one measure of the situation, in March 1944 bookkeeper Hugh McVicar received a call-up notice even though he was thirty years old and had a wife and two children.[41] He did not think he could contribute very much, but he volunteered for overseas service anyway. Canada's manpower pool was bone dry.

Things were building toward a political blow-up. Defence Minister Ralston set off to Europe on September 26 to visit military headquarters and hospitals in Britain, France, and Italy, and he was quickly convinced it was a genuine emergency. On October 13 King received a cable saying Ralston was returning to Canada urgently because he had grave concerns. King wrote in his diary, "It is a repetition of the kind of thing that led to the creation of the Union government [in the First World War].... That will not take place under me."[42] There was a rare emotional outpouring in one diary entry:

> This is going to be a trying experience for me. Indeed, Ralston has been a thorn in my flesh right along. However, I have stood firm before and shall do so again.... I could not bring myself to being the head of a government which would take that course [i.e., conscription] — a course which might, after five years of war in Europe, and preparation of a year and a half for another war in the Pacific — lead to spurts of civil war in our own country. It would be a criminal thing and would destroy the entire war record.

On October 19 Ralston, back in Ottawa, stunned the war cabinet by saying the situation was much worse than previously thought. In a top secret memo General Stuart reluctantly asked the cabinet to send fifteen thousand conscripts overseas immediately and an additional 5,300 per month after that. Suggestions such as reducing the size of each battalion from four companies to three, as the British and Germans had done, and further relaxing recruiting standards would not solve the problem, according to the army. The answer — the only answer — was full overseas conscription. King warned the cabinet that to impose conscription, Parliament would have to debate the issue and there might even have to be an election. Ralston was shocked, reminding King of his earlier promise that if conscription did become necessary, it would be imposed by an Order-in-Council.

Ralston's allies included Navy Minister Angus Macdonald, Mines and Resources Minister T.A. Crerar, the able Finance Minister James Ilsley, and the young Ontario minister, Colin Gibson. Among those on the other side were King, Justice Minister Louis St. Laurent, Anglo-Quebec's Chubby Power, and the former Saskatchewan premier and at this point agriculture minister, Jimmy Gardiner. C.D. Howe sat on the fence.

For King, St. Laurent was the key. With his support the prime minister might be able to hold on to all or at least part of Quebec. St. Laurent was the champion of French Canada in the cabinet even though he was, in reality, only half French — "a man of Gallic charm and Irish temper."[43] King was looking for any kind of middle ground. For the next two weeks he tried to prevent, at all cost, a resignation that might trigger a cabinet collapse. King polled the ministers in turn: Would you lead a conscriptionist government? There were no takers.

Finally, everyone in the cabinet realized the time for debate was over. Reconciliation or explosion, they must decide. While the cabinet was horribly split, and while some disliked King intensely, few, if any, wanted him to go. For his part, Ralston was no hater of French Canadians; rather, he was a tormented figure trying to do the right thing for the soldiers on the front lines. All of them — King allies, King haters, Ralston admirers, and everyone in between — would meet on November 1 for a showdown.

At mid-afternoon on that day, the scene was the fusty, ugly, mid-Victorian cabinet room in the East Block on Parliament Hill, all flocked wallpaper and stale air. An aged chandelier hovered. The ministers gathered in ones and twos. The prime minister took his place in his ornate chair that looked like something pinched from a ducal palace. Then, joining the circle of uncertainty was the man on whom all eyes focused — Defence Minister James Layton Ralston.

Ralston said he would agree to one more attempt at voluntary recruitment, but only if that were limited to two or three weeks and only if conscription would be implemented immediately afterward if it failed. Two or three weeks. What came next has been described as "an event unparalleled in daring, unspeakable in brutality, incredible in consequence."[44]

King spoke for less than one minute. He would not have full conscription. Ralston had submitted a letter of resignation in 1942, said King, and the letter would now be accepted. A thunderbolt. Ralston's place would be taken by General Andy McNaughton. Another thunderbolt. Secretly, King had spoken to the retired general the night before, and McNaughton thought his personal prestige might be enough to get thousands of new volunteers for the army. King had not fired his minister in private or with any measure of courtesy or tact, but rather in front of everyone else. An excruciating scene. Ralston rose, shook hands with his colleagues, including King, and left. Would others follow him out the door? Pause. Pause. No one.

It was still possible that others might have joined Ralston later, but none did. Had Ralston wanted to be prime minister, this was his moment. Some cabinet members, along with the Conservatives, would have rallied behind him, but he had no desire to be prime minister, nor to crush King. This was the real measure of the man. The next day Ottawa residents opened their newspaper to read, "RALSTON OUT — MCNAUGHTON IN."

It was now up to the legendary general to do the impossible. McNaughton was an admired figure in the army, "the very image of Canada at arms," but this was a hopeless cause.[45] Major-General Harry Letson commented later, "I shall go to my grave wondering at the unbelievable arrogance of Andy in thinking that he could solve a problem which so many able men had attempted to do without avail."[46]

In terms of public support it appears the whole issue of conscription was in a state of flux, uncertainty, and division. A poll in November 1944 showed that 57 percent of Canadians supported it and 36 percent were against.[47] Virtually all English-language newspapers favoured implementing overseas conscription. French-language papers, while applauding the appointment of McNaughton, were still dead set against it.

Many in English Canada thought the problem was "the French." They were the shirkers, the Zombies. As far back as 1942 Arthur Meighen had said the root of the conscription problem was French Canada. Meighen calculated that among Ontarians the army enlistment was 147,114, and given the population differences, Quebec enlistment should have been 125,783 but instead was only 61,247. However, that was off the mark because at that point the actual Quebec enlistments were estimated to be about eighty-three thousand.[48]

Contrary to popular belief, not all, or even most, of the NRMA soldiers in 1944 were French-speaking. The number of French or bilingual members of the army (which presumes French as a first language) changed over time, and in any event estimates varied. However, it is likely that in 1944, by place of origin, about 39 percent of NRMA men were from Quebec while 24 percent were from Ontario, and 37 percent from other provinces.[49] Quebec numbers were proportionately higher than those other provinces but were by no means a majority.

There were many reasons why the Quebec volunteer rate was lower. The language of the Canadian Army was English. The army was commanded by English Canadians, and most instruction and officer training was in English. Even disciplinary charges were in English. There was widespread prejudice in the army against French Canadians and, incidentally, against other minorities, including Jews. Compounding the problem was the chilling history of conscription in the First World War and the widespread feeling in Quebec that the present war was essentially a British conflict. Quebeckers were fundamentally more inward looking.

One of the officers in B.C. who had been trying to persuade the conscripts to volunteer, Brigadier Wilfred "Slim" Macklin, said there was a large contingent of French-speaking NRMA soldiers but added many others were simply "typical European peasants, with a passionate attachment for the land."[50] They included Germans, Poles, Italians, and Russians. Interviews with NRMA soldiers frequently mentioned fear of separation from elderly or ill family members and worries about the family farm. Still, the perception remained that conscription was necessary because too many French Canadians were hiding among the ranks of the Zombies.

McNaughton the salesman set to work planning a campaign that was intended to go on until the end of November. On November 5 he appeared at an event in Arnprior, Ontario, west of Ottawa, but was coolly received, while the next day he was booed and jeered at a Canadian Legion meeting in Ottawa. On November 14 McNaughton organized a meeting in Ottawa for senior officers from across the country. The new minister said he intended to reduce some units in Canada, and he reaffirmed the government's voluntary enlistment policy. It was the duty of all of them, he told the group, to enlist public support in a national emergency.

On November 20 began one of the most debated, confounding, and controversial episodes of the conscription crisis — "the Generals' Revolt." The issue was whether some members of the army openly defied the government to force it to accept conscription. As a result, was there a moment when Canada teetered on the edge of chaos?

The controversy began with Major-General George Pearkes, VC, General Officer Commanding-in-Chief, Pacific Command, where more NRMA men were based than anywhere else in the country. Although Pearkes had made strenuous efforts to get the conscripts to volunteer, he thought there would be no mass conversions in any new campaign. Pearkes gathered the top officers from all over British Columbia in Vancouver to bring them up to date with McNaughton's new plan. As several senior officers waited for Pearkes to arrive, some newspaper reporters appeared. They wanted to know if, indeed, the officers thought the voluntary enlistment goal could be reached. According to Pearkes's biographer, when the general arrived he found "to his surprise" that some officers were already talking to reporters.[51] It was clear that many of the officers, like their colleagues across the country, were seething about any further delay in sending conscripts overseas.

Pearkes did not hold a news conference and turned down press requests to attend the meeting, but he agreed that reporters "might ask the various Camp Commanders what the situation was in their areas." Pearkes felt that newspaper reporters would, with some digging, be able to find out the situation in the camps anyway. Reporters rummaging around for information was one thing; having five army brigadiers and lieutenant-colonels quoted in newspapers criticizing the enlistment program was something else entirely. One officer, Lieutenant-Colonel C.A. Scott, was quoted as saying, "If the government would only assume its responsibility, I am convinced this whole mess could be cleaned up."[52] Pearkes had allowed his officers to savage the government's plan in public.

Not surprisingly, the result was a firestorm in Ottawa. King, always tetchy on any kind of perceived disloyalty anyway, saw it as a conspiracy, a concerted campaign to defy the government.[53] McNaughton questioned the loyalty of Pacific Command officers, saying the army was "full of rotten stuff" and Pearkes was at the bottom of it.[54] McNaughton tepidly dispatched Lieutenant-General Ernest Sansom to Vancouver to conduct an investigation. What was to investigate? The only question was whether they were quoted accurately or not, and if they were, one might have thought they would have been fired on the spot.

With another ten days or so to go in the campaign, McNaughton was still optimistic that recruitment quotas might be met. On November 20 he reported to cabinet that there had been fewer battlefield casualties in recent fighting, and one thousand volunteers had been signed up off the street. However, on the other side of the ledger, the NRMA volunteer rate was low — thousands of enlistments had been expected but fewer than three hundred a week had materialized.

At this point Parliament had been recalled on short notice to begin sitting on November 22. King wanted a confidence vote and MPs would not have long to make up their minds. The choices were to back King or not back him, and if it were the latter choice, he would resign. A new leader, perhaps supported by a mix of Liberals and Conservatives similar to the Union government of the First World War, might carry on for a while. However, that leader would find himself arrayed against King and a significant number of MPs standing with him.

The pro-conscription ministers demanded a date to send the first drafted soldiers overseas. On November 21, the day before Parliament met, King gathered with his exhausted colleagues. Howe exclaimed at one point, "For God's sake let us make up our minds!"

King said he wanted the public appeal to continue a while longer but laid out his resignation scenario. A cohort of Quebec and English ministers said if King resigned they would, too.

At this point we are at the last page of the mystery novel and still uncertain about how it will all turn out. The date is November 22, 1944 — the most dramatic moment of King's political career. It began with a startling development. Some members of the Army Council sent McNaughton a message and subsequently visited him. The Army Council was a wartime committee of eight made up of the minister of defence as chairman plus five top generals and two civilians. It was the meeting point between the army and the government.

Those involved in the meeting were the generals on the Council led by Lieutenant-General John Murchie. The beefy Murchie was quintessentially a backroom operator, completely forgotten today but at that point was the chief of the general staff. Murchie told McNaughton, "In my considered opinion the voluntary system of recruiting through Army channels cannot meet the immediate problem."[55] In other words, the McNaughton plan had failed. Murchie recommended conscription overseas be implemented without delay.

But why the recommendation on that particular day? The enlistment campaign was supposed to run for another ten to twelve days, while the campaign in British Columbia had only been underway for two days. The point of it all was clear: Murchie and his fellow generals were trying to lever the government into accepting conscription before King could get a vote of confidence from Parliament. If they had waited until McNaughton's campaign ended, it would have been too late.

McNaughton seems to have been strangely paralyzed. One might have expected him to fight back and say that the campaign still had time to run, so why not just wait? Even more puzzling is that he soon decided to concur with their judgment. For the second time in the crisis McNaughton had acted indecisively.

Sometime before noon, as the prime minister made final preparations for the opening of Parliament, McNaughton phoned, beginning his conversation by saying, "I have terrible news for you, Chief." The defence minister relayed the information that Murchie had recommended conscription immediately, calling it a "kick in the stomach." McNaughton also said that Brigadier R.A. MacFarlane, the district officer commanding in Winnipeg, had resigned because of the government's delay in implementing conscription.

To understand what happened next, it is well to recall the enormous burden that weighed on King at that moment. He had been under excruciating pressure for weeks. There was the alarming message from Conn Smythe, Ralston's firing, and the fact that the cabinet was hours away from imploding. The Conservative Party press had been howling every day, demanding conscription immediately. The *Globe and Mail* shouted, "The government is wickedly sacrificing young men's lives to retain its governing power in Quebec."[56] The middle ground of public opinion was vaporizing. A survey of newspapers on November 20 said a majority of reports from English Canada supported overseas conscription and talked of "appeasement of Quebec." The French-language press was immovable on the other side of the battlefield. All these things would have been ricocheting around in King's mind as he finished talking to McNaughton and hung up the phone.

This was the moment of decision.

In one of the most electrifying decisions in Canadian political history, King made a 180-degree turn. He would accept conscription. His bedrock belief since the beginning of the war and something he had built his political life around disappeared in a flash. King had said as far back as 1942 that *if the time came* to implement conscription, he would do it. "Conscription if necessary." It was now necessary. It is remarkable that, having decided in mere seconds, King was not troubled, but relieved. He later wrote, "This really lifts an enormous burden from my mind."[57]

Putting aside General Murchie's message for the moment, fundamentally King changed his mind for one single reason: if he did not, half his ministers would have quit. The cabinet would have collapsed. It was the only move he had left except to resign himself. Not only that, but changing course was the shrewd thing to do. Accepting conscription meant some Quebec ministers or MPs would leave, but on the other hand, others might stay. What was their alternative? If he supported conscription, the Liberal Party's hold on English Canada would be strengthened. In politics you do what you have to do to survive and King was among the craftiest politicians ever to don a three-piece suit and sincere tie.

But there is one other thing. This cold-light-of-day political calculation was not enough for King's own peace of mind. Yes, a cabinet revolt had forced his hand, and, yes, he did what he had to do to survive. But he, a man of conviction, could not just do a flip-flop of this magnitude on his own. There had to be more to it. And this is where the "Generals' Revolt" comes in.

You can see King's mind turning: with Lieutenant-General Murchie's poisonous message, Pearkes' public attack, and MacFarlane's resignation, it all added up to a crisis in the army. It was all the evil generals' fault. It might only be a matter of days "before there would be no Government in Canada" and there might be "a situation of civil war" — a "Generals' Revolt."[58]

It was all patent hogwash. Despite what King thought, no one, neither Murchie nor anyone else, was thinking in terms of a banana republic–style coup. There was no sign whatsoever of soldiers storming Parliament Hill and arresting the offending politicians. The idea of civil war was plain silly.

No doubt Pearkes's action was completely improper, but MacFarlane's resignation was not that significant by itself. There is a question, however, about Murchie's message. Even today, there are some things about it that remain fuzzy. There has been a lot of comment, for example, on precisely what was said between the generals and McNaughton. Author Bruce Hutchison said in a 1976 book that the generals threatened they would all resign if the government did not act.[59] That view has been seconded by Richard J. Walker in a recent article "The Revolt of the Canadian Generals, 1944: The Case for the Prosecution."[60]

Despite that, a more likely rendering is that of Dawson, King's early biographer. He said there was "no explicit agreement among them" to resign if their advice was not followed.[61] They simply had an informal understanding of what might happen, but in the meantime they sat around their offices all day waiting to be fired. They thought they would be. They were simply giving their advice, although the timing of it was malicious.

There is no question that Murchie and the others acted improperly.[62] It was by definition a direct intervention in politics, but there never was a military revolt. What is important is that Mackenzie King needed to *interpret* it as a revolt. With the phone call from McNaughton he realized instinctively that he was being given a powerful argument he could use to hold his cabinet together. As Granatstein said, "For the Prime Minister, only a revolt could suffice. He had to find some way of making his *volte-face* appear credible, and only extreme urgency could justify his course both to himself and to his ministers."[63] It may well be that those around King knew he was simply justifying himself and he was not fooling anybody.[64] As to exactly what happened at the crucial meeting, according to Hutchison, "Perhaps King himself never knew, for he could believe anything he wished to believe."[65]

King called St. Laurent and laid out the generals' threat, probably rendered in the most bloodcurdling terms. St. Laurent, despite knowing what the policy reversal would mean for French Canada, sided with King. This was remarkably courageous on St. Laurent's part. The two put together a plan to enact limited conscription overseas, with sixteen thousand soldiers to be dispatched, only as many as the army said it actually needed.

Now came some complications. King had made his decision, but neither the cabinet nor the caucus nor Parliament knew. On the evening of November 22, King arrived late at the full cabinet meeting, where at least two conscriptionist ministers were set to resign and others were expected to do so shortly. However, King shocked them all by saying the voluntary system had failed and conscription would have to be implemented. He had done everything possible to avoid it, and now he had no choice. It was quickly apparent that conscription would be accepted by most ministers because it was the only possible solution. King made no mention of the trouble with the army.

The next morning King entered the caucus meeting to a tremendous ovation. Speaking for about an hour, he unveiled the same plan he had given to the cabinet. He would propose a compromise — conscription, but only limited conscription. Chubby Power told members he would have to resign, but others, while shaken, stayed put. King signed Order-in-Council PC 8891 to enact full conscription for the sixteen thousand NRMA men.

King's staff meantime had worked until five in the morning to rework a speech McNaughton planned to give to Parliament. It resumed in early afternoon with the Conservatives entirely unprepared for King's about-face. Obviously, he could not talk about the army's attitudes, nor their threats, and could not discuss the cabinet and party upheavals. He simply read the Order-in-Council and deferred to McNaughton. The defence minister was not a member of Parliament but had been given special leave, in light of the importance of the issue, to address members. It was McNaughton who outlined the new plan and the justification for it.

The news stunned the nation. The conservative *Ottawa Journal* said King "abandoned on Thursday what he said was right on Wednesday." King's main contribution to the conscription debate came on November 27 when he delivered one of the finest speeches of his career. At one point he turned his back on the opposition benches and addressed his own party members directly. He quoted Laurier, saying, "If there is anything to which I have devoted my political life, it is to promote unity, harmony and amity between the diverse elements of this country." Unlike so many dusty King speeches, this one was heartfelt. The confidence vote carried 143 to 70. Twenty-three Quebec MPs voted with King. Thirty-two French Canadians, both Liberals and opposition, were opposed, while others were absent.[66]

The government's new Order-in-Council did not go down well with the conscripts. Hundreds of them deserted or were reported absent without leave, while there were serious mutinies at some army bases in British Columbia and protests elsewhere. One thousand men marched along the streets of Vernon, B.C., shouting "Down with Conscription." On November 24, with many officers away from the base at Terrace, elements of three regiments, one of them ironically called the Prince Albert Volunteers, armed themselves. They scooped up more than fifty thousand rounds of ammunition and posted anti-tank guns to cover the approaches to the base. The worry for the government and the army was that if things really got out of hand, the only soldiers available to deal with trouble would be other NRMA troops. Sit-down strikes and protests continued for several weeks, but fortunately the mutinies petered out.

Sixteen thousand NRMA troops were authorized to be sent overseas, but only 2,463 were actually posted to units of the First Canadian Army before the war ended. They were generally welcomed by others and, by all accounts, performed well on the battlefield. In one of the great ironies of the whole affair, the fears about infantry shortages turned out to be wrong. Incredibly, the actual shortages had been overcome before the NRMA men were even sent overseas. On September 3, 1944, the 2nd Division, for example, was short 2,645 men, but by October 16, that number had been reduced to 753. Historian Terry Copp has commented of Conn Smythe that "his views were widely shared in the overseas army, but that does not mean they were accurate."[67]

The epic battle was over. But, when it was done the question remained: who were the winners and losers in the greatest conscription crisis of all?

General Murchie and his colleagues, who had a role in provoking the decision to adopt conscription, were as of December 13 banished from the Cabinet War Committee. King said they were not needed. He neither forgave nor forgot. McNaughton remained as minister of national defence, but he was ultimately unable to win a seat in Parliament and with that his political career was over.

It could be argued that the brass hats had won the battle for the Big Army. They got their wish and the First Canadian Army continued its spectacular victories late in the war. But the Canadian Army failed to get one of its most cherished dreams — postwar conscription. A document called "Plan G" surfaced in June 1945 calling for a permanent force of fifty-five thousand soldiers with a total of 178,000 troops in all, including conscripts. Plan G never saw the light of day.

Conscription itself was a loser. The affair had demonstrated that conscription simply did not work in Canada — it was too divisive. It worked elsewhere, but not here.

In the crisis English Canada got its way. Quebeckers were unhappy but realized King had done everything he could to avoid conscription. What King wanted most of all in the war and most definitely in the 1942 and 1944 conscription battles was national unity. Victory, yes, but victory while avoiding the destruction of the country in the process. In 1944 he decided limited conscription was the best way to achieve it while — *what else?* — keeping himself in office.

King's actions have been bitterly criticized. Tim Cook, for one, has said that "One can only conclude that King's concern for Quebec and its support for the Liberal Party was more important to him than any anxiety over the overseas soldiers and unnecessary combat deaths."[68] Despite that, in terms of its final outcome, in "one of the most violent and bitter public controversies in Canadian political history," King was the biggest winner of all.[69] The conscription battles of both 1942 and 1944 left his political leadership unchallenged.

While undoubtedly cynical, his complete reversal on November 22 was something few in politics could have pulled off. King was at this time nearly seventy years old, and he was most certainly under intense pressure, but there was little sign that he flagged at any time or was overwhelmed. A combination of shrewd political instincts, persuasion, nerves of steel, energy, and vitality was evident throughout. He kept most of his ministers and his caucus from bolting while at the same time not alienating the majority of people in either English or French Canada. His decision to implement overseas conscription when he did (but not a moment earlier) was one of the most far-reaching decisions of the war.

DECISION TEN

From War to Peace

May 8, 1945, marked VE Day — the end of the war in Europe. In Holland, where there were thousands of Canadian troops, the German capitulation came at the Hotel DeWereld near Arnhem, where Lieutenant-General Charles Foulkes accepted the formal surrender signed by German Colonel-General Johannes Blaskowitz. Canadians immediately moved to liberate the remaining German-held areas in the western Netherlands, including the starving cities of Amsterdam and Rotterdam. So dire was the food situation that, since April 29, aircraft from Bomber Command, including those of No. 6 Group RCAF, had been dropping supplies to the Dutch population. Even with all the hardship, on May 8, "every village, street and house," according to the record of the 1st Canadian Infantry Division headquarters, "was decked with red, white and blue Dutch flags and orange streamers." The Dutch people had heard that the Canadians would be arriving, and they were "lining the roads, [and] streets in thousands to give us a tumultuous welcome." Years later Private Frank Graham of Midland, Ontario, who had fought through Sicily, mainland Italy, and northwest Europe, remembered he could hardly believe the surrender news. "I didn't believe it to start with," he said. "When I heard them giving up? No."[1]

When the news started leaking out on May 7, some folks back home could not wait one more day to start celebrating. It turned out to be a two-day affair in many places. Granville Street in Vancouver was jammed with cars honking and people piled onto car running boards or hoods, waving flags. A paper blizzard wafted down from office buildings. Newspapers published "Extra" editions with one headline shouting, "VANCOUVER GOES WILD AS GERMANS SURRENDER." In Ottawa, main streets were filled with cars and people. A bagpiper perched himself on the front bumper of one car as it inched down Sparks Street. Jacqueline LaPlante, a member of Canadian Women's Army Corps remembered, "Every noise that could be made in the city was being made: the church bells were all clanging, the whistles on factories were blowing, what jubilation!"[2]

At the Inglis plant in Toronto, which made Bren machine guns, news of the surrender was broadcast over loudspeakers with the announcement followed by the playing of "God Save the King."[3] Regina held huge celebrations at the corner of Eleventh Avenue and Albert Street with a parade of soldiers. There were similar scenes in scores of communities, including

Celebration — They danced, cheered, kissed strangers, and threw streamers. Noisy street celebrations erupted on Bay Street in Toronto and all across the country on May 7, 1945, with the first word of Germany's surrender. The official VE-Day was May 8.

St. George, New Brunswick, west of Saint John. On a bright, sunny day it seemed as if everyone came out to watch the town's parade, led by three local ministers in their vestments. A brass band from a nearby army camp played, while following behind came students from St. George Superior High School, church choirs, Boys Scouts, First World War veterans, and a few wounded men from the Second World War. At the post office everyone stopped for an impromptu service of thanks and remembrance.[4]

An embarrassing exception to the celebrating came in Halifax, where liquor stores and restaurants had been closed so that everyone could enjoy the holiday. But as many as nine thousand rowdy sailors and others were left angry at the closures and the liquor cut off. They turned to looting and vandalism both in Halifax and Dartmouth. More than 550 businesses were damaged and two hundred shops looted. Three rioters died and numerous others ended up with jail terms. It ended the career of Rear-Admiral Leonard Murray,* the senior naval officer in charge, who was judged to have failed to intervene decisively.

In Ottawa, the government had done a lot of preparation for what would come after the celebration. It had on hand a three-part master plan: one part of it was aimed specifically at veterans, another part was made up of social programs for all Canadians, and the third part was aimed at boosting the postwar economy. Put all together, this broad plan was a landmark. It sped the transition from war to peace, helped bring on a postwar economic boom, and set new standards for social legislation. Because it reached so many Canadians and because it was ultimately so successful, the drawing up of this postwar plan constitutes one of the greatest and most far-reaching Canadian decisions of the war.

To deal with the veterans first, the vets' program was loosely referred to as the Veterans Charter, a basket of measures that included new laws, health care, and financial help. For veterans, what happened in 1945 had a lot to do with what had *not* happened in 1918.

---

* Rear-Admiral Murray was the same officer involved in selecting the corvette. He also played a significant role in the Battle of the Atlantic. He was the only Canadian during the war to become a theatre commander, appointed in 1943 as Commander-in-Chief Canadian Northwest Atlantic. After the war he retired, moved to Britain, and became a solicitor specializing in maritime law.

After the First World War it was considered groundbreaking that there was at least some help for vets. Still, it soon became apparent that the barriers they faced were much greater and the problems much deeper than anyone had realized. Soldiers did know about "shell shock," as they called it, but the real effects of what we call post-traumatic stress disorder (PTSD) today, were only dimly understood in 1918. PTSD must have affected thousands of men, which is one reason why there were hundreds of complaints about hospital and health care after the war. Many of the programs were also poorly run. Nearly 79 percent of veterans who applied for one rehabilitation program were turned down.[5] Only 5 percent qualified for the highest pension rate. Some of the trades schools set up for veterans had almost no equipment and unqualified instructors. Eighty percent of veterans who took up farming went broke within five years because the land offered by the government was so poor. The government said buying existing farms was too expensive. The net result of these failures, plus a worldwide recession after the war, led to complete alienation. Thousands of veterans became radicalized because of poor treatment.

With these failures in mind, when the Second World War began the object was, as historian Jeff Keshen described it, "to get it right the second time around."[6] For one thing it was in the interest of creating social peace. It was good defensive strategy and the way to undercut unrest and alienation. An editorial in *Maclean's* magazine in 1941 said soldiers could become "part of an inflammable, disillusioned mass" if they came home to a country offering little more than when they left. A poll early in the war showed that two-thirds of Canadians endorsed better treatment for veterans than they had had in the past.

The second part of the plan was to create a number of social programs for all Canadians. The government would support citizens in a way it had never done before. The welfare of children, for example, would not be just a private concern but would matter to everyone and not only in times of distress but at all times. Similarly, the elderly would not be shunned or forgotten, nor would the worst of the Great Depression ever again be visited on the poorest Canadians. Evidence of the change was at hand in 1945. On February 20 the federal government began mailing out the first family allowance cheques — the Baby Bonus.

The social legislation of the 1940s is generally referred to as creating the "welfare state." These days the words may have a negative connotation, but in those wartime years the legislation was unquestionably visionary. In addition to the Baby Bonus the measures included unemployment insurance and health care for poorer people. Today it is hard to imagine a modern nation without them. The legislation and benefits arrived at different times — some of them earlier, some later — but they are most closely associated with the end of the war.

The push for social reform could be dated back to a wave of new ideas percolating through Britain in the late nineteenth century. Many of them were taken up by Canadian writers, academics, and politicians. Mackenzie King wrote about them in 1918 in his door-stopping book *Industry and Humanity*. King claimed the work was still the template for legislation he began putting into place twenty-five years later.[7] Given King's fusty image it is hard to realize that his thinking was much more left wing than almost anyone in his party.

In 1927 Parliament passed an Old Age Pension Act — the first of its kind in Canada. At the time the act was a condition demanded by J.S. Woodsworth for helping to prop up King's minority government. It applied to men and women over the age of seventy, although it came with a means test and the benefits were meant to be a supplement to other savings that, in reality, did not often exist. Still, it was a start. The provinces joined the program gradually, British Columbia leading the way in 1927. A big push for social reform came with the founding in 1932 of the Co-operative Commonwealth Federation. As mentioned in Decision Nine the party became an advocate for fundamental social change. By the early 1940s it had pushed all national political parties to include social security measures in their platforms.

In 1935 Conservative R.B. Bennett wanted a national unemployment scheme, but the plan was pre-empted before it could be implemented. It was referred to the courts to sort out a huge federal-provincial jurisdictional battle. The writers of the British North America Act in 1867 had no inkling that social programs would become so important, and jurisdiction ended up being split in some areas between the provincial and federal governments. A constitutional amendment enacted in 1940 transferred jurisdiction over unemployment insurance from the provinces to Ottawa, but it was the 1950s before some disputes were settled. Disputes in other areas continued even after that.

It was only in August 1940, with King back in office, that the new unemployment insurance measure made it through Parliament. It was an important step toward a full-scale national social security umbrella even though still less than 50 percent of the labour force was to be covered. Under the 1940 Unemployment Insurance Act wage earners who were covered would gain benefits in the event of extended periods of unemployment. A fund of more than $250 million was built up to supply benefits. The scheme was financed through contributions by employees, employers, and the federal government.

It is astonishing to realize that work on new veterans' legislation, new social programs, and the postwar economy can be dated back to December 9, 1939. The cabinet set up a Committee on Demobilization led by Minister of Pensions and National Health Ian Mackenzie. The committee itself focused on veterans' issues, but setting it up showed the government's intention to act on a broad range of planning. Mackenzie was an unlikely choice to head the committee. He had been a dud as minister of national defence before that. He had signed a contract to buy Bren light machine guns before the war without ever having read it and, when questioned about it during a formal inquiry, displayed a vast ignorance about the whole deal. Mackenzie was also an out and out racist. He was outspoken in pushing for the removal of twenty-one thousand Japanese Canadians and people of Japanese descent from the British Columbia coast during the war. He declared, "It is my personal intention, as long as I remain in public life, to see they [the Japanese and Japanese Canadians] never come back here. Let our slogan be for British Columbia: No Japs from the Rockies to the seas."[8]

Somehow stepping over that mess, it must still be said that Mackenzie was no fool and, anyway, he was saved by his friendship with the prime minister. As it turned out Mackenzie was much more successful in planning for the postwar period than anyone could have imagined. He was "at the heart of the entire planning process for rehabilitation and demobilization" and played a key role in getting Prime Minister King on board.[9]

Mackenzie was among the first to push for King to lead the Liberal Party through another general election expected in 1945 and "frame" that election on the Liberals' postwar programs.

In the middle of the war there were a number of stepping stones toward new social legislation in addition to unemployment insurance. There was a groundbreaking British report in 1942 by economist Sir William Beveridge that proposed reform to deal with five "Giant Evils" in society — squalor, ignorance, want, idleness, and disease. The report became the basis for sweeping social change in Britain after the war. Beveridge's report also triggered widespread debate in Canada, with King, for his part, describing it as a "magnificent and admirable document."[10] In January 1943 King took special note of a speech by Beveridge that suggested Winston Churchill could cap his political career by putting the new proposals into effect.

From 1941 to 1943 a committee headed by Cyril James of McGill University urged setting up a social safety net for the old and the ill and called for government economic planning to promote and direct it. He also urged government to play a greater role in the economy in postwar years. Even more important was a report by Dr. Leonard Marsh, a Canadian who had been one of Beveridge's researchers and the James Committee's research director. Marsh's 1943 *Report on Social Security for Canada* has been called "the most important single document in the history of the welfare state in Canada."[11] It called for a comprehensive national system of social security, including insurance for sickness, old age, disability, and maternity. Another subject was family allowances, which many Canadians were coming to view as not simply an option, but a requirement — "a new right."

Who would pay for it all? Economist and later Liberal cabinet member Walter Gordon said Marsh had rushed to judgment without examining the cost. He termed the proposals "pie in the sky."[12] The left-leaning *Canadian Forum* called the report "the price that Liberalism is prepared to pay in order to prevent socialism."[13] The Conservative Party's Charlotte Whitton, later a mayor of Ottawa, said the cost of such a program terrified her.[14]

The battle for new social legislation was often wrapped in politics. King always presented anything he did as a quasi-crusade to save Canada from the dreaded Tories or the socialist hordes while turning aside the least suggestion that it was all about keeping himself in office. King was petrified of the CCF, and a lot of what he did was aimed at appealing to their supporters. On January 8, 1943, he told aide Jack Pickersgill that there would be four parties in contention in the next election, expected in 1945 — Liberals, Conservatives, CCF, and Social Credit. King felt that none of them would likely be able to command a majority in Parliament.[15] He thought if it came to a minority, the Conservatives would not be open to an alliance but the CCF might be. For some time before the election King actively thought about putting in a proportional representation voting system for the election, believing it would boost his chances of winning.[16]

The Conservatives, meantime, made moves of their own. In September 1942 an unofficial Conservative conference in Port Hope, Ontario, drafted a forward-looking social policy platform. The man behind it was J.M. Macdonnell, the president of the National Trust Company and, many years later, a minister in the Diefenbaker government. In speeches and articles Macdonnell called for the party to keep the key elements of free enterprise but adopt a progressive social policy to undercut the CCF.[17] At a convention in Winnipeg in December 1942 the party endorsed policies calling for social security, full employment, collective bargaining, and medical insurance. At the same time it adopted a new name, the Progressive Conservative Party.

The CCF edged closer to the political mainstream with its reaction to Canada's declaration of war in 1939. The party had a pacifist foreign policy, but in 1939, while party leader J.S. Woodsworth opposed the war declaration, other CCF members, including MP Tommy Douglas, voted in favour of it. By 1943 the CCF led the Liberals and Conservatives in a federal Gallup poll. The lead was narrow and short-lived, but it was clear that the CCF had arrived as a major party.

August 1944 would mark twenty-five years for King as Liberal leader and his thoughts were turning to his legacy. An election was coming up in 1945 and a win would be the glory of his career. He had been working toward innovative social legislation since the First World War, and with another election victory and a list of new progressive legislation he would be up there with Laurier and Macdonald, among the greats.

Up and coming Montreal Liberal MP Brooke Claxton outlined a path to victory in a memo to his boss. What was required, said Claxton, was to turn people's attention away from the government's tired image and the brutal conscription battle and instead highlight postwar plans. At one point the Wartime Information Board did a survey that gave people a list of twelve things to consider and asked, "What would you like to hear more about?" The most popular choice was "post-war plans."[18]

The Speech from the Throne on January 11, 1944, was a landmark. The heart of it was setting up three new departments: Reconstruction, Veterans Affairs, and National Health and Welfare. These departments mirrored the three broad areas that had been the centre of government planning since the beginning of the war. Veterans Affairs would look after demobilizing and re-establishing the veterans; Reconstruction would oversee converting the war economy into a postwar economy and providing protection against a major recession; and National Health and Welfare would look after social legislation. In addition the government pledged to work with the provinces to sort out what the federal government would do and what the provinces would do on social issues. Those shocked by the enormity of it all included cabinet minister Ilsley, who said the government was "seeking to outdo the CCF."[19]

When the war in Europe finally ended in 1945 the first priority was to get the veterans home. Labour Minister Humphrey Mitchell (a labour leader corralled by the Liberals) said, "They have served Canada. It is Canada's turn to serve them."[20] They could not, obviously, all return at once. The plan for getting them back included a point system that was supposed to allow for "first in–first out," but there was interminable wrangling. In the end, along with those who did have long service, married men and prisoners of war got priority, with family emergencies taken into account. Nevertheless, there were simply not enough ships, especially with tens of thousands of Americans trying to get home, too. It took most of a year to finish the job.

On a January evening in 1946 a train pulled onto a siding at the Canadian National Exhibition grounds in Toronto, packed with soldiers from the Toronto area — including members of the Governor General's Horse Guards — all home from the battlefields of Europe. The Coliseum on the Exhibition grounds was jammed with excited friends and relatives. "The din was terrific," said one officer as the troops got off the train and formed up.[21] It was an emotional, thrilling moment, and as the soldiers marched through the doors, the Coliseum "fairly shook to the rafters with cheer after cheer." It was hard to make out much of the welcoming address by Toronto Mayor Robert Saunders or that by Major-General Arthur Potts, the commander of the Toronto Military District, but when the speeches were over the parade was dismissed and "the mad scramble started." Children jumped and hugged, wives and husbands embraced, parents beamed. Everyone cried. It had been a long, long time.

The scenes were repeated in many other cities and towns. Three trainloads of men, as many as one thousand in all, arrived in Calgary on one single day — June 28, 1945. In Windsor there was such a throng on hand to welcome the Essex Scottish that the troops could hardly march up Ouellette Street.[22]

Russ Bannock, having just left the air force, returned to Edmonton later than many others, in mid-May 1946. Bannock had been offered a new job as chief test pilot at de Havilland Aircraft of Canada, but he first went to Alberta to visit his parents.[23] Jim Bessey, who had been commissioned from the lower decks in the Royal Canadian Navy, was happy it was all over, but there were emotional glances over his shoulder. When he left the corvette HMCS *Lethbridge* for the last time he admitted he cried like a baby.[24]

Some homecomings were more sombre. Sergeant-Major George MacDonell stepped ashore from a passenger ferry in Victoria in October 1945, "not only free, but on Canadian soil at last."[25] After the fall of Hong Kong in December 1941, MacDonell had survived terrible brutality and starvation as a prisoner of war in Japan. He said that if the war had gone on even a few months longer, he would not have made it and, as it was, too many from Hong Kong and from the battlefields in Europe had not. One veteran commented, "When you see your friends blown to bits around you, it makes you think the post-war world ... better be good."[26] In all, 395,013 men and women were discharged from the armed forces in 1945; another 381,031 in 1946.

On their return home veterans who did not want to remain in the forces were, after the usual paper work, released to civilian life. Veterans

Affairs provided them with $100 for new clothes plus $7.50 for each month of service and a range of other bonuses. Since regular deductions had been made for government bonds, many had a tidy wad of cash. Bannock was able to pay eight hundred dollars from his savings for a new (and very hard to come by) Plymouth car.

Former Lancaster tail gunner Bill Milne of Barrie, Ontario, who was only eighteen when he enlisted, remembers he had more than two thousand dollars when he returned, which included extra pay because he had been a prisoner of war in Germany.[27] Some parents and others on the home front had little understanding of what a lot of men had gone through and how much they had changed during the war. When Pilot Officer Milne decided he was going to visit the Officers' Mess at nearby Camp Borden, his father asked, "Will they be serving alcohol?" After two years in Bomber Command J.K. Chapman returned to his wife in Fredericton as something of a stranger. She might have been alarmed by his appearance. In his

Showroom Star — Automakers including Packard in the U.S. began producing civilian cars again in 1946. Despite flashy advertising, most Canadian- and American-built cars were simply updated 1942 models. There was so much demand that automakers did not need to spend money on new designs.

final tour of operations he had lost thirty pounds because of insomnia.[28] Bernard Finestone, a tank officer in British Columbia Dragoons, was haunted by the war for years afterward. He reflected, "There isn't anybody who was in real battle who came out unmarked."[29]

One important benefit was a low-cost life insurance program of up to ten thousand dollars that did not require a medical examination for most veterans. The Department of Veterans Affairs established more than thirty hospitals and other care facilities across the country. There were rehabilitation programs for the wounded and the psychologically traumatized. More than twenty-nine thousand veterans would require long-term medical care. Some men with burns would need years of skin grafts. Most Hong Kong vets endured lifelong illnesses, often going blind at an early age and dying prematurely. Their situation was especially dire and in 1976, after prolonged criticism, the federal government provided a further compensation program for them. Forty-eight percent of Dieppe prisoners of war had problems adjusting to life back home.

For the hundred thousand men who wanted to take up farming or return to it, the Veterans Charter provided land grants and low-cost mortgages. Rules about land selection would keep in mind the problems experienced in 1918. There were business loans. Veterans were welcomed at colleges and universities across the country even though most campuses had to scramble to make room. The University of British Columbia started up new programs in pharmacy, medicine, and law to meet demand. Before the war it had been just too expensive for most Canadians to go to university, but by 1947 almost thirty-five thousand veterans were enrolled in post-secondary programs. In that same year, half of the students at University of Toronto were ex-service members. Tuition was free for veterans and there was a sixty-dollar-a-month living allowance. Money was tight, but most got by.

MacDonell, after his return from the Japanese POW camp, joined a crash program to finish high school and then went to university. Later in life he became a deputy minister in the Ontario government and, in a strange irony, went back to Japan to negotiate the opening of a Japanese-owned car plant in Ontario. Former POW Tom Brandon of Regina enrolled at a makeshift campus of the University of Toronto in

Ajax, Ontario, where the classrooms had earlier been used to assemble artillery explosives.

In the first year after the war, 86 percent of returning veterans got jobs within two months of discharge.[30] For one thing, white-collar employment increased sharply, providing jobs for many new college and university graduates or those who had had leadership experience in the military. Some used their military background, perhaps as mechanics, paymasters, or pilots, to get new jobs, while others leaned on what they had gone through in a completely different way. Earle Birney, an army personnel officer, turned his experiences into the 1949 novel *Turvey* and then went on to become an award-winning poet. Farley Mowat wrote about his miraculous survival in combat in his book *And No Birds Sang*, which remains even today one of the great Canadian books of the war. He then turned to full-time writing.[31]

Some of the forty-five thousand women who had served in the armed forces also took advantage of the Veterans Charter. At the University of Toronto Judy LaMarsh, a Canadian Women's Army Corps member and army linguist, earned her Bachelor of Arts degree in thirteen months, then went to Osgoode Hall Law School. Later she took up a political career in

Young Captain — Farley Mowat was among those who stormed ashore in Sicily in 1943 and later fought on the Italian mainland and in northwest Europe. Later he was the author of more than forty books, including Never Cry Wolf *and* The Regiment.

Ottawa and became a minister in the Lester Pearson government. One woman commented, "We were the pioneers. We were the ones who could show them that women could take on any serious assignment."[32]

However, the situation for women in 1945, whether veterans or not, was complicated. The 1942 Civil Employment Act guaranteed that veterans could return to pre-enlistment jobs and many did. The federal civil service was told to hire veterans where possible. The priorities were those with war-related disabilities, then those who had served overseas, and last, widows of personnel who had been killed while in the armed services. Certainly there were jobs available. But a sign of the times was a survey of two hundred Canadian servicemen done just before the end of the war. The survey asked whether or not they agreed with the statement "A woman's place is in the home?" Fifty-six percent agreed with it while only 21 percent disagreed.[33] Another survey in 1950 asked if men should have first chance at jobs and two-thirds of those polled said yes, men should.[34]

About 750,000 women had worked in war industries. While most of the jobs were strictly for the duration of the war, married women in many companies and in government were laid off at the end of the war simply to make room for men. There was no account taken of ability or seniority. If women were veterans, accommodation would have to be made, but that was exceptional. At one point Burrard Dry Dock, the Vancouver shipbuilder, had a work force of thirteen thousand that included one thousand women. In December 1945 Burrard laid off the last of its female employees. With the end of war undoubtedly most would have been laid off anyway, but when the time came, they were all laid off.

All in all, the Veterans Charter was better than its British equivalent and at least as good as the American "GI Bill." However, there was a conspicuous failure in the treatment of twelve thousand members of the Canadian Merchant Marine, who were not provided benefits. In the Battle of the Atlantic the cargo ships and tankers were the real targets of the U-boats. The merchant sailors took risks every bit as great as those in the corvettes and were even described by RCN sailors as being among the bravest of the brave. In what must be one of the most astonishing survival stories of the war, Allan Harvie, a chief steward, was aboard nine ships that were torpedoed. Twice he was the sole survivor.[35] About 1,500 Canadian merchant sailors died in the war, including eight women, while seventy-two Canadian and Newfoundland-owned cargo ships and tankers were sunk. The Canadian Legion (later Royal Canadian Legion) opposed benefits for merchant mariners for some years but finally took up their cause.[36] It was only in 1992 that merchant seamen were finally granted official status as veterans but, of course, by that time thousands of them had already died.

It was not only veterans who were looking forward to new lives after the war. Donald Hings, aged thirty-eight, a sharp-minded inventor and acclaimed developer of the "Walkie-Talkie" portable radio, wrapped up his war work in Ottawa and moved back to Burnaby, B.C. He was set to open his own research and development company, Electronic Laboratories of Canada. Olive Renaud was a "Bomb Girl," one of the six thousand employees at the Bouchard ammunition factory in Blainville, northwest of Montreal. When the war ended, she had just resigned from work to get married.[37] Canadians, both veterans and non-veterans alike, were counting on a new start to their lives. This is where the Department of Reconstruction came in.

The new minister of reconstruction was a familiar face. He was C.D. Howe, the "Minister of Everything" but now with new responsibilities added. Howe commented, "Memories of the depressed thirties were on everyone's mind."[38] He was determined to clear away any and all obstacles to rebuilding the economy. He, more than anyone else, seemed to understand the problems that had to be addressed.[39]

Howe was in a strong position to act because the federal government had become much more powerful during the war years. The number of federal employees expanded from 46,000 in 1939 to about 116,000 by 1945. Howe also took swift action to wind up wartime controls over timber, coal, motor vehicle distribution, and in some areas, natural gas.

One of Howe's "big levers" was to give generous tax writeoffs to companies that had spent a lot of money on new buildings and equipment. Howe thought the main challenge was not a shortage of factories or of industrial capacity — the factories existed because of the war. The real job was to convert them to civilian use and to do so quickly. Factories, instead of producing artillery shells, could now begin turning out consumer goods, home building materials, transportation equipment, or furniture. Among the greatest shortages were items such as refrigerators, cars, electric stoves, and farm equipment. It may be surprising that retail sales actually rose through the war because so many more people were working, but many consumer goods were still hard to find.

Some of the federal government's ideas about growth and expansion were echoed by the provinces. As early as October 2, 1944, the Ontario Highways Department had among its first postwar projects building a "modern two lane" highway between Toronto and Barrie, to the north. The cost was estimated at $5 million.[40]

With the government moves, and with economic trends that were taking place anyway, results were dramatic. Beatty Brothers Limited based in Fergus, Ontario, the first in Canada to use a clothes washing machine agitator in 1927, quickly returned to making washers and related products. Sears provided competition with the first Kenmore top-loading automatic washer going on sale at $239.95. During the war Canadian General Electric made searchlights and radar for ships, among other products, but it opened up a new factory in Barrie, Ontario, to make toasters, kettles, and clothes irons. Textile companies in Quebec, including Dominion Textile, found new demand for their products, including such famous names as Wabasso sheets and Caldwell towels. Canada had become a major producer of uranium during the war, and that continued. Potash from Saskatchewan added to export revenues. Labrador and Quebec developed one of the largest iron industries in the world in the Ungava region. Prairie wheat production provided steady growth across western Canada, despite Europe's economic upheaval.

Most municipal transit systems in the country had not updated their streetcars or buses since 1929. Canada Car and Foundry, in what is now Thunder Bay, returned to its roots as a railcar manufacturer. But it also made a successful leap into the streetcar business, supplying Montreal, Toronto, Regina, Calgary, Vancouver, Edmonton, and the Brazilian cities of Rio de Janeiro and São Paulo with streetcars.

In 1945 Canadian industry was also poised to take advantage of some new ideas. Consolidated Mining and Smelting (Cominco), which operated the world's largest lead-zinc smelter in Trail, B.C., had turned to producing more fertilizers. During the war Cominco plants near Calgary produced nitric acid and ammonium nitrate for explosives, but newer explosives did not use them, so Cominco switched the plants to making fertilizer-grade nitrogen for gardens and farms.

There were dramatic changes in the aircraft industry, which had grown to employ thousands during the war. In 1945 de Havilland Aircraft of Canada began work on the DHC-2 Beaver bush plane. In time, and despite the fact that there were hundreds of war surplus aircraft available, it became a workhorse in Canada and a tremendous international success. Russ Bannock, the former Mosquito pilot and new Plymouth car owner, was at the controls as the first Beaver took to the air on August 14, 1947. C.D. Howe knew, however, that much of the industry could not survive without foreign technology. He sold Victory Aircraft to A.V. Roe and Canadair to the Electric Boat Company (which despite its name was also in the aircraft business). One result was the production of the Canadair North Star passenger aircraft. It used a basic Douglas DC-4 fuselage but incorporated a pressurized cabin and a DC-6 nose and added power with the famous (but deafening) Rolls-Royce Merlin engine. The aircraft was faster than the original DC-4.

Apart from the Veterans Charter, and C.D. Howe's focus on the economy, new social legislation was a key part of the government's postwar program. The best known of those measures was the family allowance — the Baby Bonus, which applied to all Canadians. Wartime wage limits had been especially hard on low-income earners, so a recommendation in 1943 suggested that the government start family allowances as a counter balance. There would be a payment of $5 to $8 a month for each child so that over a year a family of four might get $250 or more. It became the first universal social security program that did not include a means test. In January 1944 the cabinet agreed to it. The plan ran into opposition from the Progressive Conservatives, who called it a bribe to Quebec because of its traditionally large families. Certainly, Mackenzie King would have been the last person to overlook the political implications of it. The Duplessis government in Quebec joined the Conservatives' chorus, arguing that it was a threat to provincial autonomy. The allowance was paid to the mother in each family except in Quebec, where the provincial government insisted that the allowance be paid to the father.

The federal government plans for further postwar social legislation included public health insurance, but those plans faced a jurisdictional fight. A federal-provincial conference in 1945 tried to resolve key issues but failed mainly because of opposition from both Ontario and Quebec. So in 1947 Saskatchewan introduced public hospital insurance itself while Newfoundland had a measure of public health insurance when it entered Confederation in 1949. It was not until 1957, with the support of a majority of provinces, that the House of Commons unanimously enacted the Hospital Insurance and Diagnostic Services Act.

The final verdict on the government's three-point program of veterans' assistance, economic recovery, and advanced social legislation came with the 1945 general election. It marked the end of the wartime period politically. Canadians had to decide: were they willing to put all the upheavals of war and the bitterly divisive conscription battles behind them, and were they satisfied with the government's postwar program? To a large extent it was a referendum on Mackenzie King.

Things looked bad for the Liberals. There had been two years of federal and provincial disasters. In 1943 Ontario Progressive Conservatives under George Drew defeated a Liberal government with the Grits reduced to third place. There was a big CCF breakthrough in Saskatchewan in June 1944 when Tommy Douglas was elected head of the first socialist government in North America. In Quebec a Liberal government was defeated by Maurice Duplessis. Federal Liberals fared badly in a series of by-elections in 1943. In Selkirk, Manitoba, the CCF defeated a Liberal candidate by nearly five thousand votes and in Humbolt, Saskatchewan, by three thousand. The Liberals lost two by-elections in Quebec. It appeared as if the conscription battles were taking a toll. As if all that were not enough, then came the Grey North by-election on February 5, 1945, in which Andy McNaughton was trounced. Cabinet ministers, including Navy Minister Angus Macdonald, were pessimistic about the coming general election, blaming King for all the problems.

In early 1945, after being told another six weeks of brutal fighting might still be at hand in Europe, Mackenzie King stalled on calling an election, determined that conscription would *not* be the defining campaign issue. Only when he saw the way clear did he name the election date as June 11. That would be the day to determine whether King the magician could — in some prestidigitous and wizardly way — pull one more victory from his sleeve. Already journalist Grant Dexter was wondering whether this would be the "goodbye" election for the Liberals.[41]

The party's central pitch was, as its campaign literature and advertising outlined, that it would "Build a New Social Order" for Canada. The platform was based around the plan it had already unveiled and was, even then, implementing. There was the Veterans Charter, but also $750 million for jobs, businesses, and reconstruction, $250 million for family allowances, and $400 million for new housing.

The Progressive Conservatives had long attacked the Liberals for their conscription failures and for coddling Quebec, especially with the Baby Bonus. The Conservatives were strong in Ontario, but John Bracken, the party's leader since late 1942, had failed to really take command. Confusingly, Ontario voters would be bombarded with campaigning for two elections at the same time because an Ontario election was set for June 4. The CCF proposed a national commission made up of economists, engineers, and statisticians to further economic planning. It pushed a list of social welfare programs, calling for Canada to "Left turn, CCF." Social Credit, the fourth party in the race, had burst onto the political scene as a populist movement advocating sweeping monetary reform, but its appeal was mostly limited to Alberta.

Prior to the election King's cabinet had taken a beating. Ralston had been fired, Power had quit, and Angus Macdonald (as an ardent conscriptionist) was fed up with both King and Ottawa and went back to Nova Scotia. Others chose to retire. At least that allowed King to bring in some dynamic younger Liberals including Paul Martin, Lionel Chevrier, and Doug Abbott. All went on to become prominent cabinet ministers in the next decade. King himself was at this time past seventy years old but still an energetic campaigner. In a radio address he said it was up to Canadians to determine if a trusted government should be turned over to "unknown and untried hands."[42] King was featured prominently in party advertising in Quebec but, interestingly, the Liberals chose to downplay his role in English Canada. Instead, advertisements proclaimed the party's "New Housing Plan" and "Liberal Family Allowances."[43] The party told Ontario Liberals that the next year, family allowances would pour $153,891 into Welland, for instance, while they would add up to a total of $6 million in the province.[44]

John Bracken's speeches returned again and again to the conscription controversy and King's "cowardly manpower policy." In Calgary Bracken asked if it was Canada's wish to have 46 percent of available men from one part of the country sent to war while another part sent only 22 percent. The Liberal policies were all "a frantic desire to satisfy Quebec."

When voting day arrived the verdict shocked many. Despite everything King won 118 seats out of 245. Eight "Independent Liberals" were also elected and with their support he would have a small majority.* The Conservatives won sixty-seven seats, the CCF twenty-eight, and Social Credit thirteen.

Most remarkable of all was the verdict of the armed forces. Many men and women had not yet been demobilized and took part in voting at their bases or wherever they were stationed. Despite the conscription crisis more members of the armed forces voted for the Liberals than any other party, and without those votes King could not have won. It was noted earlier that historian Tim Cook was scathing in his criticism of King in the 1944 conscription crisis, but the men and women in uniform in June 1945 either forgave or forgot.[45] On election night, to the consternation of his opponents, Mackenzie King, the old magician, stepped dramatically into the spotlight to take one final bow.

It might have been expected that with the Germans defeated and with the first veterans returning home, there would have been smooth sailing in the summer of 1945. However, that was not the case. The war against Japan still had weeks to go. President Roosevelt was dead, Churchill defeated, and Europe in tatters. The defection of Soviet cipher clerk Igor Gouzenko in Ottawa on September 5, 1945, marked the start of the Cold War. Meat rationing was lifted and then had to be

---

* Seven of the Independent Liberals were from Quebec. Some candidates there were trying to put distance between themselves and conscription.

reintroduced. A ninety-nine-day strike at the Ford Motor Company in Windsor teetered on the edge of violence. Massive strikes in the auto industry in the United States continued until March 1946.[46] Canada was in dire need of three hundred thousand new homes, and, in desperation, some former barracks had to be turned into emergency housing. The government offered support for homebuyers, but 50 percent of people rented so that was no help to them. Unions and others called for building public housing, but it was not a priority.

Still, by March 1946 the last of the troops had returned home. The washing machines, the toasters, and the cars soon appeared, and the postwar boom went on to become the longest sustained run of prosperity in Canadian history. Unemployment remained below 6 percent until 1957. It was good fortune, but it was good fortune assisted by plans that had been years in the making.

Despite the fears of Walter Gordon and others that social programs would bankrupt the country, the growing economy generated enormous tax revenues. The Baby Bonus and other social programs were sustainable. While the social changes were important in themselves, even more, they were catalysts for reforms in other areas as diverse as housing, schooling, urban police forces, labour legislation, and juvenile justice.[47]

For his part Mackenzie King had rightly judged the mood of Canadians. Canada had been transformed by the Depression and the war and there would be no going back. All by itself the Veterans Charter has been called "one of the most significant groupings of legislation ever passed" in Canada.[48] The planning for veterans, for broad social benefits, and for the economy paid off.

CONCLUSION

The New Canada

In 1945 Canada was a nation transformed. It was more outward looking, confident, and optimistic than it had been before. The war had "opened eyes and widened horizons."[1] An immense crisis had been faced and fears had been conquered. Historian Desmond Morton said that with the entry of thousands of civilians into wartime factories, suddenly people who had been poor farmers or labourers had enough money to put the necessities of life together. "People had jobs and therefore could stand up for themselves and have opinions."[2]

The numbers reflected some of it. The nation's population jumped from eleven million to more than twelve million in the war years. Importantly, the birth rate rose by 20 percent, revealing a genuine optimism for the times ahead. The Gross National Product, the total of goods and services produced, grew from $5.6 billion in 1939 to $11.8 billion in 1945 and was set to expand far past that.

The war had completely changed the role of government. After the war it never really let go of some fields — regulating transport, train, air, road and rail, petroleum products, hydro-electricity, and construction materials. It continued to be involved in such companies as the Canadian Broadcasting Corporation and Canadian National Railway. Provincial governments, too, would become more involved in health and education than they ever had been. Highways would soon open up previously inaccessible communities.

The war provided a vast new human resource: thousands of people skilled in the use of machines. There would be little need for tank drivers in the postwar world, but there would be need for heavy equipment operators. Men who had spent five years working on or repairing trucks, radios, radar equipment, and aircraft had new skills for a new era. The nation was also on the edge of an education revolution. It could expand in engineering, construction, architecture, nursing, and dozens of other fields with a well-trained work force.

There was a new-found patriotism. Men and women overseas were dismayed when they thought their homeland had been belittled or overlooked. "God help the Yanks who called us Brits," said David Gordon, a stretcher-bearer with the 24th Field Ambulance.[3] After the war senior naval officers wanted to remove the "Canada" flashes from naval uniforms so they would be the same as British uniforms. There was a furious outcry and the navy backed down.

Dan McCaffery, in his book *Dad's War*, wrote about his father, James, who had been a crew member on a Lancaster bomber.[4] Dan said his father had "gone to war as an Irish Catholic and had emerged as a Canadian." In sharing the dangers of bombing missions, James McCaffery had made close friends with people from other religious backgrounds, "something that would have been highly improbable had they not served together."

Ordinary Canadians could take satisfaction for having had a role in the struggle against tyranny, however humble. When the British Commonwealth Air Training Plan was being established, many communities were eager to have a training base built near their town. They wanted jobs, of course, but just as much, they wanted the feeling that they were making at least a small contribution to victory. P.J. Rawlinson, the Secretary Treasurer of Mossbank, Saskatchewan, believed that a training base in his community would bolster a feeling of national pride among the citizens. In a letter to Defence Minister Norman Rogers he wrote, "The work and presence amongst us of many members of the Air Force would give our people a new spirit, make them conscious they are directly interested in the successful issue of the war, stimulate recruiting, [and] arouse their national feelings."[5]

Wartime patriotism pushed Parliament to pass the Canadian Citizenship Act in 1946. Until that time a person in Canada was a "British Subject," but with the new act they could officially proclaim, "I am a Canadian."

Canada played a much bigger military role in the Second World War than anyone could have possibly imagined in 1939. In all, 1,086,343 Canadian men and women served in the army, navy, and air force, approaching one in ten of the entire population. About forty-two thousand Canadian service members died. The battles at Dieppe and Hong Kong showed that courage was never in short supply, but the legacy of neglect from the pre-war years took a long time to overcome. For a while in 1945 the armed forces of Canada were among the largest in the world. At the end of the war the First Canadian Army was a battlefield force "at least as effective as any Allied force of comparable size anywhere."[6] It is unlikely there will ever be another like it.

The Royal Canadian Navy had ninety-five thousand men and women in uniform and 434 vessels in commission in 1945, including cruisers, destroyers, frigates, corvettes, and auxiliaries. Its role in winning the Battle of the Atlantic had been fundamental to victory, but it also participated in many other engagements including Operation Husky in Sicily and Operation Neptune leading up to D-Day.

The Royal Canadian Air Force reached a total strength of 215,000 men and women. RCAF squadrons or members served in Britain, in northwest Europe and in operations in Egypt, Sicily, mainland Italy, Malta, Ceylon, India, and Burma. They had a powerful role in Bomber Command. Then there was the tremendous scope of the British Commonwealth Air Training Plan. Also, a total of twelve thousand men and women served in Canada's Merchant Navy, making more than twenty-five thousand ship voyages, mostly across the Atlantic.

One thing did not change. C.P. Stacey said at heart Canada was and remained an unmilitary nation even after the war. "Warlike her people have often been forced to be; military they have never been."[7] Despite their achievements in war, most veterans could not wait to go home and take up civilian lives.

Canadians in 1945 looked out on an international order that had been completely transformed.

Among the greatest changes was Canada's relationship to Britain. There were still treasured links, especially with the Crown, but things were never the same. The "Canadianization" of the RCAF had shown some of that taking place. By the end of the war, a new order for the RCAF was not so much welcomed as it was demanded. For its part, the British Commonwealth Air Training Plan has been described as "the Empire's last hurrah." There could never again be a program that funnelled Canadians into the Royal Air Force in the way the BCATP had.

As for the United States, the Ogdensburg Agreement was the very definition of change. Canada would trade much more with the United States in the coming years. It would engage more with the United States. For one thing, the United States was one of the few nations that had escaped devastation and could afford to buy Canadian goods. The Ogdensburg Agreement showed Canada was open to new international agreements. In 1945 it was also eager to join in world affairs. On April 25, 1945, seven Canadians were among 282 official delegates in San Francisco at the founding of the United Nations. Canada was ready to accept an important role as a middle power in the postwar world.

The Naval Service Headquarters in Ottawa showed it could solve a naval impossibility. How could the RCN find a warship that could be built quickly in a nation without a shipbuilding industry worthy of the name? How could you find crews and train them even if the ships magically appeared? The navy did.

The industrial war effort gave a glimpse of the country's stupendous potential. Never mind all the other tools of victory, the production of eight hundred thousand trucks in just a few years was little short of miraculous.

The ten major decisions of the war covered here included an incredibly broad range — politics, the military, diplomacy, and the economy. Sometimes two or three of them at once. Some decisions had an enormous impact on others. Canada could have an immense industrial war effort, but could it have a Big Army at the same time? It is sometimes thought that politicians have a wide choice among possible policy alternatives, but the conscription crises showed they often operate in an extremely narrow range.

There is greatness among us. The men and women of the armed forces were the equal to any. J.L. Granatstein has pointed out that high enlistment standards in the Canadian Army were one factor contributing to the outstanding achievement of the Canadian soldiers on the battlefield.[8] The achievements of men and women in the Royal Canadian Navy, the Royal Canadian Air Force, and the Merchant Marine were no less. Lieutenant-General Simonds demonstrated that a Canadian could be among the best commanders of the war. It is easy to forget that those Allied corps commanders included Sir Richard O'Connor, the early victor in North Africa, and Brian Horrocks, one of the greatest Allied soldiers of the war. C.D. Howe could stand among any of the world industrial leaders. Elsie MacGill, the aircraft engineer, showed glimpses of what women would achieve if given a chance. Many leaders — men and women — were inspired by their wartime experiences to take on greater challenges in the postwar world.

Greatness came in many shapes and disguises, but perhaps the most effective disguise of all was that worn by Mackenzie King. What a strange man to have become the greatest vote getter in Canadian history. There is about him what might be called the "Great Mackenzie King Paradox." The Paradox is the result of putting his achievements next to his personality. It is best summed up by Professor Stephanie Bangarth of Western University, who said, "I both loathe and admire William Lyon Mackenzie King."[9] One article on Canada's greatest prime ministers lists Sir John A. Macdonald as one of them and refers to him as "flawed but magnificent." The description of King was that he was "Slippery, unpleasant, selfish, dogged, ruthless, far-sighted, and crazy like a fox."[10] Upon King's death on July 22, 1950, civil servant Norman Robertson, who worked with him every day for years, said "I never saw a touch of greatness in him."[11] In June 1946 King exceeded Sir John A's record for longevity in office, although, sadly, in his last two years King became a liability to his colleagues. His memory was failing but no one dared tell him.

King's two supreme aims in the Second World War were to win victory and to keep the country together. He achieved both. In political terms, he effectively balanced majority rule and minority rights. His views on conscription were not based on emotion or theory. Canadians delivered a resounding verdict on King's wartime leadership in the 1945 election. Britons did not do the same even for Winston Churchill.

There were other King achievements. He cultivated a personal relationship with Roosevelt that helped cement the Canadian–American continental relationship. He founded the welfare state. "Social welfare had been one of the guiding principles of Mackenzie King's life," said J.L. Granatstein.[12] He made the Liberals the government party. By the time he retired he had left a "prouder and more prosperous nation than the one he inherited."[13]

King was a nationalist. He raged for days after a speech in Toronto in 1944 by Lord Halifax, at the time the British ambassador to Washington. Halifax had floated the idea that after the war there might be four major powers at the United Nations: the United States, China, the Soviet Union, and the British Commonwealth. King said Canada, and not Britain, would make Canadian foreign policy. There would be no "Commonwealth foreign policy" that included Canada. Curiously, this was the same thought King had expressed at an Empire prime ministers meeting in 1923.

Finally, on King, Patrick Brennan of the University of Calgary has commented, "He was, after all the spiritualist and other jokes about his private life, our greatest prime minister. He tried to understand the country, he was capable of intellectual flexibility and change, and he attracted and held able colleagues. He was an intellectual who was sympathetic to ideas — our first!"[14]

Some questions about the war remain with us even today. How could Dieppe have happened? Can Canada have defence co-operation with the United States and economic integration without becoming a colony? The Second World War is now more than seventy years behind us, and those who experienced it first-hand are vanishing before our eyes. While much about the story of the war can be placed in some kind of perspective or perhaps put at some distance, for Canadians not all of it can.

Among the red and blue flowers strewn through the Canadian War Cemetery at Ortona in Italy, there are graves with a maple leaf design etched on them and the simple inscription "A Soldier of the 1939–1945 War." How can one visit that cemetery, or the one at Bény-sur-Mer in

Normandy, or the one at Sai Wan Bay in Hong Kong, and not be moved to tears. How can one see the wreaths float gently in the waters off Halifax on Battle of the Atlantic Sunday or witness the missing man formation in a flypast on Remembrance Day and not feel an ache? How can one stand on the beach at Dieppe, knowing that on August 19, 1942, so many young men, with lives still to live and with family longing for them, were cut down on that very spot? What happened in those years is not simply history; it cannot simply be confined to the past. It whispers to us yet.

NOTES

CANADA IN 1939: ON THE EDGE OF WAR

1. There were nominally about fifty-thousand in the reserves, but half the number was made up of names on a list. Extensive examination of Canada's being unprepared for war in Larry D. Rose, *Mobilize!: Why Canada Was Unprepared for the Second World War* (Toronto: Dundurn, 2013).
2. John English, *The Canadian Army and the Normandy Campaign* (Mechanicsburg, PA: Stackpole, 2009).
3. In addition to the schools and buildings named for the King, there were dozens more named for his father, King George V, and many after his great-grandmother, Queen Victoria.
4. Dominion Bureau of Statistics, *Canada Year Book 1943–44* (Ottawa: King's Printer, 1944), 40, 103.
5. Bruce Hutchison, *The Incredible Canadian* (Toronto: Longmans, 1953), 228.
6. J.L. Granatstein, *Canada's War: The Politics of the Mackenzie King Government, 1939–1945* (Oakville, ON: Rock Mills Press, 2016), 107.
7. J.L. Granatstein, *The Ottawa Men* (Oakville, ON: Rock Mills Press, 2015), 159–60.
8. John MacFarlane, *Ernest Lapointe and Quebec's Influence on Canadian Foreign Policy* (Toronto: University of Toronto Press, 1999), 11.
9. Ibid.

DECISION ONE: TO GO TO WAR

1. The exception among English-Canadian MPs was J.S. Woodsworth, the leader of the Co-operative Commonwealth Federation, a pacifist.
2. House of Commons, *Debates*, 18th Parliament, 5th Session, vol. 1, September 9, 1939 (Ottawa: King's Printer, 1939), 69.
3. Ibid., September 7, 1939.
4. Desmond Morton, *A Military History of Canada* (Edmonton: Hurtig, 1985), 178.
5. Eric Brown and Tim Cook, "The 1936 Vimy Pilgrimage," *Canadian Military History Journal* 20, no. 2 (2011): 37–54.
6. *Maclean's*, April 15, 1936.
7. John Thompson and Allen Seager, *Canada 1922–1939: Decades of Discord* (Toronto: McClelland & Stewart, 1985).
8. Quoted in Morton, *A Military History of Canada*, 174.
9. *Winnipeg Free Press*, March 13, 1937.
10. *L'Action Catholique*, quoted in Thompson and Seager, *Canada 1922–1939*, 317. The magazine carried fifty similar editorials.
11. Comment by J.N.O. Laroque of Montreal, *Financial Post*, June 26, 1937.
12. Germany became a member in 1926. The Soviet Union joined in 1934.
13. C.P Stacey, *Canada and the Age of Conflict*, vol. 2, *The Mackenzie King Era* (Toronto: University of Toronto Press, 1981), 215.
14. Hutchison, *The Incredible Canadian*, 239.
15. Ibid.
16. J.W. Dafoe wielded the kind of influence that has rarely been seen since his time. He was a strong Liberal although reserved about Mackenzie King until later in the war. The *Free Press* played a role in national unity at the time of the war declaration in 1939.
17. *Le Devoir*, March 30, 1936.
18. Morton, *A Military History of Canada*, 178.
19. Blair Neatby, *William Lyon Mackenzie King*, vol. 3, *The Prism of Unity: 1932–1939* (Toronto: University of Toronto Press, 1976), 294.
20. William Lyon Mackenzie King, *The Diaries of William Lyon Mackenzie King*, November 14, 1938, MG26J13, Library and Archives Canada.

21. An excellent examination of King's campaign is in Gordon Case, "The Lessons of Munich: Mackenzie King's Campaign to Prepare Canada for War," *Canadian Military Journal* 3, no. 4 (2004): 73–82.
22. J.L. Granatstein and R. Bothwell, "A Self-Evident National Duty: Canadian Foreign Policy 1935–1939," *Journal of Imperial and Commonwealth History* 3, no. 2 (1975): 213–21.
23. King, *Diary*, January 30, 1939.
24. Stacey, *Canada and the Age of Conflict*, 2:237.
25. King, *Diary*, January 27, 1939.
26. Case, "The Lessons of Munich," 79.
27. Wesley Wark, "Diplomatic Revolution in the West: 1939, The End of Appeasement and the Origins of the Second World War," in *A Country of Limitations: Canada and the World in 1939*, eds. Norman Hillmer et al. (Ottawa: Canadian Committee for the History of the Second World War, 1996), 35–49.
28. Stuart Soward, *A Formidable Hero* (Toronto: Canav Books, 1987), 12–14.
29. King, *Diary*, March 20, 1939.
30. Hutchison, *Incredible Canadian*, 242.
31. *Globe and Mail*, April 1, 1939.
32. King, *Diary*, March 31, 1939.
33. Case, "The Lessons of Munich," 82.
34. Hutchison, *Incredible Canadian*, 244.
35. Granatstein, *Canada's War*, 19.
36. Stacey, *Canada and the Age of Conflict*, 2:234.
37. King, *Diary*, September 12, 1939.

DECISION TWO: THE UNLOVED CORVETTE

1. Mac Johnston, *Corvettes Canada* (Mississauga, ON: Wiley, 2008), 6.
2. Donald Graves, *In Peril on the Sea: The Royal Canadian Navy and the Battle of the Atlantic* (Toronto: Canadian Naval Memorial Trust/Robin Brass Studio, 2003), 73.
3. Tony German, *The Sea Is at Our Gates* (Toronto: McClelland & Stewart, 1990), 71.

4. Graves, *In Peril on the Sea*, 94.
5. Ralph Hennessy interview with Larry D. Rose, May 7–8, 2008.
6. S.E. Morison, *History of United States Naval Operations in World War Two: The Battle of the Atlantic 1939–43* (New York: Castle Books, 2001), 76–80.
7. Marc Milner, *North Atlantic Run: The Royal Canadian Navy and the Battle for the Convoys* (St. Catharines, ON: Vanwell, 2006), 80.
8. In May 1942 the navy threw caution to the wind and did order two Tribals to be built in Halifax. They were not finished until after the war ended.
9. Milner, *North Atlantic Run*, 82.
10. Rear-Admiral L.W. Murray, Interview, May 1970, by Department of History and Heritage. PAC, MG 30, E 307, v 4.
11. Schull, *Far Distant Ships* (Ottawa: Queen's Printer, 1956), 427.
12. Marc Milner, *Canada's Navy: The First Century* (Toronto: University of Toronto Press, 1999), 82.
13. Mac Johnston, *Corvettes Canada*, 85.
14. Ken Macpherson and Marc Milner, *Corvettes of the Royal Canadian Navy 1939–1945* (St. Catharines, ON: Vanwell, 2000), 30.
15. Johnston, *Corvettes Canada*, 87.
16. During the war, most RN and RCN ships would have known sonar as "asdic," but "sonar" — an American term — has become accepted and is used here. "Asdic" supposedly stood for "Anti-Submarine Detection Investigation Committee," the group that first developed it. "Sonar" stands for Sound Navigation and Ranging.
17. Schull, *Far Distant Ships*, 58–59.
18. Macpherson and Milner, *Corvettes of the Royal Canadian Navy*, 30.
19. W.A.B. Douglas, Roger Sarty, and Michael Whitby, *No Higher Purpose: The Official Operational History of the Royal Canadian Navy in the Second World War, 1939–1943*, vol. 2 (St. Catharines, ON: Vanwell, 2004), 80.
20. King, *Diary*, January 29, 1940.
21. Rear Admiral L.W. Murray, Interview, May 1970, by Department of History and Heritage.

22. Robert Halford, *The Unknown Navy* (St. Catharines, ON: Vanwell, 1995), 13.
23. James Pritchard, "Fifty-Six Minesweepers and the Toronto Shipbuilding Company During the Second World War," *Northern Mariner* 16, no. 4 (2006): 29–31.
24. Milner, *Canada's Navy*, 86.
25. Schull, *Far Distant Ships*, 26.
26. Johnston, *Corvettes Canada*, 10.
27. Frank Curry, *War at Sea: A Canadian Seaman on the North Atlantic* (Toronto: Lugus, 1990), 66.
28. Macpherson and Milner, *Corvettes of the Royal Canadian Navy*, 30.
29. Graves, *In Peril on the Sea*, 91.
30. Johnston, *Corvettes Canada*, 17.
31. Graves, *In Peril on the Sea*, 80–81.
32. Macpherson and Milner, *Corvettes of the Royal Canadian Navy*, 28.
33. Curry, *War at Sea*, 66.
34. Milner, *North Atlantic Run*, 206–10.
35. Marc Milner, "Over the Side: The Courageous Boarding of U-94," *Legion*, January 15, 2015.
36. Marc Johnston, "Scrappy Little Corvettes," *Legion*, January 5, 2010.
37. Milner, *Canada's Navy*, 80.
38. Ibid.
39. Johnston, *Corvettes Canada*, 47.
40. Schull, *Far Distant Ships*, 427.
41. Ibid., 426.
42. Curry, *War at Sea*, 25.

DECISION THREE: CANADA'S AIR TRAINING COLOSSUS

1. The numbers in this section based on F.J. Hatch, *Aerodrome of Democracy: The British Commonwealth Air Training Plan* (Ottawa: Department of National Defence, 1983) and W.A.B. Douglas et al., *Creation of a National Air Force: The Official History of the Royal Canadian Air Force Volume II* (Toronto: University of Toronto Press/ Department of National Defence, 1986).

2. Douglas et al., *Creation of a National Air Force*, 204-05.
3. J.W. Pickersgill, *The Mackenzie King Record* (Toronto: University of Toronto Press, 1960), 40.
4. King, *Diary*, October 17, 1939.
5. Hatch, *Aerodrome of Democracy*, 16.
6. C.P. Stacey, *Arms, Men and Governments: The War Policies of Canada 1939-1945* (Ottawa: Queen's Printer, 1970), 29.
7. Hatch, *Aerodrome of Democracy*, 1.
8. Russ Bannock, Interview with Larry D. Rose, March 29, 2010.
9. Christopher Cole and Frank Cheesman, *The Air Defence of Britain 1914-1918* (London: Putnam, 1984), 436-45.
10. Spencer Dunmore, *Wings For Victory: The Remarkable Story of the British Commonwealth Air Training Plan in Canada* (Toronto: McClelland & Stewart, 1995), 60.
11. Flying Officer Robert English, *Letters*, Grant Penwill Collection, Mississauga, ON. Robert English wrote seventy letters home that are in the possession of the next of kin, the Penwill family.
12. Douglas et al., *Creation of a National Air Force*, 280. MacKenzie became a Spitfire pilot. He was also a Sabre jet pilot in Korea, where he was shot down and spent two years as a Chinese prisoner.
13. Harry Furniss, "Reminiscences of Harry Furniss," in Normand Marion, ed., *Camp Borden: Birthplace of the RCAF* (Borden, ON: 16 Wing RCAF, 2004), 84.
14. Howard Hewer, *In For a Penny, In For a Pound* (Toronto: Anchor Books, 2004). Hewer remained in the air force after the war and retired as a wing commander.
15. Douglas et al., *Creation of a National Air Force*, 245.
16. Ibid., 278-79.
17. C.G. Power, *A Party Politician: The Memoirs of Chubby Power* (Toronto: Macmillan, 1966).
18. Douglas et al., *Creation of a National Air Force*, 280.
19. Extensive treatment of casualty figures in Jean Martin, "The Great Canadian Air Battle: The British Commonwealth Air Training Plan and RCAF Fatalities During the Second World War," *Canadian Military Journal*, Spring 2002, 65-69.

20. English, *Letters*.
21. Peter Conrad, *Training for Victory: The British Commonwealth Air Training Plan in the West* (Saskatoon, SK: Western Producer Prairie Books, 1989), 43.
22. R.V. Manning "Graduation of the First Pilot Course, BCATP," in Marion ed., *Camp Borden*, 97.
23. John Golley, *Aircrew Unlimited: The Commonwealth Air Training Plan in World War 2* (London: Patrick Stephens, 1993), 71.
24. English, *Letters*.
25. Paul Hellyer, *Damn the Torpedoes: My Fight to Unify Canada's Armed Forces* (Toronto: McClelland & Stewart, 1990), 2–4.
26. Bill Milne, Interview with Larry D. Rose, February 13, 2016. Milne was in a Lancaster that was shot down over Berlin in February 1945.
27. Douglas et al., *Creation of a National Air Force*, 640.
28. Ibid., 293.
29. Ibid., 270.
30. Ibid., 269, 272–73.
31. Ibid., 251.
32. Golley, *Aircrew Unlimited*, 78.
33. Douglas et al., *Creation of a National Air Force*, 293.

DECISION FOUR: PUTTING "CANADIAN" IN "ROYAL CANADIAN AIR FORCE"

1. Jorg Friedrich (trans.) and A. Brown, *The Fire: The Bombing of Germany 1940–1945* (New York: Columbia University Press, 2008), 210.
2. F.H. Hitchens, *RCAF Overseas: The Sixth Year* (Toronto: Oxford University Press 1949), 37.
3. Richard Overy, *The Bombers and the Bombed* (New York: Penguin, 2013), 103.
4. Arthur Harris, *Bomber Offensive* (London: Collins, 1947), 63–65.
5. Quoted in Brereton Greenhous et al., *The Crucible of War, 1939–1945, The Official History of the Royal Canadian Air Force*, vol. 3 (Toronto: University of Toronto Press, 1994), 18. The British message said Canadian squadrons could be formed "later."

6. Quoted in Stacey, *Arms, Men, and Government*, 25.
7. Greenhous et al., *The Crucible of War*, 18.
8. Ibid., 19–21.
9. Ibid., 13.
10. Leslie Nuttall, "Canadianization and the No. 6 Bomber Group RCAF" (Ph.D. thesis, University of Calgary, 1990).
11. Morton: *A Military History of Canada*, 180.
12. The defence minister was Norman Rogers and, after Rogers was killed in a plane crash, Layton Ralston. The minister nominally oversaw all three services, but in reality mainly focused on the army. Power was responsible for the RCAF while Nova Scotian Angus Macdonald was Minister for Naval Services.
13. C.G. Power, *A Party Politician: The Memoirs of Chubby Power* (Toronto: Macmillan, 1966).
14. Greenhous et al., *The Crucible of War*, 36.
15: Ibid., 38.
16. Ibid., 47.
17. Ibid.
18. Vincent Rigby, "Air Marshal Edwards," *Canadian Defence Quarterly* 16, no. 3, 41.
19. Rigby, "Air Marshal Edwards," 41.
20. Greenhous et al., *The Crucible of War*, 52.
21. Ibid., 68.
22. Ibid., 60.
23. Ibid., 69.
24. Tim Cook, *The Necessary War V1, Canadians Fighting the Second World War 1939–1945* (Toronto: Penguin, 2014), 310.
25. Robert Collins, *The Long and the Short and the Tall: An Ordinary Airman's War* (Saskatoon: Western Producers Prairie Books, 1986), 80.
26. David Bashow, *No Prouder Place: Canadians and the Bomber Command Experience 1939–1945* (St. Catharines, ON: Vanwell, 2005), 85.
27. William Carter, "Anglo-Canadian Wartime Relations 1939–1945: RAF Bomber Command and No. 6 (Canadian) Group" (Ph.D. thesis, McMaster University, 1989), 122.
28. Greenhous et al., *The Crucible of War*, 51, 67.

29. Ibid., 36.
30. William Carr, Interview with Larry D. Rose, January 19, 2008.
31. Carter, *Anglo-Canadian*, 117.
32. Greenhous et al., *The Crucible of War*, 84.
33. Cook, *The Necessary War*, 310.
34. Ibid., 311.
35. Historical Section Army Headquarters, *Manpower Problems of the Royal Canadian Air Force During the Second World War, Report No. 67* (Ottawa: Dept. of National Defence, 1954), 32.
36. Iain Johnston, "The British Commonwealth Air Training Plan and the Shaping of National Identities in the Second World War," *Journal of Imperial and Commonwealth History*, Vol. 43, No. 5, 915.
37. Suzanne Edwards, "The Leadership of Air Marshal Harold (Gus) Edwards," *Canadian Aerospace Power Studies, Vol. 1*, 2009. www.airforce.gc.ca.
38. Greenhous et al., *The Crucible of War*, 82.
39. Carter, *Anglo-Canadian Wartime Relations, 1939–1945*, 168–83.
40. Bashow, *No Prouder Place*, 182.
41. Ibid., 115.
42. Richard Overy, *Bomber Command 1939–1945* (London: HarperCollins, 1997), 7.
43. Bashow, *No Prouder Place*, 130.
44. Nuttall, *Canadianization*, 351.
45. Ibid., 344.
46. See, for example, Greenhous et al., *The Crucible of War*, 44.
47. Johnston, "The British Commonwealth Air Training Plan," 916.

DECISION FIVE: APPOINTMENT OF THE MINISTER OF EVERYTHING

1. Robert Bothwell and William Kilbourn, *C.D. Howe: A Biography* (Toronto: McClelland & Stewart, 1979), 128.
2. J.L. Granatstein, "Arming the Nation: Canada's Industrial War Effort 1939–1945," written for the Canadian Council of Chief Executives, Ottawa, 2005, 4.

3. Matthew Bellamy, "The Rush for Rubber," *Legion*, January 28, 2012.
4. Maury Klein, *A Call to Arms: Mobilizing America for World War II* (New York, Bloomsbury Press, 2013), 234.
5. Klein, *A Call To Arms*, 235.
6. Ibid., 509.
7. Jeffrey Keshen, *Saints, Sinners and Soldiers: Canada's Second World War* (Vancouver: University of British Columbia Press, 2007), 97.
8. Howe did not enlist in the army or navy because he considered what he was doing to be vital war work.
9. Bothwell and Kilbourn, *C.D. Howe: A Biography*, 47.
10. Ibid., 79.
11. *Department of Munitions and Supply Act*, Statutes of Canada 3, George VI, Chapter 3. Assented to September 13, 1939, and proclaimed on April 9, 1940.
12. *National Resources Mobilization Act 1940*, Statutes of Canada 4, George VI, Chapter 13. Assented to June 21, 1940.
13. James Crandall, "Careful Attention Is Given Gigantic Task of Supplying Vital Needs for War Effort," *Hamilton Spectator*, August 30, 1940.
14. Bothwell and Kilbourn, *C.D. Howe: A Biography*, 153.
15. Peter C. Newman, *The Canadian Establishment*, vol. 1 (Toronto: McClelland & Stewart, 1975), 315.
16. Bothwell and Kilbourn, *C.D. Howe: A Biography*, 133.
17. Quoted in Robert Bothwell, "A Curious Lack of Proportion: Canadian Business and the War," in Sidney Aster, ed., *The Second World War as a National Experience* (Ottawa: Canadian Committee for the History of the Second World War, 1981), 27.
18. Frederick Gibson and Barbara Robertson, eds., *Ottawa At War: The Grant Dexter Memoranda 1939–1945*, vol. 11 (Winnipeg: Manitoba Record Society Publications, 1994), 67.
19. Figures from Granatstein, *Arming the Nation*, 10.
20. Robert Halford, *The Unknown Navy: Canada's World War II Merchant Navy* (St. Catharines, ON: Vanwell, 1995), 138.
21. Canadian vehicle production detailed in William Gregg, *Blueprint for Victory* (Rockwood, ON: Canadian Military Historical Society, 1981).
22. Granatstein, *Arming the Nation*, 9.

23. Ibid., 8.
24. J.L. Granatstein and Desmond Morton, *Canada and the Two World Wars* (Toronto: Key Porter, 2003), 193.
25. No author cited, "Manitoba Industrial Topics," Booklet (Winnipeg: Industrial Development Board of Manitoba, February 1942, Vol. 1 No. 10), 14 ff.
26. Bentley's personal story is remarkable. His family, the Bloch-Bauers, were owners of one of the largest sugar mills in Austria. Bentley changed his name after arriving in British Columbia. Other Bloch-Bauer family members gained international attention for their long and finally successful attempt to recover the famous Klimt painting *The Lady in Gold*.
27. Jay White, "Pulling Teeth: Striking for the Check Off in the Halifax Shipyard, 1944," *Acadiensis* XIX, no. 1 (Fall 1989), 116ff.; in Brian Palmer, ed., *The Character of Class Struggle: Essays in Canadian Working-Class History, 1850–1985* (Toronto: McClelland & Stewart, 1986).
28. David Roth, "A Union on the Hill" (master's thesis, Simon Fraser University, 1991).
29. Valerie Knowles, "Women's Work," *Legion*, May 15, 2012.
30. Richard Bourgeois-Doyle, *Her Daughter the Engineer: The Life of Elsie Gregory MacGill* (Ottawa: NRC Research Press, 2008).
31. Stephen Kimber, *Sailors, Slackers and Blind Pigs: Halifax at War* (Toronto: Doubleday, 2002), 159–66.
32. Keshen, *Saints, Sinners and Soldiers*, 160.
33. Granatstein, *Arming the Nation*, 8.
34. Bothwell and Kilbourn, *C.D. Howe: A Biography*, 32.
35. Gibson and Bentley, *Ottawa at War*, Dexter Memo, 63.
36. Hutchison, *The Incredible Canadian*, 266.
37. House of Commons *Debates*, February 26, 1941.
38. Newman, *The Canadian Establishment*, vol. 1, 327.
39. C.P. Stacey, *Canada in the Age of Conflict, Vol. 2, The Mackenzie King Era* (Toronto: University of Toronto Press, 1984), 316.
40. Later cabinet minister Mitchell Sharp commented that the civil servants were "active promoters of new ideas" in wartime Ottawa. J.L. Granatstein, *The Ottawa Men: The Civil Service Mandarins*

1935–1957 (Oakville, ON: Rock Mills Press, 2015), 246.
41. Bothwell and Kilbourn, *C.D. Howe*, 148.
42. Granatstein, *Arming the Nation*, 4.
43. Bothwell and Kilbourn, *C.D. Howe*, 350.
44. Hutchison, *Incredible Canadian*, 280.
45. Newman, *The Canadian Establishment Vol. 1*, 321.

DECISION SIX: THE OGDENSBURG AGREEMENT — CANADA TURNS TO AMERICA

1. R.G. Trotter and A.B. Corey, eds., *Proceedings of the Conference on Canadian-American Affairs, 1941* (Toronto: Ginn, 1941), 227.
2. King, *Diary*, May 24, 1940.
3. J.L. Granatstein, *How Britain's Weakness Forced Canada into the Arms of the United States* (Toronto: University of Toronto Press, 1989), 14; also see J.L. Granatstein, "Mackenzie King and Canada at Ogdensburg, August 1940," in Joel J. Sokolsky and Joseph T. Jockel, eds., *Fifty Years of Canada–United States Defense Cooperation* (Lewiston, NY: Edwin Mellen Press, 1992).
4. Walter Lippmann, "Wake Up America!" *Readers Digest*, July 1940. His comments were written before the final defeat of France and actually referred to both the British and French fleets.
5. P.B. Waite, *The Man from Halifax: Sir John Thompson, Prime Minister* (Toronto: University of Toronto Press, 1985), 357.
6. James Eayrs, *In Defence of Canada, Appeasement and Rearmament* (Toronto: University of Toronto Press, 1965), 176.
7. Aaron Plamondon, *Canada and the Ogdensburg Agreement: The Historical Analysis of a Logical Progression* (Kingston: Royal Military College of Canada, undated master's thesis).
8. *Ottawa Citizen*, August 19, 1938.
9. David Beatty, "The 'Canadian Corollary' to the Munroe Doctrine and the Ogdensburg Agreement of 1940," *Northern Mariner*, no. 1, January 1991, 4.
10. Tim Cook, *Warlords: Borden, Mackenzie King and Canada's World Wars* (Toronto: Penguin, 2012), 247.

11. Stanley Dziuban, *Military Relations Between the United States and Canada 1939-1945* (Washington, DC: Center for Military History, United States Army, 1990), 15.
12. Beatty, "The 'Canadian Corollary' to the Munroe Doctrine," 11.
13. Dziuban, *Military Relations*, 18.
14. Quoted in Granatstein, *How Britain's Weakness*, 27.
15. Beatty, "The 'Canadian Corollary' to the Munroe Doctrine," 12.
16. U.S. historian Stanley Dziuban concludes that surviving documents are simply not clear on who first suggested the meeting. See footnote in Dziuban, *Military Relations*, 21. Hugh Keenleyside claimed much later on that the meeting between King and Roosevelt was actually King's idea, sent to Washington via the U.S. minister. Stacey thought "it was evidently Mr. Roosevelt's own idea." *Arms, Men, and Governments* (Ottawa: Queen's Printer, 1970), 337n.
17. King, *Diary*, August 17, 1940.
18. Ibid.
19. Quoted in Stacey, *Arms, Men, and Governments*, 339.
20. Henry Stimson, *Diary*, August 17, 1940, Stimson Papers, Historical Manuscript Collection, 1940–1943, Yale University, quoted in Dziuban, *The Military Relations Between the United States and Canada*, 23–24.
21. Quoted in Stacey, *Arms, Men, and Governments*, 338–39.
22. Dziuban, *Military Relations Between the United States and Canada*, 25.
23. C.P. Stacey, "The Canadian-American Permanent Joint Board on Defence, 1940–1945," *International Journal* 9, no. 2 (1954): 112.
24. Stacey, *Arms, Men and Governments*, 340.
25. Hutchison, *Incredible Canadian*, 284.
26. Quoted in Granatstein, *How Britain's Weakness*, 30.
27. Quoted in J.L. Granatstein, "The Conservative Party and the Ogdensburg Agreement," *International Journal* 22, no. 1 (1966–67): 74.
28. Hutchison, *Incredible Canadian*, 283.
29. Cook, *Warlords*, 248.
30. Stacey, *Arms, Men and Governments*, 340.
31. George Grant, *Lament for a Nation* (Montreal: McGill-Queen's University Press, 1965).
32. Paul Romney, *Getting It Wrong: How Canadians Forgot Their Past and*

Imperilled Confederation (Toronto: University of Toronto Press, 1999), 236.
33. Donald Creighton, *Canada's First Century* (Toronto: Oxford University Press, 2012), 352–53.
34. "Bulky St. George," quoted in Granatstein, *How Britain's Weakness*, 23; "puppet" in Donald Creighton, *The Forked Road: Canada 1939–1957* (Toronto: McClelland & Stewart, 1976), 43.
35. Ibid., 44.
36. W.L. Morton, *Kingdom of Canada* (Toronto: McClelland & Stewart, 1963); Charles Lynch, *Ottawa Citizen*, December 18, 1974.
37. Greg Donaghy. *Tolerant Allies: Canada and the United States, 1963–1968* (Montreal: McGill-Queen's University Press, 2002), 4.
38. Granatstein, *How Britain's Weakness*, 3.
39. Ibid., 61.
40. Ibid., 3.
41. Ibid., 6.
42. Hutchison, *Incredible Canadian*, 284.
43. Stephane Roussel, *The North American Democratic Peace* (Montreal: McGill-Queen's University Press, 2004), 182.
44. Granatstein, *How Britain's Weakness*, 30.
45. Desmond Morton, *A Military History of Canada* (Toronto: McClelland & Stewart, 2007) 232.
46. A "symbol," the description of former Canadian PJBD secretary Ronald W. MacDonnell in letter to David Beatty, "The 'Canadian Corollary' to the Munroe Doctrine," 22.

DECISION SEVEN: DIEPPE

1. David O'Keefe, *One Day in August: The Untold Story Behind Canada's Tragedy at Dieppe* (Toronto: Knopf Canada, 2013). One skeptical review is that of Tim Cook, *Globe and Mail*, November 2, 2013.
2. Quoted in Philip Ziegler, *Mountbatten: The Official Biography* (London: Collins, 1985), 186.
3. Tim Cook, *Warlords: Borden, Mackenzie King and Canada's World Wars* (Toronto: Penguin, 2012), 290.

4. Arthur Bryant, *The Turn of the Tide* (New York: Doubleday, 1957), 300.
5. John A. English, *The Canadian Army in the Normandy Campaign: A Study of Failure in High Command* (Westport, CT: Praeger, 1991), 132.
6. Michelle McQuigge, Canadian Press, August 19, 2012.
7. The description in David Bercuson, *Our Finest Hour: Canada Fights the Second World War* (Toronto: HarperCollins, 2015), 93.
8. Nigel Hamilton, *Monty: The Making of a General 1887–1942* (New York: McGraw-Hill, 1981), 546–47.
9. C.P. Stacey, *Six Years of War: The Official History of the Canadian Army in the Second World War* (Ottawa: Queen's Printer, 1955), 399.
10. German records do not show that they were warned. After the war, Churchill stated unequivocally he believed that they were not warned. W.S. Churchill, *The Hinge of Fate Vol. 4, The Second World War* (Boston: Houghton Mifflin, 1950), 510. Stacey said the same in *Six Years of War*, 355. However, Stanley Lovell, in *Of Spies and Stratagems* (New York: Prentice-Hall, 1967) claims the Germans were warned by mistake by Britain's Secret Intelligence Service.
11. Catharine Goodier, *Blind Veterans UK Magazine.*
12. Brian Loring Villa, *Unauthorized Action* (Toronto: Oxford University Press, 1998), 16.
13. Robin Neillands, *The Dieppe Raid* (London: Aurum Press, 2005), 169.
14. Quoted in Paul Dickson, *A Thoroughly Canadian General* (Toronto: University of Toronto Press, 2007), 206.
15. Donald Wolfe, "The Memory Project," undated, www.thememoryproject.com/search/?query=dieppe.
16. Caroline D'Amours, "Les Fusiliers Mont-Real Au Debarquement De Dieppe" (master's thesis, Laval University, 2009), 37.
17. A good study of the tanks' role is in Hugh Henry, "The Calgary Tanks at Dieppe," *Canadian Military History Journal,* 4, no. 1, 1995, 61ff.
18. Alan Saunders, *Blind Veterans UK Magazine* (2013).
19. Neillands, *The Dieppe Raid*, 264.
20. Stacey, *Six Years of War*, 386.
21. Timothy Balzer, "In Case the Raid Is Unsuccessful …: Selling Dieppe to Canadians," *Canadian Historical Review* 87, no. 3, 412.

22. Villa, *Unauthorized Action*, 17.
23. John Keegan, *Six Armies in Normandy* (London: Jonathan Cape, 1982), 120–21.
24. Quoted in Villa, *Unauthorized Action*, 3.
25. Henry, "The Calgary Tanks at Dieppe," 70.
26. Lieutenant-Colonel James Goodman, "Operation *JUBILEE*: The Allied Raid on Dieppe (1942) — A Historical Analysis of a Planning Failure," Marine Corps University, Quantico, VA, March 6, 2008, v–20.
27. Neillands, *The Dieppe Raid*, 209.
28. Quoted in Goodman "Operation Jubilee," 20.
29. John S. Edmondson and R. Douglas Edmondson, "Memories and Reflections of the Dieppe Raid of 19 August 1942," *Canadian Military History Journal*, Autumn 2004, 48.
30. Neillands, *The Dieppe Raid*, 215.
31. Nigel Hamilton, *The Full Monty: Montgomery of Alamein 1887–1942* (London: Penguin, 2002), 441.
32. Philip Ziegler, *Mountbatten: The Official Biography* (London: Collins, 1985), 188.
33. Hamilton, *Monty: The Making of a General 1887–1942*, 546–47.
34. Villa, *Unauthorized Action*, 18.
35. Andrew Roberts, *Eminent Churchillians* (London: Weidenfeld & Nicholson, 1994), 67.
36. Winston Churchill, *The Second World War*, vols. 1–6 (London: HoughtonMifflen, 1948–53).
37. David Reynolds, *In Command of History* (New York: Random House, 2005), 345ff.
38. Villa's view has been challenged by British historian Peter Henshaw, who argued the commanders often deliberately did not write decisions down. "The Dieppe Raid: A Product of Misplaced Canadian Nationalism?" *Canadian Historical Review* 77, no. 2 (1996): 250–66; also Brian Villa and Peter Henshaw, "The Dieppe Raid Debate," *Canadian Historical Review* 79, no. 2 (1998): 304–15.
39. Roberts, *Eminent Churchillians*, 66.
40. Henshaw, "The Dieppe Raid: A Product of Misplaced Canadian Nationalism," 250ff.

41. Villa, *Unauthorized Action*, 191.
42. LAC, RG 24 Vol 10, Crerar to McNaughton, August 11, 1942, quoted in Dickson, *A Thoroughly Canadian General*, 205.
43. Henshaw, "The Dieppe Raid: A Product of Misplaced Canadian Nationalism," 250–66.
44. Villa, *Unauthorized Action*, 191.
45. Henshaw, "The Dieppe Raid: A Product of Misplaced Canadian Nationalism," 250–66. Also, for example, see Bercusson, *Our Finest Hour*, 93.
46. Dickson, *A Thoroughly Canadian General*, 209.
47. Granatstein, *The Generals*, 103.
48. J.L. Granatstein, "Dieppe: They Didn't Have to Die," *Legion*, July 1, 2012.

DECISION EIGHT: SIMONDS APPOINTED TO COMMAND II CANADIAN CORPS

1. Vokes in Granatstein, *The Generals*, 159.
2. Douglas Delaney, *Corps Commanders: Five British and Canadian Generals at War, 1939–1945* (Vancouver: University of British Columbia Press, 2011), 195.
3. E.A.C. Amy interview with Larry D. Rose, April 8, 2008.
4. "Did brilliantly" in Granatstein, *The Generals* 151; "outstanding," Dominick Graham, *Price of Command: A Biography of General Guy Simonds* (Toronto: Stoddart, 1993), 43.
5. See for example Captain G.G. Simonds, "An Army That Can Attack — A Division That Can Defend," *Canadian Defence Quarterly* 15, no. 4, (1938): 413. Simonds debated future warfare with Lieutenant-Colonel E.L.M. Burns, which was extraordinary considering both were future corps commanders.
6. Granatstein, *The Generals*, 72.
7. Roman Jarymowycz, "General Guy Simonds: The Commander as Tragic Hero," in Bernd Horn and Stephen Harris, eds., *Warrior Chiefs* (Toronto: Dundurn, 2001), 107–41.
8. Quoted in G.W.L. Nicholson, *The Canadians in Italy 1943–1945* (Ottawa: Minister of National Defence, 1956), 75.

9. *Winnipeg Free Press*, May 19, 1943, quoted in Granatstein, *The Generals*, 71.
10. Nicholson, *The Canadians in Italy*, 125–26.
11. Graham, *Price of Command*, 96; Geoffrey Hayes, "The Canadians in Sicily Sixty Years On," *Canadian Military History* 12, no. 3 (2003): 1–17.
12. Quoted in Granatstein, *The Generals*, 158.
13. John English, *The Canadian Army and the Normandy Campaign* (Mechanicsburg, Pennsylvania: Stackpole, 2009), 145.
14. Ibid.
15. In any event, McNaughton would never have served under Montgomery in Normandy because of what McNaughton called Monty's "well known arrogance." John Sweetenham, *McNaughton*, vol. 2 (Toronto: Ryerson, 1969), 334.
16. English, *The Canadian Army and the Normandy Campaign*, 146.
17. Paul Dickson, *A Thoroughly Canadian General: A Biography of General H.D.G. Crerar* (Toronto: University of Toronto Press, 2007), 222.
18. Jarrymowycz, "General Guy Simonds: The Commander as Tragic Hero," 114.
19. See Larry D. Rose, "Tank Ace Began Stellar Career in Normandy," Obituary of Brigadier-General Sydney Radley-Walters, *Globe and Mail*, April 23, 2015.
20. English, *The Canadian Army and the Normandy Campaign*, 141.
21. Tim Cook, *Fight to the Finish: Canadians in the Second World War 1944–1945*, vol. 2 (Toronto: Allen Lane, 2015), 250.
22. Jarymowicz, "General Guy Simonds: The Commander as Tragic Hero," 122.
23. Unnamed officer in Cook, *Fight to the Finish*, 254.
24. It was in this counterattack that one of Germany's greatest tank aces, Michael Wittmann was killed, likely by tanks of the Sherbrooke Fusilier Regiment.
25. Quoted in J.L. Granatstein, *Best Little Army in the World: The Canadians in Northwest Europe 1944–1945* (Toronto: HarperCollins, 2015), 115.
26. Cook, *Fight to the Finish*, 267; Chester Wilmot, *The Struggle for Europe* (London: Wordsworth Edition, 1997), 424.

27. Omar Bradley, *A General's Life: An Autobiography by General of the Army Omar N. Bradley* (New York: Simon and Schuster, 1983), 299.
28. Cook, *Fight to the Finish*, 264.
29. For example, Wilmot, *Struggle for Europe*, 424.
30. Granatstein, *Best Little Army in the World*, 122.
31. Wilmot, *Struggle for Europe*, 417–19.
32. Terry Copp, *Cinderella Army* (Toronto: University of Toronto Press, 2006), 5.
33. Larry D. Rose, "Six months. Three sons. All Dead," *National Post*, November 10, 2014. A fourth son, unable to enlist because of his medical history, survived, along with two daughters.
34. Jeffrey Williams, *The Long Left Flank: The Hard Fought Way to the Reich* (Toronto: Stoddart, 1988), 114–15.
35. Delaney, *Corps Commanders*, 234.
36. William "Bill" Davis, undated, www.thememoryproject.com/stories/70:william-bill-davis.
37. Copp, *Cinderella Army*, 178.
38. Ibid., 126.
39. Howard Hisdal, "Lieutenant-General Guy Simonds and the Battle of the Scheldt: A Study in Generalship" (master's thesis, Carleton University, 1994), 96ff.
40. Campaign description outlined in Granatstein, *Best Little Army in the World*, 136ff.; Cook, *Fight to the Finish*, 338ff.
41. Simonds was joined in advocating the bombing by the Naval Commander-in-Chief, Admiral Ramsey. Copp, *Cinderella Army*, 88.
42. Brigadier Ted Beament quoted in Granatstein, *Best Little Army*, 144.
43. Williams, *The Long Left Flank*, 118.
44. Delaney, *Corps Commanders*, 246.
45. Stephen A. Hart, *Second World War 60th Anniversary: The Clearing of the Scheldt Estuary*, no. 8 (London: U.K. Ministry of Defence, 2004), 6.
46. Delaney, *Corps Commanders*, 247.
47. Mark Zuehlke, "A Perfectly Engineered Killing Ground," *Journal of Military and Strategic Studies* 16, no. 3 (2015): 64ff.

48. Bernard Montgomery, *Memoirs of Field Marshal Montgomery* (London: Collins Edition, 1958), 294.
49. Ibid., 294–95.
50. Delaney, *Corps Commanders*, 250.
51. Graham, *Price of Command*, 189.
52. John English, *Lament for an Army: The Decline of Canadian Military Professionalism* (Toronto: Irwin, 1988), 44.
53. Brian Horrocks, *A Full Life* (London: Collins, 1960), 254.
54. Granatstein, *The Generals*, 145–78.
55. Graham, *The Price of Command*, 151. Interestingly, Graham said in Sicily Simonds "had an artilleryman's mindset," p.94.
56. English, *The Canadian Army and the Normandy Campaign*, 45ff.
57. Cook, *Fight to the Finish*, 275–76.
58. Ibid., 276.
59. "Superb," Granatstein, *Best Little Army in the World*, 238; "acme of Canadian generalship," Jarymowicz, "General Guy Simonds: The Commander as Tragic Hero," 128; "brilliant examples," Copp, *Cinderella Army*, 289.
60. Hisdal, "Lieutenant-General Guy Simonds and the Battle of the Scheldt: A Study in Generalship," 96ff.
61. Cook, *Fight to the Finish*, 264.
62. Jarymowycz, "General Guy Simonds: The Commander as Tragic Hero," 107.
63. Brigadier James Roberts quoted in Granatstein, *The Generals*, 265.
64. Granatstein, *The Generals*, 172–73.
65. Jarymowycz, "General Guy Simonds: The Commander as Tragic Hero," 107.
66. Graham, *Price of Command*, 2.
67. Delaney, *Corps Commanders*, 22.
68. Granatstein, *The Generals*, 172.
69. Ibid.

DECISION NINE: THE GREATEST POLITICAL CRISIS OF THE WAR

1. Barry Broadfoot, *Six Years of War, 1939–1945: Memories of Canadians at Home and Abroad* (Toronto: Doubleday, 1974), 334–35.
2. Reginald Roy, *Ready for the Fray* (Vancouver: Evergreen Press, 1958), 147–48.
3. The treatment was probably common but not universal. Recruits from Le Régiment de Hull in Nanaimo, B.C., learned some English and were generally welcomed. Daniel Byers, *Zombie Army* (Vancouver: University of B.C. Press, 2016), 156–57.
4. The term "Big Army" was first used by Grant Dexter of the *Winnipeg Free Press* in 1941. The question covered in detail in Richard Walker "The Revolt of the Canadian Generals, 1944: The Case for the Prosecution," in Howard Coombs, ed., *The Insubordinate and the Noncompliant* (Toronto: Dundurn, 2007).
5. J.L. Granatstein and J.M. Hitsman, *Broken Promises: A History of Conscription In Canada* (Toronto, Oxford University Press, 1977), 156.
6. R. MacGregor Dawson, *The Conscription Crisis of 1944* (Toronto: University of Toronto Press, 1961), 28. Dawson was a noted political scientist. He intended to write a multi-volume biography of King and was given access to King's vast archive. However, Dawson died after writing the volume on the conscription crisis.
7. E.L.M. Burns, *Manpower in the Canadian Army 1939–1945* (Toronto: Clark, Irwin, 1956), 28.
8. Walker, "The Revolt of the Canadian Generals, 1944," 61.
9. Ibid., 63.
10. Ibid., 70.
11. Quoted in Ibid., 57.
12. Ibid., 61.
13. Ibid., 64–65.
14. King, *Diary*, December 3, 1941.
15. Grant Dexter Memorandum, January 12, 1942, Dexter Papers, Queen's University.
16. Dexter Memorandum, January 12, 1942.

17. Walker, "The Revolt of the Canadian Generals, 1944," 71.
18. Granatstein and Hitsman, *Broken Promises*, 158.
19. J.L. Granatstein, *Conscription in the Second World War 1939-1945* (Toronto: McGraw-Hill Ryerson, 1969), 36.
20. *Canadian Forum* 21(December 1941), 260.
21. House of Commons *Debates*, May 12, 1941.
22. Quoted in Granatstein and Hitsman, *Broken Promises*, 162.
23. Granatstein, *Conscription in the Second World War*, 45.
24. Ibid., 42.
25. Quoted in Granatstein, *Canada's War*, 243.
26. Tim Cook, *Warlords*, 287.
27. According to the Minutes quoted in Granatstein and Hitsman, *Broken Promises*, 210.
28. Granatstein, *Best Little Army In The World* (Toronto: HarperCollins, 2015), 128–29.
29. Terry Copp, *Cinderella Army* (Toronto: University of Toronto Press, 2006), 9.
30. Granatstein, *Best Little Army in the World*, 129.
31. J.L. Granatstein, *Weight of Command* (Vancouver: University of British Columbia Press, 2016), 76, 98.
32. Kitching in Granatstein, *Weight of Command*, 38, 82; Megill in Granatstein, *Best Little Army*, 130.
33. Burns, *Manpower in the Canadian Army 1939-1945*.
34. Ibid., 18. To some extent the U.S. formations had fewer administrative troops because their number could be divided over a large number of divisions while the Canadian army was much smaller.
35. Dawson, *The Conscription Crisis of 1944*, 32–33.
36. Granatstein and Hitsman, *Broken Promises*, 195.
37. In Granatstein, *Weight of Command*, 48.
38. English, *The Canadian Army in the Normandy Campaign*, 45.
39. Granatstein and Hitsman, *Broken Promises*, 194.
40. Various figures are used. Of course the number at any one time did not match the total number. The figures are from C.P. Stacey, *The Canadian Army 1939-1945: An Official Historical Summary* (Ottawa: King's Printer, 1948), 324.

41. Byers, *Zombie Army*, 187.
42. King, *Diary*, October 13, 1944.
43. James Eayrs, *In Defence of Canada, Peacemaking and Deterrence* (Toronto: University of Toronto Press, 1972), 14.
44. Hutchison, *Incredible Canadian*, 358.
45. Ibid., 355.
46. Walker, "The Revolt of the Canadian Generals, 1944," 78.
47. Granatstein and Hitsman, *Broken Promises*, 223.
48. Quoted in Granatstein, *Conscription in the Second World War 1939–1945*, 32. That number was about fifteen thousand higher than French-Canadian enlistments in 1916.
49. Byers, *Zombie Army*, 128.
50. Reginald Roy, *For Most Conspicuous Bravery* (Vancouver: University of British Columbia Press, 1977), 215.
51. Ibid., 225.
52. *Globe and Mail*, November 21, 1944.
53. King, *Diary*, November 20, 1944.
54. Roy, *For Most Conspicuous Bravery*, 226.
55. Dawson, *The Conscription Crisis of 1944*, 85.
56. *Globe and Mail*, November 7, 1944.
57. Granatstein and Hitsman, *Broken Promises*, 229.
58. King, *Diary*, November 22, 1944.
59. The officer who made the statement was identified later as Major-General Hugh Young. Hutchison, *Far Side of the Street* (Toronto: Macmillan, 1976), 225–26.
60. Walker, "The Revolt of the Canadian Generals, 1944."
61. Dawson, *The Conscription Crisis of 1944*, 90–91.
62. Walker adds "even outrageously" in "The Revolt of the Canadian Generals 1944," 86.
63. Granatstein, *Canada's War*, 367.
64. J.W. Pickersgill, a long-time aide to King, believed that, except for Pearkes, the army did not conspire or revolt. J.L. Granatstein, *Weight of Command*, 209.
65. Hutchison, *Incredible Canadian*, 375.
66. Figures in Ibid., 398.

67. Copp, *Cinderella Army*, 179, 297.
68. Cook, *Warlords*, 335.
69. Stacey, *The Canadian Army 1939–1945*, 235.

DECISION TEN: FROM WAR TO PEACE

1. Quoted in Bruce Campion-Smith, *Toronto Star*, May 5, 2015.
2. Lisa Banister, ed., *Equal to the Challenge* (Ottawa: Department of National Defence, 2001), 21.
3. *Globe and Mail*, May 9, 1945.
4. David Goss, *New Brunswick Telegraph-Journal*, May 6, 2005.
5. Keshen, "Getting It Right the Second Time Around: The Re-Integration of Canadian Veterans of World War II," in *The Veterans Charter and Post-World War II Canada*, eds. Peter Neary and J.L. Granatstein (Montreal: McGill-Queen's University Press, 1998,) 63.
6. Keshen, "Getting It Right the Second Time Around," 62–94.
7. William Lyon Mackenzie King, *Industry and Humanity: A Study in the Principles of Industrial Reconstruction* (Toronto: Thomas Allen, 1918).
8. Granatstein, *Canada's War*, 211–12. Despite the fact that Mackenzie King signed the authorization to remove the Japanese, he was far more tolerant than most of his contemporaries.
9. Ibid., 249–54.
10. Raymond Blake, *From Rights to Needs: A History of Family Allowances in Canada 1929–1992* (Vancouver: University of British Columbia Press, 2009), 53.
11. Ibid., 53.
12. Robert Bothwell, Ian Drummond, and John English, *Canada Since 1945: Power, Politics and Provincialism* (Toronto: University of Toronto Press, 1989), 68.
13. *Canadian Forum* 12 (1943), 292. The magazine was a platform for many leftist writers including Frank Underhill and F.R. Scott.
14. *Toronto Telegram*, September 17, 1943; Granatstein, *Canada's War*, 261.
15. Ibid., 250.

16. Frederick Gibson and Barbara Robertson, *Ottawa at War: The Grant Dexter Memoranda, 1939–1945* (Winnipeg: Manitoba Records Society, 1984), Memorandum, September 17, 1944, 480.
17. Alvin Finkel, *Social Policy and Practise in Canada: A History* (Waterloo, ON: University of Waterloo Press, 2006), 127.
18. Granatstein, *Canada's War*, 250.
19. Ibid., 275.
20. Humphrey Mitchell, CBC Trans-Canada Network broadcast, July 30, 1945.
21. The unnamed officer's description in J. Marteinson, *The Governor General's Horse Guards: Second to None* (Toronto: Robin Bass Studio, 2002), 250–51.
22. Keshen, *Saints, Sinners and Soldiers*, 29.
23. Russ Bannock, e-mail to author, October 24, 2016.
24. Mac Johnston, *Corvettes Canada*, (Mississauga, ON: Wiley, 2008), 220.
25. George MacDonell, *One Soldier's Story* (Toronto: Dundurn, 2002), 157; interview with Larry D. Rose, March 31, 2011.
26. Jeff Keshen, "Getting It Right the Second Time Around," 67.
27. Bill Milne, interview with Larry D. Rose, October 28, 2016.
28. Cook, *Fight to the Finish*, 420.
29. Ibid., 422.
30. Keshen, *Saints, Sinners, and Soldiers*, 273.
31. Farley Mowat, *And No Bird Sang* (Toronto: McClelland & Stewart, 1979).
32. Cook, *Fight to the Finish*, 420.
33. Keshen, *Saints, Sinners, and Soldiers*, 269.
34. Ibid., 167.
35. John Boileau, "Canada's Merchant Navy: The Men That Saved the World," *Legion*, July 14, 2010.
36. The main argument against merchant mariners was that they were civilians, not members of the armed forces. Typical of the experiences was that of merchant sailor Clayton Stones, who had hearing difficulties and went to a veterans' facility in 1946, where he was told, "You guys are only … civilians." Stones had volunteered for the navy but was turned down because his work as a sailor was considered

vital to the war. Matthew Moore, "The Kiss of Death Bestowed with Gratitude: The Postwar Treatment of Canada's Second World War Merchant Navy" (master's thesis, Carleton University, 2015), 58.
37. Banister, ed., *Equal to the Challenge*, 169.
38. Granatstein, *Canada's War*, 277.
39. Bothwell et al., *Canada Since 1945*, 65.
40. *Maple Leaf*, October 2, 1944.
41. Dexter, in Granatstein, *Canada's War*, 265.
42. Ibid., 403.
43. Ibid., 397.
44. Ibid., 406.
45. Cook, *Warlords*, 335.
46. There had been many strikes during the war, but patriotism had held others back. Also, union membership during the war years doubled. Many union members felt it was time to regain wages and benefits lost during the Depression.
47. Keshen, *Saints, Sinners and Soldiers*, 286.
48. Cook, *Fight to the Finish*, 419.

CONCLUSION: THE NEW CANADA

1. Granatstein, *Canada's War*, 421.
2. Morton quoted in Ingrid Perlitz, *Globe and Mail*, November 8, 2013. Morton was specifically referring to Quebec, but the comments could apply to the entire country.
3. Cook, *Fight to the Finish*, 434.
4. Dan McCaffery, *Dad's War* (Toronto: James Lorimer, 2004), 217.
5. P.J. Rawlinson to Norman Rogers, 11 January 1940, 5168-803, RG 12, vol. 2332, Library and Archives Canada. Quoted in "The British Commonwealth Air Training Plan," *Veterans Affairs Canada*, www.veterans.gc.ca/eng/remembrance/history/second-world-war/british-commonwealth-air-training-plan.
6. Granatstein, *The Generals*, xiii.
7. Stacey, *Six Years of War*, 3.
8. J.L. Granatstein, e-mail to Larry D. Rose, January 15, 2017.

9. Stephanie Bangarth, quoted in Stephen Azzi and Norman Hillmer, "Ranking Canada's Best and Worst Prime Ministers," *Maclean's*, October 7, 2016.
10. Ibid. The article divides prime ministers into "short-term" and "long-serving" categories. It lists King as first among the long-serving prime ministers, with Laurier second and Sir John A. Macdonald third. The lists were compiled from responses by 123 scholars and journalists.
11. Allan Levine, *King: William Lyon Mackenzie King: A Life Guided by the Hand of Destiny* (Vancouver: Douglas & McIntyre, 2011), 404.
12. Granatstein, *Canada's War*, 422.
13. Cook, *Fight to the Finish*, 435.
14. Quoted in Azzi and Hillmer, *Maclean's*.

IMAGE CREDITS

Author's collection: 104

BCATP Museum: 74 (top), 80

Bomber Command Museum: 88

Brigadier-General Garry Thomson: 173

Canadian Science and Technology Museum: 245

City of Toronto Archives: 236

Directorate of History and Heritage: 157

Lenore Wagner Floyd Collection: 193 (top and bottom)

Library and Archives Canada: 29, 31, 38, 48, 62, 114, 130, 136, 153, 172 (left and right), 182, 198, 247

McCord Museum: 210

Mike Bechthold: 186, 195

Penwill Family Collection: 82

Public domain: 74 (bottom), 124

INDEX

Abbott, Doug, 253
Acadia, HMCS, 47
Adams, Ernie, 42
air cover, for the Atlantic, 60
aircraft, 72–73, *74*, 76, 78, *80*, *88*, 96, 103, *104*, 105, 121–23, 125, 251
aircraft carriers, 45
Alaska highway, 134–35
Alberni, HMCS, 50, 57, 59
Algoma, HMCS, 51
Algonquin Regiment, 189
aluminum, 124, 126
Ambler, HMCS, 47
Amherst, HMCS, 51
amphibian vehicles, *198*
Amy, Ned, 176
anti-war activism. *See* pacifism
appeasement, 32, 34, 37
Ark Royal, 45
armoured vehicles, 123, 187
arms production, 116–17, 119, 128
Armstrong Whitworth Atlas (plane), 16
army, 132, 156, 177, 180–81, 209, 218–21, 225
  and conscription, 207–08, 225–26
  encouragement to enlist in, 83, 206–08, 222
  plans for, 211–12
  shortage, 218–20
  statistics, 15
Army Council, 228
army officers, problems with, 15
asdic. *See* sonar
Athenia, SS, 45
Athlone, Earl of, 140
Austria, 30, 32
avoidance, as policy, 17–18, 30, 35

Baddeck, HMCS, 58
Bailey, John, 107–08
Balfour, Harold, 95
Bangarth, Stephanie, 260
Bannock, Russ, 70, 77, 86, 244–45
Barnes, Morley, 63
Barter, George, 86
Bashow, David, 99
Battle of Berlin, 103
Battle of Britain, 132

Battle of the Atlantic, 42–43, 154, 248–49
Battle of the Scheldt, 192–93, *195*, 196–200, 203
Battleford, HMCS, *48*, 61
Beatty, David, 139
Beetham, Michael, 106
Bell, Ralph, 122
Bennett, Richard B., 25, 28, 239
Bentley, Poldi, 125, 273n26
Berlin, *31*
Bessey, Jim, 244
Bethune, Norman, 27
Beveridge, William, 241
Biggar, Oliver, 145
Birney, Earle, 247
Black Watch, 163, 184, 200–01
Blaskowitz, Johannes, 235
Borden, Robert, 23–24
Bracken, John, 254
Bradley, Omar, 191
Brandon, Tom, 246–47
Bras d'Or, HMCS, 47
Breadner, Lloyd, 92, 95, 101, 102
Bren guns, 128, 218, 236
Brennan, Patrick, 261
Britain
    Canada and, 21, 259
    Canadians in, 98–99
    intelligence from, 35
    shipbuilding, 46–48
British 11th Armoured Division, 191
British 52nd Division, 201
British Army
    No. 3 Commando, 162
    No. 4 Commando, 162
British Columbia, 214
    Vancouver, 40, 236
    Victoria, 40–41
British Columbia Tank Regiment, 189

British Commonwealth Air Training Plan (BCATP), 65, 67–68, 71, 76, 79–85, 90–92, 121, 132, 257
Brooke, Alan, 155, 170, 177
Brookes, George, 103
Brophy, Pat, 108
Bruce, Herbert, 214
Bruce, Stanley, 66
Buchan, John, 21–22n
Burns, Tommy, 209, 220
    Manpower in the Canadian Army 1939–1945, 220
Burrard Dry Dock Ltd., 55, 248
Burwash, Ray, 64

Cadbury, Egbert, 71
Cagney, James, 73, *74*
Calgary Highlanders, 192, 194, 201
Calgary Regiment, 165, 178
Camp Borden, 77, 245
Campbell, Archibald, 99
Campbelltown, HMS, 152
Canada, 65
    citizenship in, 258
    declaration of war, 21–23, 49
    employment in, 122, 125–26, 131
    flag of, 16
    government during the war, 19, 117–18, 126–30, 143, 207, 225–32, 242–43, 251–52, 256–57
    National Research Council, 49
    political parties in, 28–29, 130, 242, 253–54
    population of, 16, 221–22
    prairies, 81
    rearmament of, 32, 34, 45–46
    and the U.S., 133–35, 139–42, 145–48

Canada 1922–1939: Decades of Discord (Thompson and Seager), 25
Canada's First Century (Creighton), 147
Canadian Army and the Normandy Campaign, The (English), 15
Canadian Bomber Group, 102–03
Canadian Forum, 214, 241
Canadian Institute of International Affairs, 139
Canadian Merchant Marine, 248–49
Canadian Military Pattern (CMP) trucks, 123, *124*
Canadian Scottish Regiment, 198
Canadian Vickers, 55
Canadianization, 88–89, 93–95, 97–100, 108–09
Captains of the Clouds (film), 73, *74*
Carey, N.T., 27
Cariboo, HMCS, 47
Carmichael, Harry, 119
Carr, William, 99–100
Carrington, Charles, 168
cars, *245*
Cartier, HMCS, 47
Casa Maury, Marquis "Bobby" de, 169
Case, Gordon, 40
casualties, 192, 220
    Battle of the Scheldt, 196, 200, 202
    Black Watch Regiment, 163, 184, 200
    Bomber Command, 82, 106–07
    Dieppe raid, 151, 163, 166, 168, 170
    Operation Spring, 184
    Operation Totalize, 189
    Operation Tractable, 189–91
    overall, 258
    in RCAF training, 79–80

Regina Rifles Regiment, 199
Sicily, 179
Catto, Douglas, 163
Chamberlain, Neville, 31–33, 37, 39, 66
Chambly, HMCS, 58–59
Chapman, J.K., 100, 245–46
Cheshire, Leonard, 107
Chevrier, Lionel, 253
Chicago Tribune, 138
Chilliwack, HMCS, 61
Church, Tommy, 100
churches, on WWII, 26–27, 37
Churchill, Winston, 33, 37, 50, 133, 138, 144–45, 154–55, 170, 254
    Second World War, The, 171
Clark, Clifford, 129
Clark, Gregory, 24
Claxton, Brooke, 243
Co-operative Commonwealth Federation (CCF), 28–29, 215, 239, 242, 254
Cold War, the, 254
Coldwell, M.J., 130
Collingwood Shipyard, 46, 48, 55
Collins, Robert, 98–99
conscription, 233
    English Canada on, 207, *210*, 215, 224–25
    French Canada on, 22, 36, 215, 224–25
    plebiscite on, 215–16
    WWI and, 19, 23–24, 214
    WWII and, 17, 20, 26, 36, 39, 40, 207–08, 213, 217–18, 223–25, 229–32, 254
convoys
    Arctic, 160–61
    corvettes escorting, 53, 56, 58–61, 63

sinkings of, 56, 59, 161
Cook, Tim, 137, 146, 153, 185, 191, 203, 217, 234, 254
Copp, Terry, 233
corvettes, *48*, 49–58, 63–64, 117, 123
Coughlin, Charles, 27
Cousins, Howard, 51
Creighton, Donald, 147
    Canada's First Century, 147
Crerar, Harry, 159–60, 171, *172*, 173–74, 176, 180–81, 184–85, 202, 204, 209, 211
Croil, George, 90, 92
Currie, David, 190
Curry, Frank, 58, 60–61, 64
Curtis, Wilfred, 96, 98
Czechoslovakia, 32–33, 36–37

D-Day, 180–81, 183–84
Dad's War (McCaffrey), 257
Dafoe, J.W., 33–34, 41, 264*n*16
    "What's the Cheering For?," 33–34
Davie Shipbuilding, 46, 54–55, 57
Dawson, R. MacGregor, 209, 221, 230, 283*n*6
Decades of Discord. See *Canada 1922–1939: Decades of Discord*
declaration of war, 21–23, 35–36, 49
defeat, planning for possible, 133
Delaney, Douglas, 199
Department of Munitions and Supply, 117–18, 129
depth charges, 51–52, 60*n*, 61
desertion, 232
destroyers, 15, 43, 45–47, 53, 61, 123
    tribal class, 46, 53
    See also individual ships
destroyers-for-bases, 56, 141, 145
Deutsch, John, 129

Dexter, Grant, 116, 121, 213, 221, 253
Diefenbaker, John, 130, 146
Dieppe, 192
Dieppe raid, 151–52, *153*, *157*, 158–60, 162–71, *173*, 174, 277*n*10, 278*n*38
Dill, John, 155
disarmament, 25
"dollar-a-year" men, 119, *130*
Donitz, Karl, 45, 56
Douglas, Tommy, 242
Drew, George, 252
Dufferin Shipbuilding, 55
Duisberg, 87–88
Duncan, Andrew, 120
Duplessis, Maurice, 27, 251–52

Easton, Alan, 58
Edmonson, John, 169
Edward VIII, King, 25
Edwards, Gus, 96–102, 108
Edwards, James "Stocky," 86
"Edwards controversy," 101–02
elections, 116, 133, 138, 147, 215–16, 223, 241–42, 252–53
Elizabeth, Queen (wife of George VI), 16, 41
England, Les, 167
English Canada, 16, 18
    on conscription, 207, 233
    on declaration of war, 22, 30–31, 36
    support for Britain, 25, 36, 41
English, John, 15, 202
    Canadian Army and the Normandy Campaign, The, 15
English, Robert, 73, 79, *82*, 86
Essex Scottish, 151, 156, 164–65, 220, 244

expansion
    naval problems with, 42–44
    of the RCAF, 73, 77–78, 83, 121
    RCN vs. Britain and the U.S., 62–63

fake guns, 42–43
Falaise Gap, 185, 189–91
Fauquier, John, 108
5th Canadian Armoured Division, 180
51st Infantry Division, *186*
53rd Division, 191
59th Division, 191
Financial Post, 27, 129
Finestone, Bernard, 246
First Canadian Army, 185, 190, 192, 196, 202, 219–21, 233, 258
1st Canadian Army Tank Brigade, 177
1st Canadian Division, 177, 180–81, 235
1st Polish Armoured Division, 185, *186*, 188, 190
First World War, 15, 21, 100, 115–16, 205
    Canadian air force in, 89
    numbers of dead, 24
    riots and, 22–24
    veterans, 238
Fishermen's Reserve, 16
flails, 187–88
    See also tanks
Foote, John, 164
Fort Cataraqui, 202
Fort Romaine, 123
49th Infantry Division, *186*
Foulkes, Charles, 184–85, 235
4th Armoured Division, 183–85, *186*, 188, 197, 199, 200
Fox, Charley, 79, 86
France, 76, 92, 104–05, 118, 158
    Vimy Memorial, 24–25
Franceschini, James, 55

French Canada, 225
    declaration of war and, 23, 35–36
    King's government and, 18, 28–29
    on war in Europe, 16–17, 27, 30, 34, 37
frigates, 61
Fulton, John "Moose," 94, 107
Fulton, Ken, 73

Galloway, Strome, 156
Garrod, A.G.R., 84
Generals, The (Granatstein), 203
George VI, King, 16, 30, 137, 263*n*3
German, Tony, 44
Germany, 104–05
    blitzkrieg, 55–56
    Duisberg raids, 87–88
    Kriegsmarine, 44–45
Gilfouy, Ella, 127
Globe and Mail, 22, 39, 100, 213, 218–19, 229
Goebbels, Joseph, 106
Gordon, David, 257
Gordon, Walter, 241, 255
Gouzenko, Igor, 254
Graham, Frank, 235
Graham, Howard, 179
Granatstein, J.L., 41, 112, 146, 148–49, 174, 191, 203, 205, 213, 231, 260–61
    Generals, The, 203
    How Britain's Weakness Forced Canada into the Arms of the United States, 148–49
Grant, George, 146–47
    Lament for a Nation, 146, 147
Grant, Harold, 57
Gray, Hampton, 37, *38*
Great Depression, the, 17, 28, 46, 65, 125, 238

Great Pipeline Debate, 130
ground crews, 65, 82, 88, 88–89, 93, 95, 98, 108
guns
    fake, 42–43
    WWI, 52

Haase, Konrad, 152
Halifax, HMCS, 61
Halifax, Nova Scotia, 43, 236–37
Hamilton, Henry, 22
Hamilton, Nigel, 158, 170
Hanson, Richard, 144, 207, 213*n*
Harris, Arthur, 78, 89, 98, 101, 103–04, 158
Harvie, Allan, 248–49
Hedgehog weapons, 60
Hellayer, Paul, 83
Hendsbee, Dorothy, 127
Hennessey, Ralph, 44
Hepatica, HMCS, 42–43
Hepburn, Mitch, 112
Heydte, Augustus von der, 199
Hickson, G.A., 167
Hings, Donald, 249
Hitler, Adolf, 22–23, 27, 30–31, 36–37
Hobart, Percy, 202
Hoffmeister, Bert, 204
Horrocks, Brian, 177, 203–04, 260
Houde, Camillien, 207
How Britain's Weakness Forced Canada into the Arms of the United States (Granatstein), 148–49
Howe, C.D., 19, 111–13, *114*, 115–16, 118–20, 124, 126–31, 212, 249, 251, 260
Husky, HMCS, 47
Hutchinson, Bruce, 17, 39, 40, 128, 131, 145, 230
Hyde Park Agreement, 150

Ilsley, James, 128
Industry and Humanity (King), 239
isolationism, 25–28, 37, 138, 144

James, Cyril, 241
Japan, 214
Jarymowycz, Roman, 204
Johnston, Iain, 109–10
Jones, G.C. "Jetty," 44

Kamsack, HMCS, 57–58, 61, 64
Keegan, John, 168
Keenleyside, Hugh, 139
Keller, Rod, 184, 188
Kennedy, Lionel, 42
Kenogami, HMCS, 59, 61
Kent, Johnny, 89–90
Keshen, Jeff, 238
Kincardine, HMCS, 63
King, Carlyle, 26
King, William Lyon Mackenzie, 17–18, 21, 21–22*n*, 28, *29*, 30, *31*, 32–35, 38–41, 45–46, 53–54, 66, 89–91, 111–12, 126, 128, 131–34, *136*, 137–42, 144–46, 156, 178, 206, 212–13, 215–17, 222, 227–34, 239, 242, 253–54, 260
    Industry and Humanity, 239
    Kingdom of Canada (Morton), 147
Kitching, George, 191, 220
Krupp armament works, 105–06, 116

Labatt, Robert, 167
LaGuardia, Fiorello, 145
LaMarsh, Judy, 247–48
Lament for a Nation (Grant), 146, 147
LaPlante, Jacqueline, 236
Lapointe, Ernest, 18–19, 22, 33, 35, 36, 39–40, 217
Laurier, Wilfrid, 18, 35

Lawrence, Hal, *62*
Lay, Robert, 140
Le Devoir, 34
Lea, USS, 62
League of Nations, 29–30
Leckie, Robert, 70–71, 84
Leese, Oliver, 179–80
Leigh-Mallory, Trafford, 98
Les Fusiliers Mont-Royal, 165
Letson, Harry, 224
Lincoln and Welland Regiment, 190
Lippman, Walter, 133
Luke, E.C., 71–72
Lynch, Charles, 147–48

Macdonald, Angus, 19, 213, 223, 253
MacDonell, George, 244, 246
Macdonnell, J.M., 242
MacFarlane, R.A., 229
MacGill, Elsie, 127, 260
MacKenzie, Andy, 73, 75
Mackenzie, Ian, 30, 240–41
Macklin, Wilfred, 225–26
Maclean's, 25, 118, 238
MacMillan, H.R., 128–30
Macpherson, Ken, 59
Magee, John Gillespie, 75–76
Manion, Robert, 39, 213*n*
Manning, Ralph, 79–80
Manpower in the Canadian Army 1939–1945 (Burns), 220
Marine Industries Ltd., 55
Marsh, Leonard, 241
  Report on Social Security for Canada, 241
Marston, Joe, 58
Martin, Paul, 253
Massey, Vincent, 66
Matthews, Bruce, 221
May, Doug, 63

McCaffrey, Dan, 257
  Dad's War, 257
McCaffrey, James, 257
McCool, Brian, 152, 168
McEwen, Mike, 103
McNaughton, Andy, 159, 171, *172*, 174, 176–77, 181, 183, 224, 226, 228, 232–33
McVicar, Hugh, 222
Megill, Bill, 220
Meighen, Arthur, 144, 213–16, 225
Melville, Saskatchewan, 40
Merrett, Cecil, 164
Meyer, Kurt, 188
Military Service Act, 23–24
Miller-William, Denis, 85
Milne, Bill, 83, 245
Milner, Mark, 47, 59, 61, 63
minesweepers, 15, 43, 48, 55
minorities, in Canada, 17, 225
Minton, Saskatchewan, 17
Mitchell, Humphrey, 243
Moffat, Jay Pierrepont, 140, 144
Moncel, Robert, 183
Montgomery, Bernard, 158–60, 175, 179, 181, 184, 191, 199, 202
Montreal, Quebec, 23
Montreal Gazette, 101
Moose Jaw, HMCS, 59
Morgan, Frederick, 159
Morrison, Les, 100
Morton, Desmond, 23, 34, 150, 256
Morton, W.L., 147
  Kingdom of Canada, 147
Mountbatten, Louis "Dickie," 155–56, 158, 160–61, 170–71
Mowat, Farley, *247*
multiculturalism, 17
Munich Crisis, 32–33
Munro, Ross, 163, 168

Murchie, John, 228–31, 233
Murphy, Harvey, 126
Murray, L.W., 20, 49, 54–55, 237
Mussolini, Benito, 27, 30
mutinies, 232
Mynarski, Andrew, *88*, 108

Napanee, HMCS, 61
National Resources Mobilization Act (NRMA), 118, 207
Naval Colleges, 44
navigational improvements, 78
Neatby, Blair, 34
Neillands, Robin, 168
Nelles, Percy, 46, 49–50, 53, 54
Nelson, HMS, 45
Newman, Peter C., 111*n*, 120
nickel, 124
1942 Civil Employment Act, 248
North Shore Regiment, 189
Nova Scotia, Halifax, 43
NRMA recruits, 226–27, 231–33
Nuttall, Leslie, 91, 109

Oakville, HMCS, 61–62
O'Connor, Richard, 260
Ogdensburg, New York, 140
Ogdensburg Agreement, 141–46, 148–50, 259, 275*n*16
Old Age Pension Act, 239
O'Leary, Gratton, 129–30
Ontario Regiment, 178
Operation Atlantic, 184
Operation Husky, 177
Operation Jubilee, 161–62, 168, 171–73
Operation Market Garden, 194, 196, 199
Operation Overlord, 183
Operation Spring, 184
Operation Switchback, 197

Operation Totalize, 185, *186*, 187–89, 203–04
Operation Tractable, 189–90
Orillia, HMCS, 59
Ottawa, Ontario, 237
Ottawa Citizen, 101
Ottawa Journal, 101, 232

pacifism, 25–28
Padlock Law (1937), 27
patriotic groups, 25
Pearkes, George, 226–27, 230
Pearl Harbor, 214
Pearson, Lester B., 132
Permanent Joint Board on Defence, 141–42, 145–46
Perry, Bill, 57
Piat anti-tank guns, 219
Pickersgill, Jack, 242
Poland, 41
Polk, James, 133
Poltoon, Jack, 174
Polymer Corporation, 113–15
Port Arthur Shipbuilding, 55
Portal, Charles, 102, 170
postwar Canada, 256–62
postwar industries, 249–51
postwar plans, 237–38, 243, 249, 253, 255
Potts, Arthur, 244
Pound, Dudley, 56, 159, 170
Powell, A.J., *62*
Power, Charles Gavin "Chubby," 19, 41, 76–77, 85, 92, 94–95, 97, 101, 108–09, 116, 231, 253
Prentice, Chummy, 59
Pressey, Arthur, 44
Prince David, HMCS, 57
Prince Henry, HMCS, 57
Prince Robert, HMCS, 57

Princess Louise Dragoon Guards, 219
Pritchard, James, 55

Quebec
    headlines in, 34
    Montreal, 23
    Quebec City, 23
Queen's Own Rifles, 199

Radley-Walters, Sydney, 184
Ralston, James, 19
Ralston, Layton, 92, 128, 140, 167–68, 181, 211, 213, 217, 220–24, 253
Ralston-Sinclair Agreement, 93–94
Ramsay, Bertram, 201
rationing, 254–55
Régiment de Maisonneuve, 201
Regina, Saskatchewan, 236
Regina Rifles Regiment, 198–99
Renaud, Olive, 249
Report on Social Security for Canada (Marsh), 241
Rhineland, 25, 30, 202
Rigby, Vincent, 96
riots, and WWI, 22–24
Riverdale, Lord, 66–67
Roberts, Hamilton, 159–60, 165, 167, 171–73
Roberts, James, 204
Robertson, Norman, 260
Robertson, Owen, 44
Rogers, Norman, 90, 211
Roosevelt, Franklin, 112, 133–35, *136*, 137–41, 254
Rossell, Arthur, 156
Royal Air Force, 66–69, 78, 89–93, 97, 109, 187, 197
Royal Canadian Air Force, 34, 53, 66, 93–94, 121, 132, 187
    Britain and, 67–69, 92–93, 96–97

Canadianization of, 88–89, 93–95, 97–102, 108–09
ground crews, 65, 82, 88, 93, 95, 98, 108
No. 6 Group, 87–89, 102–06, 235
statistics for, 16, 84–85, 258
training schools, 69–70, 72, 75–81, 83
women in, 78–79
See also British Commonwealth Air Training Plan (BCATP)
Royal Canadian Navy, 34, 62–63, 132, 258
    corvettes, *48*, 49–58, 63–64, 117, 123
    destroyers, 15, 43, 45, 53, 61, 123
    lack of trained manpower, 42–43, 46–47, 56–58
    minesweepers, 15, 43, 48, 55
    ship numbers, 15
Royal Canadian Navy Reserve (RCNR), 16, 263n1
    frigates, 61
Royal Canadian Navy Volunteer Reserve (RCNVR), 16, 57, 64
Royal Hamilton Light Infantry, 151, 163, 219
Royal Montreal Regiment, 198–99
Royal Navy, 45, 47–48
    corvettes, 49–50, 57
    submarines, 44
Royal Regiment of Canada, 174, 219
Royal Tour of May (1939), 16–17, 40–41, 137
Royal 22e Régiment, 220
rubber, 112–15
Russia, 153–54

Sackville, HMCS, 50
Salmon, Harry, 177

Sansom, Ernest, 181, 227
Saskatchewan
    Melville, 40
    Minton, 17
    Regina, 236
Saunders, Alan, 161, 166–67
Saunders, Robert, 244
Schumacher, J.E., 51
Scott, C.A., 227
Scott, Frank, 26
Scott, Gordon, 120
2nd Armoured Brigade, 180, 183–84
II Canadian Corps, 181, 183–84, 188, 204
2nd Canadian Infantry Division, 159, 177, 184, *186*, 190, 192, 199
II SS Panzer Corps, 190
Second World War, 93
    Canada's declaration of war, 21–23, 35–36, 49
    remembrance of, 261–62
Second World War, The (Churchill), 171
70th Infantry Division, 201
79th British Armoured Division, 187, 202
Shadforth, H.G., 58
Shediac, HMCS, 60–61
ship exchanges, 53–54, 57
shipbuilding, 46–47, 49, 61, 123, 126
Sicily, 177–78, 184, 203
Sifton, Victor, 211
Simonds, Guy, 175–80, *182*, 183–87, 189, 191, 200–01, 203–05, 260
Sinclair, Archibald, 92–93
Skeena, HMCS, 59
Skelton, Oscar, 35, 144
Sledgehammer plan, 154
Smythe, Conn, 218–19
Snowberry, HMCS, 61

social programs, 238–40, 251–54, 261
Solo, Robert, 112
sonar, 52–53, 266*n*16
South Alberta Regiment, 190
South Saskatchewan Regiment, 169
Southern Pride, HMS, 49
Spry, Dan, 197–98
St. George, New Brunswick, 236–37
St. Laurent, HMCS, 61
St. Laurent, Louis, 19, 217, 223, 231
Stacey, C.P., 32, 140, 143, 167, 258
Stalin, Joseph, 153–54
Stanford, Bob, 81
Statute of Westminster, 21
Stedman, E.W., 68
Stevenson, Leigh, 99
Stimson, Henry, 140–41
strikes, 125–26, 255, 288*n*46
Stuart, Ken, 212, 219–21, 223
sub-contracting, 128
submarines, 15–16, 44–45, 56
    See also U-boats
superstitions, 107
Surface Warning 1st Canadian (SW1C) radar, 60
synthetic rubber, 112–15, 124

tanks, 165–66, 178, 187, 189
Taylor, Edward Plunket, 119, *130*
3rd Canadian Infantry Division, 180
Thompson, John, 133
Three Rivers Regiment, 178
Timmerman, Nelles, 94
Toronto, *236*
Toronto Star, 131, 217
Toronto Telegram, 100
torpedoes, German, 45
training schools, 69–70, 72, 75–81, 83
Treaty of Versailles (1919), 25–26
Truscott, Lucian, 169

Turner, Phyllis, 127
Tweedsmuir, Lord, 21–22
12th SS Division, 191
21st Army Group, 188

U-boats, 45, 53, 55–56, 61, 178
   See also submarines
Unauthorized Action (Villa), 171
Unemployment Insurance, 125, 239–40
unionization, 125
United States of America, 30, 41, 47, 56, 61, 69n, 70, 75–76, 81, 119, 133–38, 140–42, 148, 154, 214, 255
universities, 26, 246
uranium, 124–25
U.S. Eighth Air Force, 188
U.S. Third Army, 190

Valour and the Horror, The (CBC), 106
Vancouver, British Columbia, 40, 236
Vansittart, Robert, 32
VE Day, 235, *236*
veterans, 243–44, 246–49, 255, 287n36
Veterans Affairs, 244–46
Veterans Charter, 237, 246–49, 251, 253, 255
Victoria, British Columbia, 40–41
Victory Loans, 127
Villa, Brian, 171, 173, 278n38
   Unauthorized Action, 171
Villeneuve, Jean-Marie-Rodrigue, 41
Vimy Memorial, 24–25
Vokes, Chris, 175

Wagner, Bruce, 192, *193*
Wagner, Harry, 192, *193*
Wagner, Ivan, 192, *193*

Wagner, Nora, 192, *193*
Walker, Richard, 209, 213
Warspite, HMS, 200
Wavy Navy. *See* Royal Canadian Navy Volunteer Reserve (RCNVR)
Welland, Robert, 52
Western Prince (ocean liner), 120
"What's the Cheering For?" (Dafoe), 33–34
Whitaker, Denis, 151
Whitton, Charlotte, 241
Williams, Jeffery, 192, 194
Willkie, Wendell, 138
Wilmot, Chester, 191–92
Winnipeg Free Press, 23, 33–34, 41, 179
Wolfe, Donald, 163
women, 78–79, 126–27, 247–48
Woods, J.R., 75
Woodsworth, J.S., 26, 239, 242, 264n1
Woodward, Billy, 119
worker shortages, 42–43, 46–47, 55–58, 70, 125
World Disarmament Conference, 25
World War One (WWI). *See* First World War
World War Two (WWII). *See* Second World War
Worthington, Don, 189
Worthington, Frank, 183

Yorkshire, 102–04

zombies, 208, *210*, 225–26, 283n3
Zuehlke, Mark, 201

dundurn.com
dundurnpress
@dundurnpress
dundurnpress
dundurnpress
info@dundurn.com

Find us on NetGalley & Goodreads too!

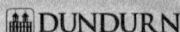